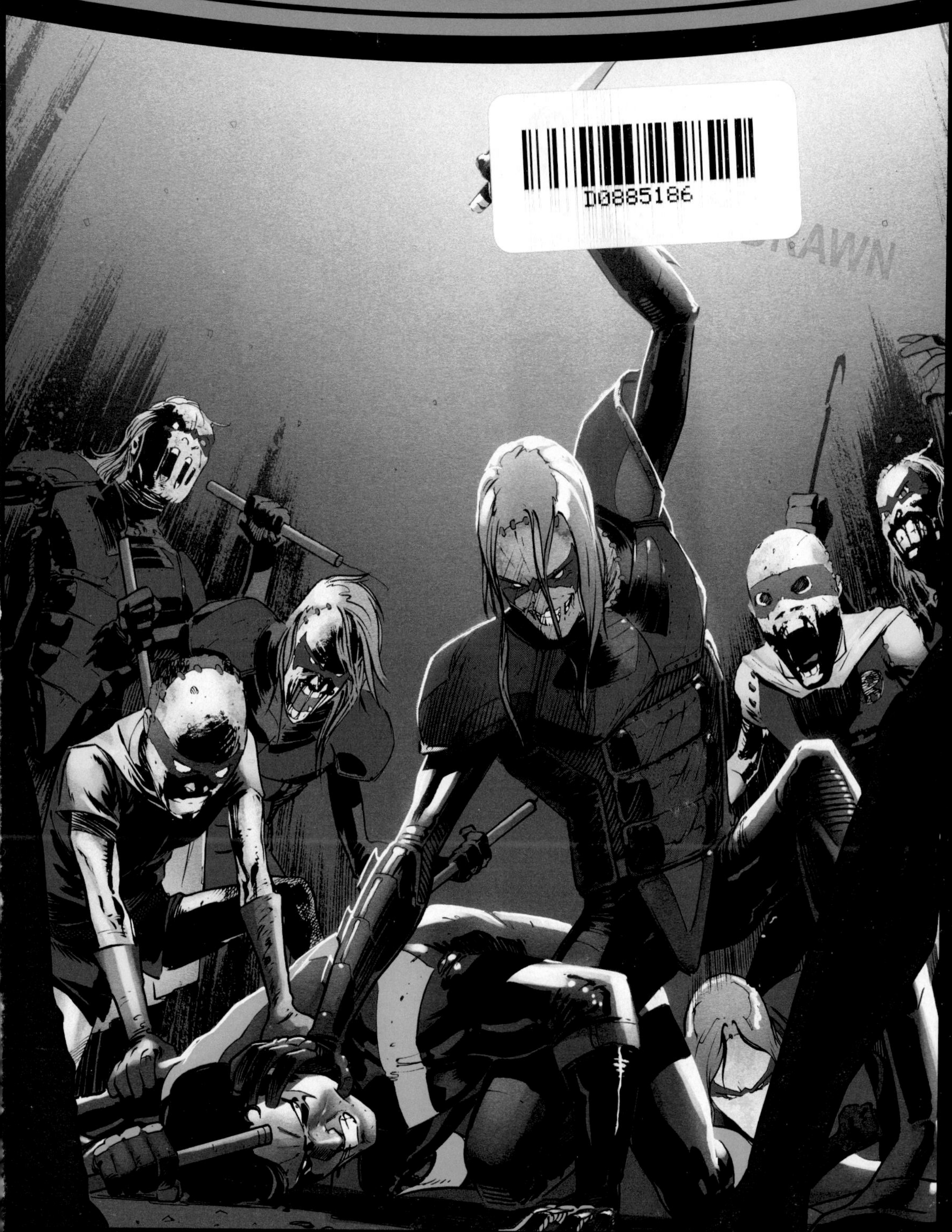

NIGHTWING

VOL.3 NIGHTWING MUST DIE!

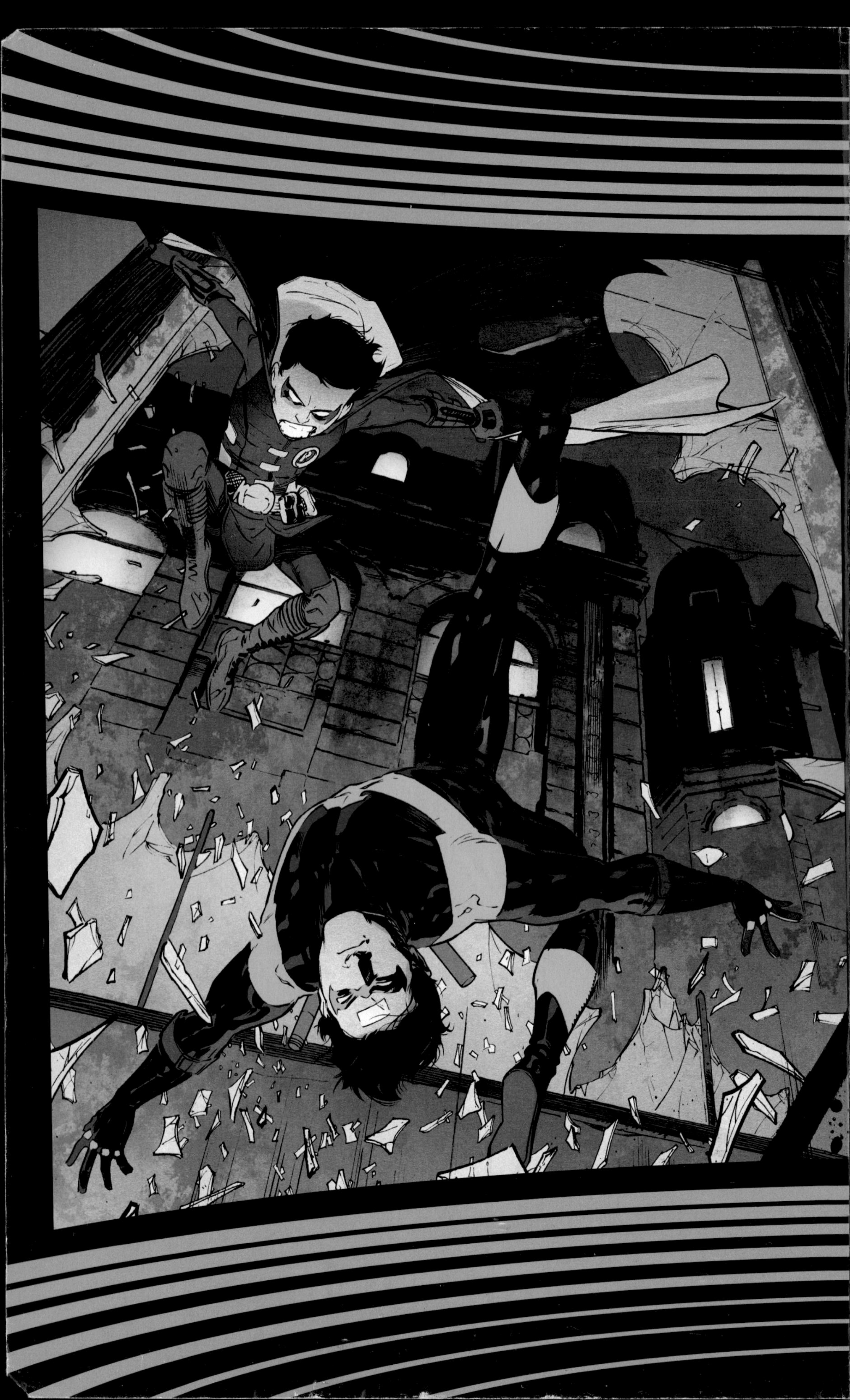

NIGHTWING
VOL.3 NIGHTWING MUST DIE!

TIM SEELEY
MICHAEL McMILLIAN
writers

JAVIER FERNANDEZ
MINKYU JUNG * CHRISTIAN DUCE
artists

CHRIS SOTOMAYOR
colorist

CARLOS M. MANGUAL
letterer

JAVIER FERNANDEZ and CHRIS SOTOMAYOR
collection cover artists

NIGHTWING created by MARV WOLFMAN and GEORGE PÉREZ
PROFESSOR PYG created by GRANT MORRISON, ANDY KUBERT and FRANK QUITELY
SUPERMAN created by JERRY SIEGEL and JOE SHUSTER
By special arrangement with the Jerry Siegel family

REBECCA TAYLOR Editor - Original Series * DAVID WIELGOSZ Assistant Editor - Original Series
JEB WOODARD Group Editor - Collected Editions * LIZ ERICKSON Editor - Collected Edition
STEVE COOK Design Director - Books * MONIQUE GRUSPE Publication Design

BOB HARRAS Senior VP - Editor-in-Chief, DC Comics

DIANE NELSON President * DAN DiDIO Publisher * JIM LEE Publisher * GEOFF JOHNS President & Chief Creative Officer
AMIT DESAI Executive VP - Business & Marketing Strategy, Direct to Consumer & Global Franchise Management * SAM ADES Senior VP - Direct to Consumer
BOBBIE CHASE VP - Talent Development * MARK CHIARELLO Senior VP - Art, Design & Collected Editions
JOHN CUNNINGHAM Senior VP - Sales & Trade Marketing * ANNE DePIES Senior VP - Business Strategy, Finance & Administration
DON FALLETTI VP - Manufacturing Operations * LAWRENCE GANEM VP - Editorial Administration & Talent Relations
ALISON GILL Senior VP - Manufacturing & Operations * HANK KANALZ Senior VP - Editorial Strategy & Administration
JAY KOGAN VP - Legal Affairs * THOMAS LOFTUS VP - Business Affairs
JACK MAHAN VP - Business Affairs * NICK J. NAPOLITANO VP - Manufacturing Administration
EDDIE SCANNELL VP - Consumer Marketing * COURTNEY SIMMONS Senior VP - Publicity & Communications
JIM (SKI) SOKOLOWSKI VP - Comic Book Specialty Sales & Trade Marketing * NANCY SPEARS VP - Mass, Book, Digital Sales & Trade Marketing

NIGHTWING VOLUME 3: NIGHTWING MUST DIE!

Published by DC Comics. Compilation and all new material Copyright © 2017 DC Comics. All Rights Reserved.
Originally published in single magazine form in NIGHTWING 16-21. Copyright © 2017 DC Comics. All Rights Reserved.
All characters, their distinctive likenesses and related elements featured in this publication are trademarks of DC Comics.
The stories, characters and incidents featured in this publication are entirely fictional.
DC Comics does not read or accept unsolicited ideas, stories or artwork.

DC Comics, 2900 West Alameda Ave., Burbank, CA 91505
Printed by LSC Communications, Kendallville, IN, USA. 8/18/17. First Printing.
ISBN: 978-1-4012-7376-7

Library of Congress Cataloging-in-Publication Data is available.

PEFC Certified

Printed on paper from
sustainably managed
forests, controlled
sources

PEFC/29-31-337   www.pefc.org

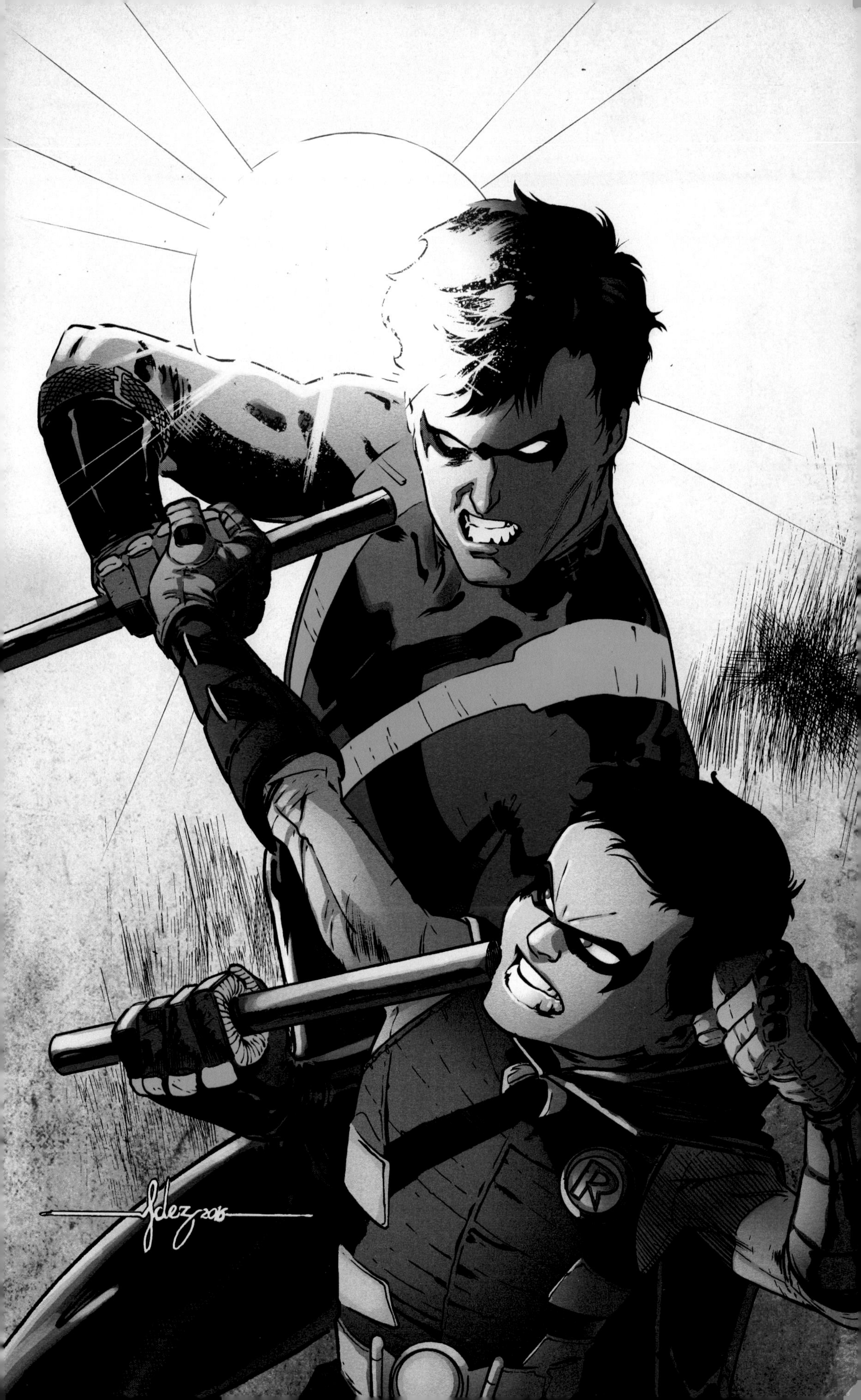

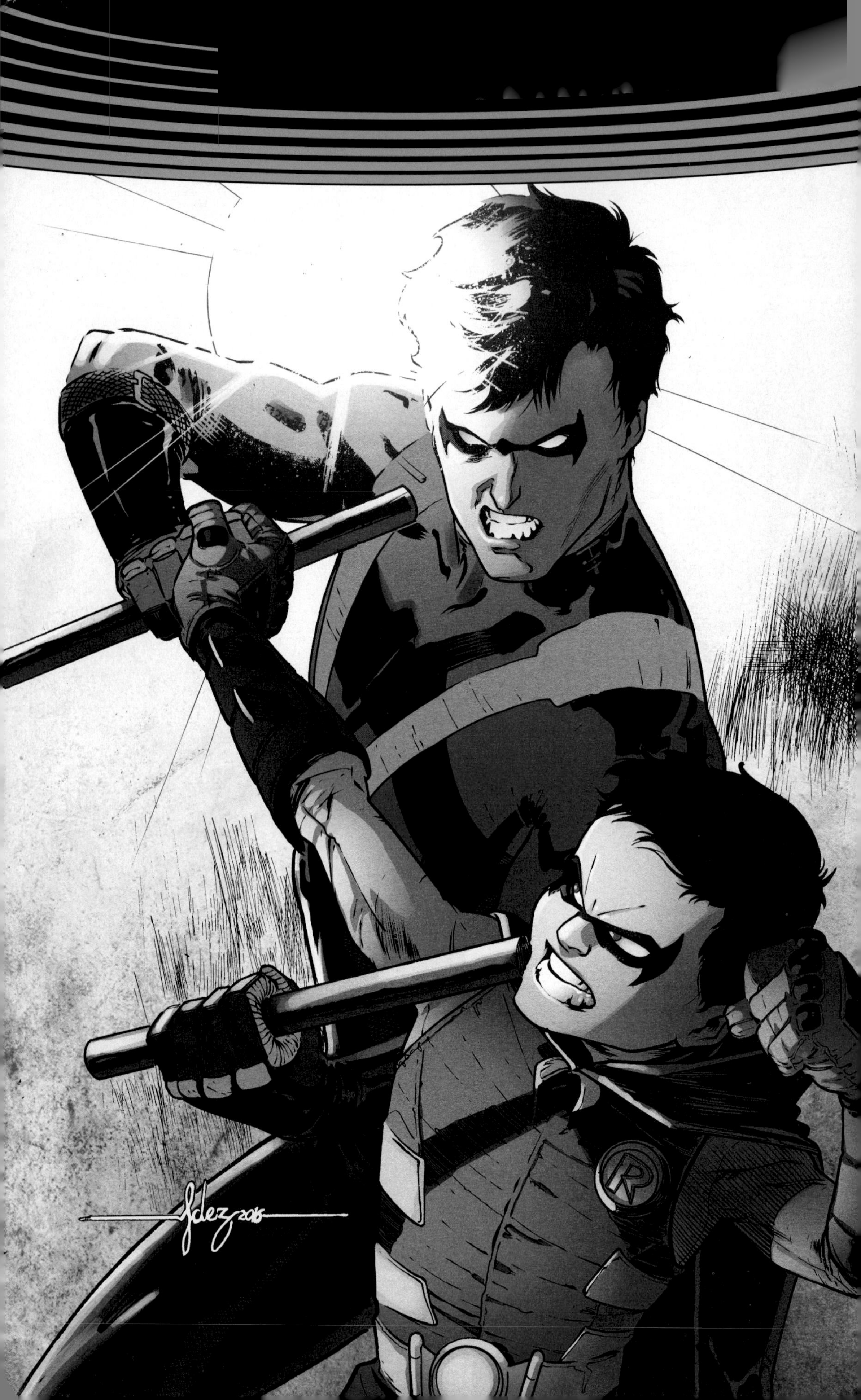

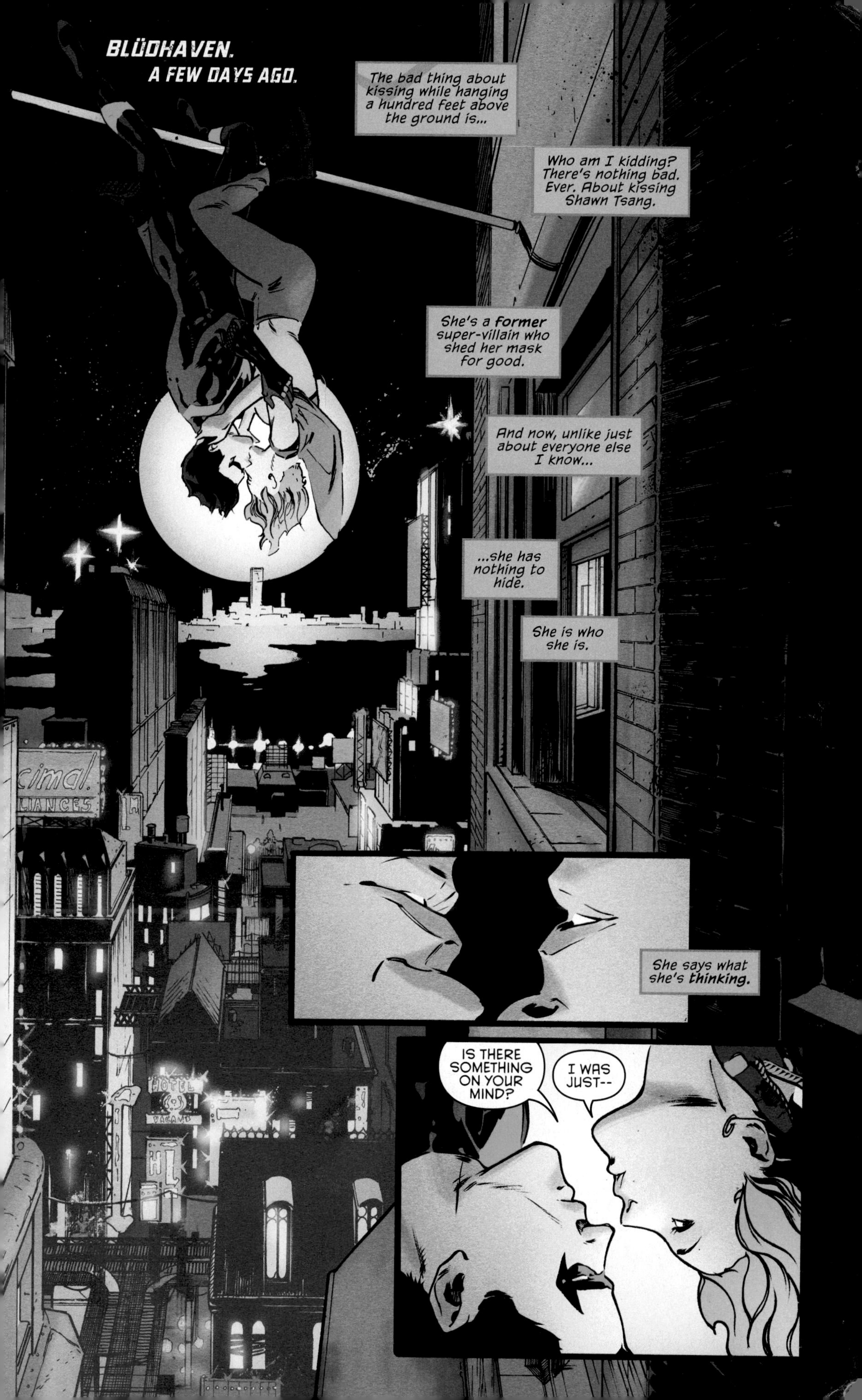
BLÜDHAVEN.
A FEW DAYS AGO.
The bad thing about kissing while hanging a hundred feet above the ground is...
Who am I kidding? There's nothing bad. Ever. About kissing Shawn Tsang.
She's a **former** super-villain who shed her mask for good.
And now, unlike just about everyone else I know...
...she has nothing to hide.
She is who she is.
She says what she's **thinking.**
IS THERE SOMETHING ON YOUR MIND?
I WAS JUST--

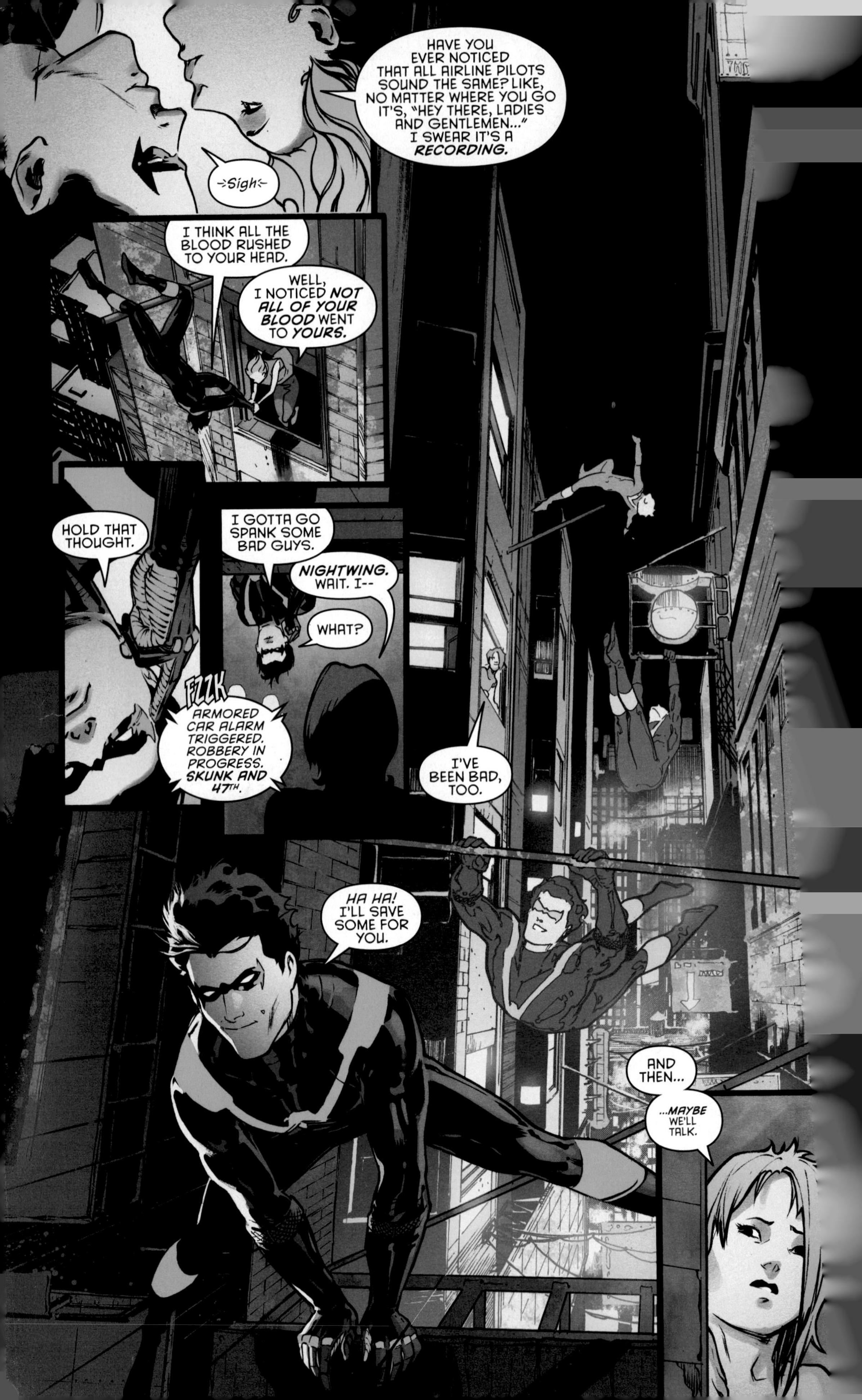
HAVE YOU EVER NOTICED THAT ALL AIRLINE PILOTS SOUND THE SAME? LIKE, NO MATTER WHERE YOU GO IT'S, "HEY THERE, LADIES AND GENTLEMEN..." I SWEAR IT'S A *RECORDING.*
Sigh
I THINK ALL THE BLOOD RUSHED TO YOUR HEAD.
WELL, I NOTICED ***NOT ALL OF YOUR BLOOD*** WENT TO ***YOURS.***
HOLD THAT THOUGHT.
I GOTTA GO SPANK SOME BAD GUYS.
NIGHTWING. WAIT. I--
WHAT?
FZZK
ARMORED CAR ALARM TRIGGERED. ROBBERY IN PROGRESS. ***SKUNK AND 47TH.***
I'VE BEEN BAD, TOO.
HA HA! I'LL SAVE SOME FOR YOU.
AND THEN...
...***MAYBE*** WE'LL TALK.

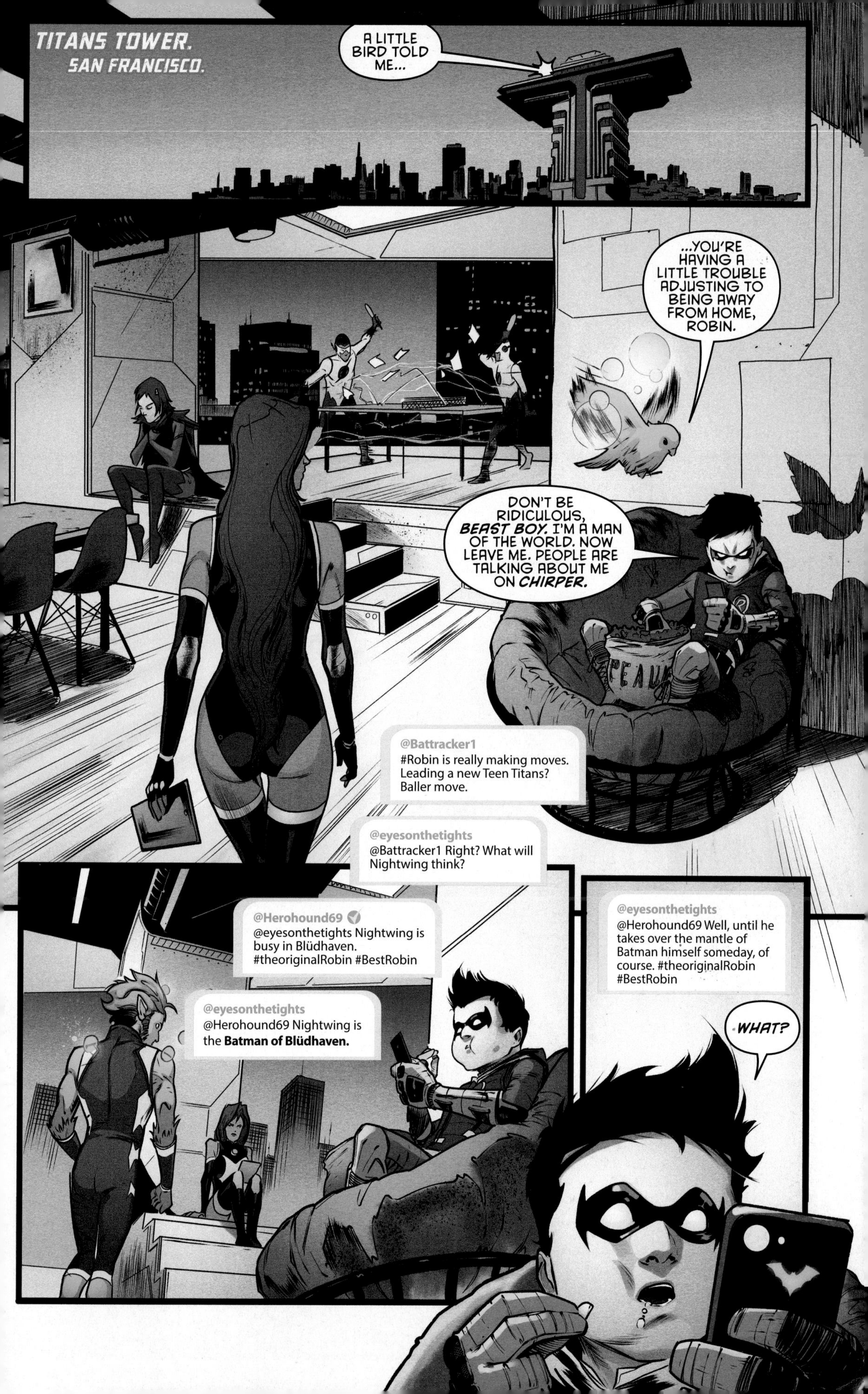
TITANS TOWER.
SAN FRANCISCO.
A LITTLE BIRD TOLD ME...
...YOU'RE HAVING A LITTLE TROUBLE ADJUSTING TO BEING AWAY FROM HOME, ROBIN.
DON'T BE RIDICULOUS, BEAST BOY. I'M A MAN OF THE WORLD. NOW LEAVE ME. PEOPLE ARE TALKING ABOUT ME ON CHIRPER.
@Battracker1
#Robin is really making moves. Leading a new Teen Titans? Baller move.
@eyesonthetights
@Battracker1 Right? What will Nightwing think?
@Herohound69
@eyesonthetights Nightwing is busy in Blüdhaven. #theoriginalRobin #BestRobin
@eyesonthetights
@Herohound69 Nightwing is the Batman of Blüdhaven.
@eyesonthetights
@Herohound69 Well, until he takes over the mantle of Batman himself someday, of course. #theoriginalRobin #BestRobin
WHAT?

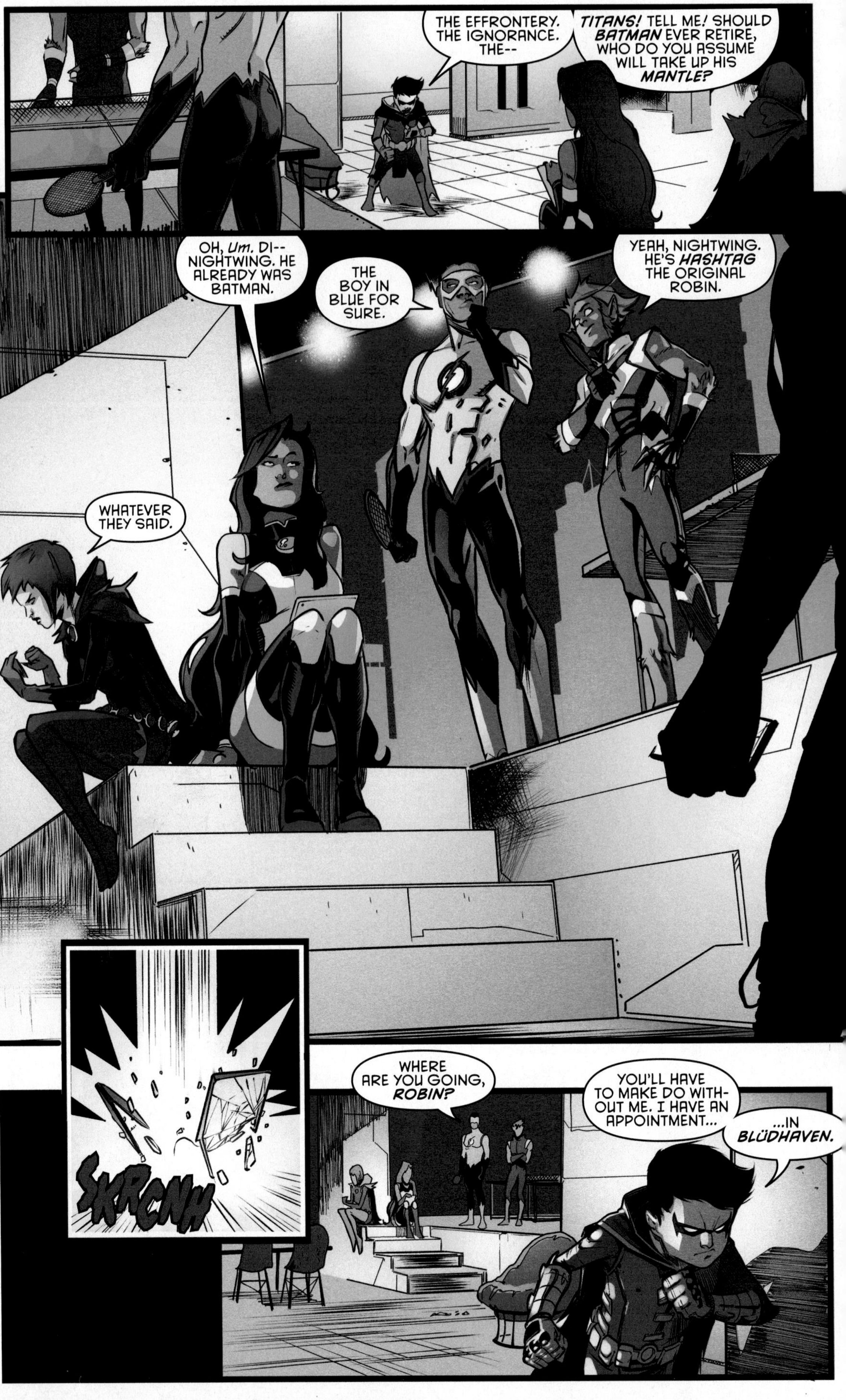
THE EFFRONTERY. THE IGNORANCE. THE--
TITANS! TELL ME! SHOULD BATMAN EVER RETIRE, WHO DO YOU ASSUME WILL TAKE UP HIS MANTLE?
OH, UM. DI-- NIGHTWING. HE ALREADY WAS BATMAN.
THE BOY IN BLUE FOR SURE.
YEAH, NIGHTWING. HE'S HASHTAG THE ORIGINAL ROBIN.
WHATEVER THEY SAID.
SKRCNH
WHERE ARE YOU GOING, ROBIN?
YOU'LL HAVE TO MAKE DO WITH-OUT ME. I HAVE AN APPOINTMENT...
...IN BLÜDHAVEN.

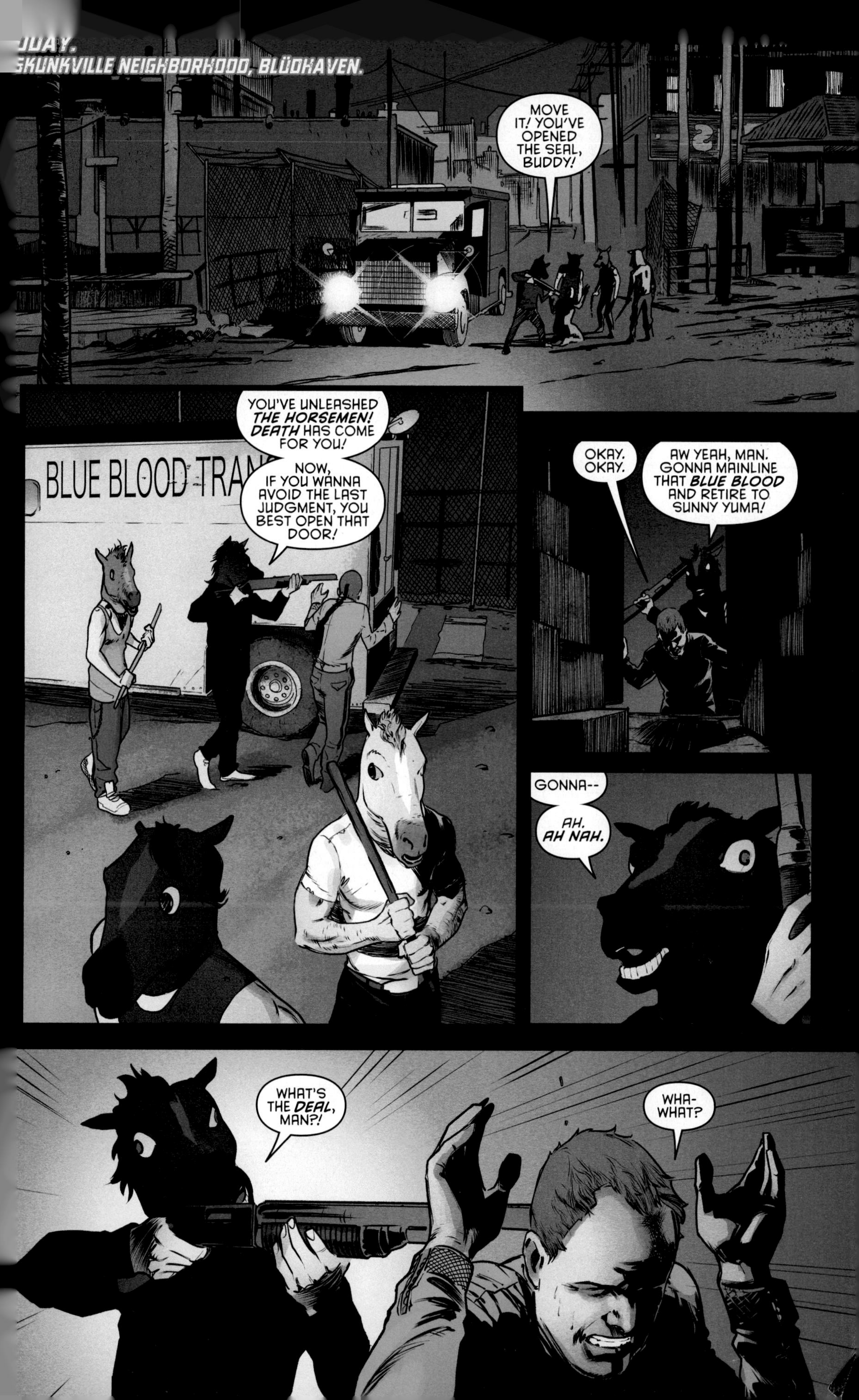

UDAY.
SKUNKVILLE NEIGHBORHOOD, BLÜDHAVEN.
MOVE IT! YOU'VE OPENED THE SEAL, BUDDY!
YOU'VE UNLEASHED THE HORSEMEN! DEATH HAS COME FOR YOU!
NOW, IF YOU WANNA AVOID THE LAST JUDGMENT, YOU BEST OPEN THAT DOOR!
OKAY. OKAY.
AW YEAH, MAN. GONNA MAINLINE THAT BLUE BLOOD AND RETIRE TO SUNNY YUMA!
GONNA--
AH. AH NAH.
WHAT'S THE DEAL, MAN?!
WHA- WHAT?

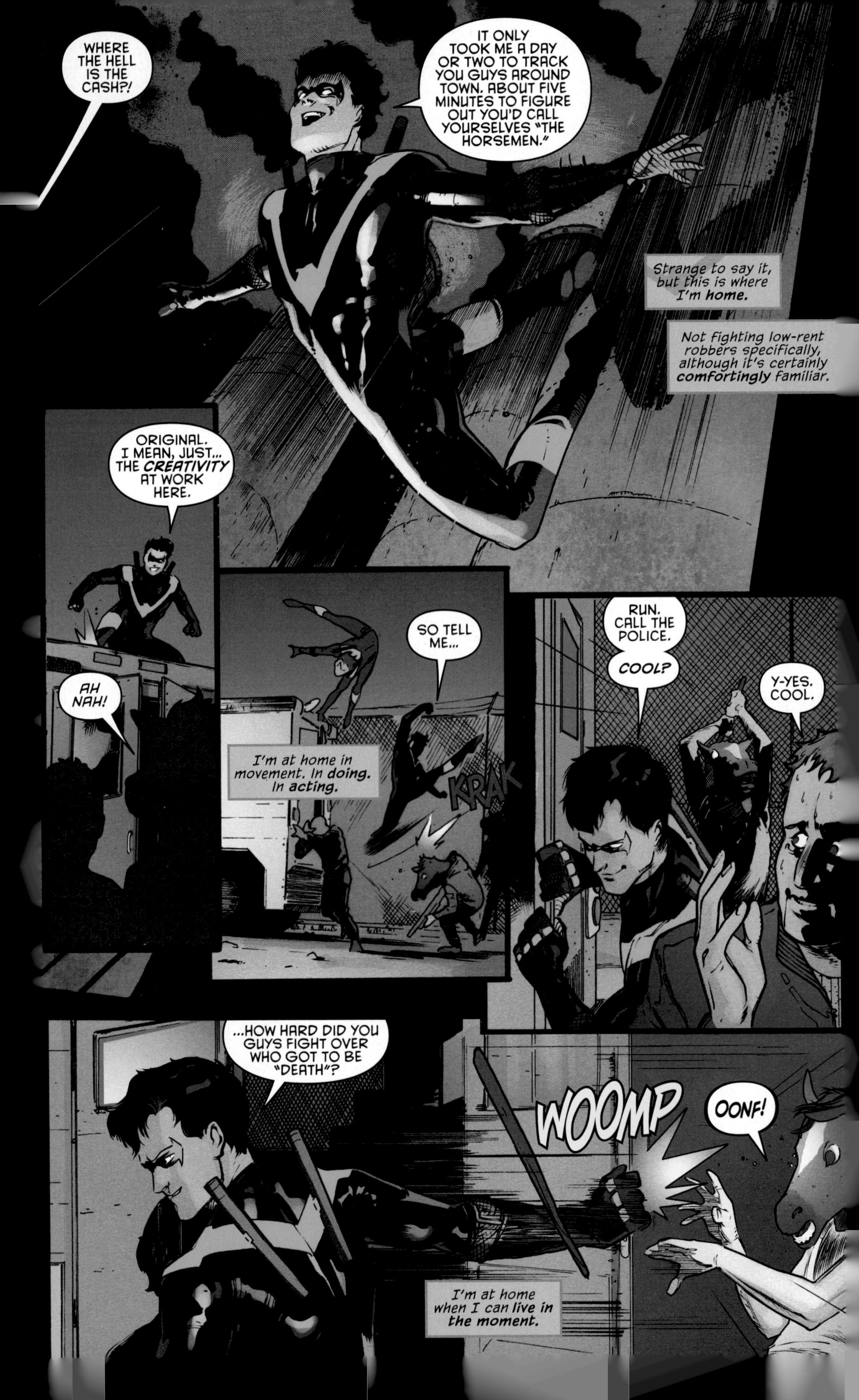

WHERE THE HELL IS THE CASH?!
IT ONLY TOOK ME A DAY OR TWO TO TRACK YOU GUYS AROUND TOWN. ABOUT FIVE MINUTES TO FIGURE OUT YOU'D CALL YOURSELVES "THE HORSEMEN."
Strange to say it, but this is where I'm home.
Not fighting low-rent robbers specifically, although it's certainly comfortingly familiar.
ORIGINAL. I MEAN, JUST... THE CREATIVITY AT WORK HERE.
AH NAH!
SO TELL ME...
I'm at home in movement. In doing. In acting.
KRAK
RUN. CALL THE POLICE.
COOL?
Y-YES. COOL.
...HOW HARD DID YOU GUYS FIGHT OVER WHO GOT TO BE "DEATH"?
WOOMP
OONF!
I'm at home when I can live in the moment.

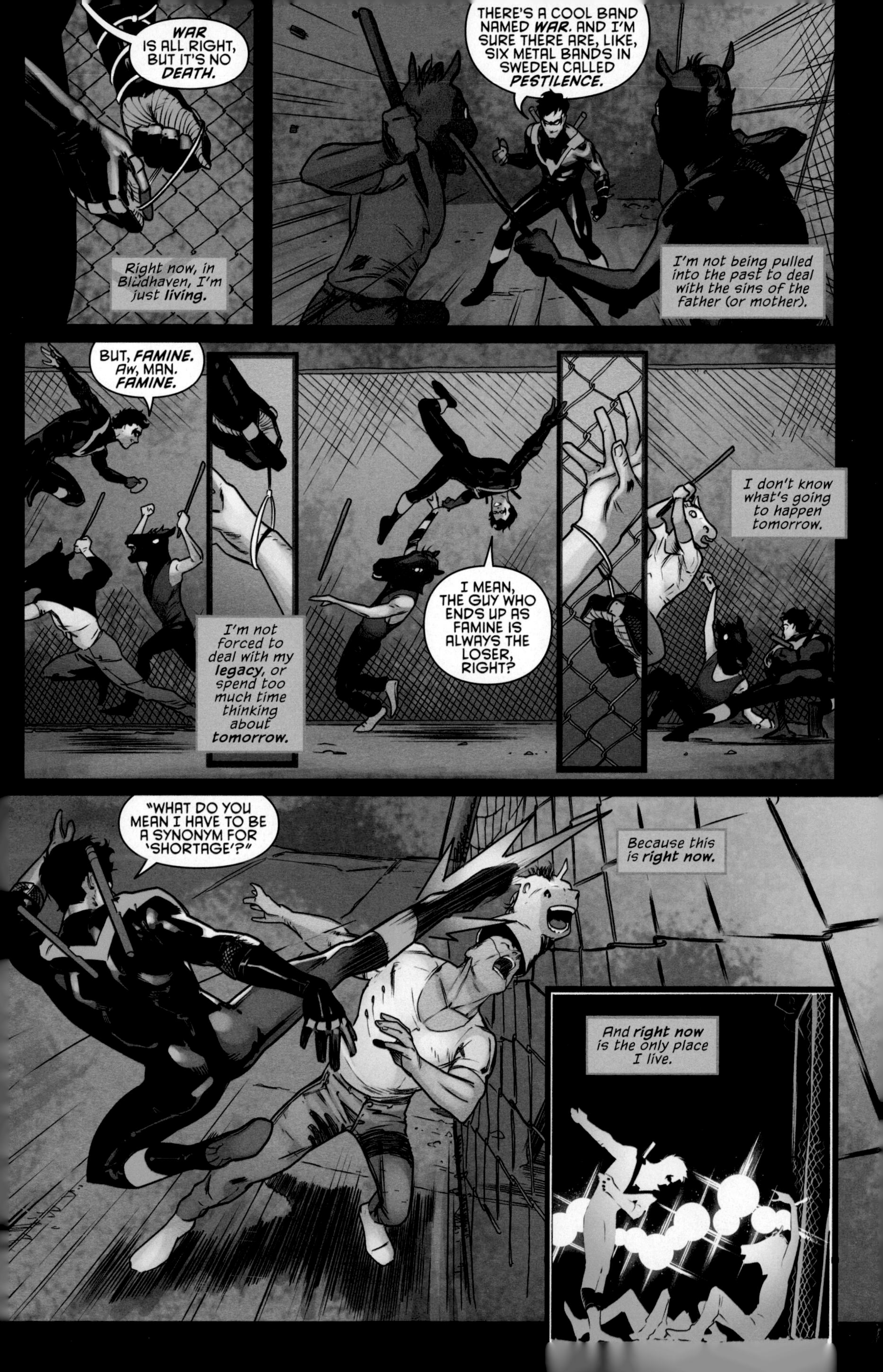
WAR IS ALL RIGHT, BUT IT'S NO DEATH.
Right now, in Blüdhaven, I'm just living.
THERE'S A COOL BAND NAMED WAR. AND I'M SURE THERE ARE, LIKE, SIX METAL BANDS IN SWEDEN CALLED PESTILENCE.
I'm not being pulled into the past to deal with the sins of the father (or mother).
BUT, FAMINE. AW, MAN. FAMINE.
I'm not forced to deal with my legacy, or spend too much time thinking about tomorrow.
I MEAN, THE GUY WHO ENDS UP AS FAMINE IS ALWAYS THE LOSER, RIGHT?
I don't know what's going to happen tomorrow.
"WHAT DO YOU MEAN I HAVE TO BE A SYNONYM FOR 'SHORTAGE'?"
Because this is right now.
And right now is the only place I live.

AAHHHHH!

KRAKK

-tt-

"BATMAN OF BLÜDHAVEN."

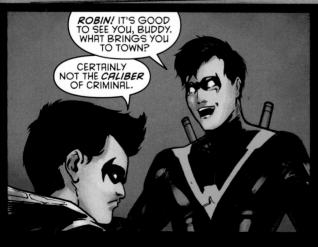

ROBIN! IT'S GOOD TO SEE YOU, BUDDY. WHAT BRINGS YOU TO TOWN?

CERTAINLY NOT THE *CALIBER* OF CRIMINAL.

BLUE BLOOD. Heh. IT'S ALMOST LIKE ALL THE SMART BLÜD CROOKS ARE ON VACATION.

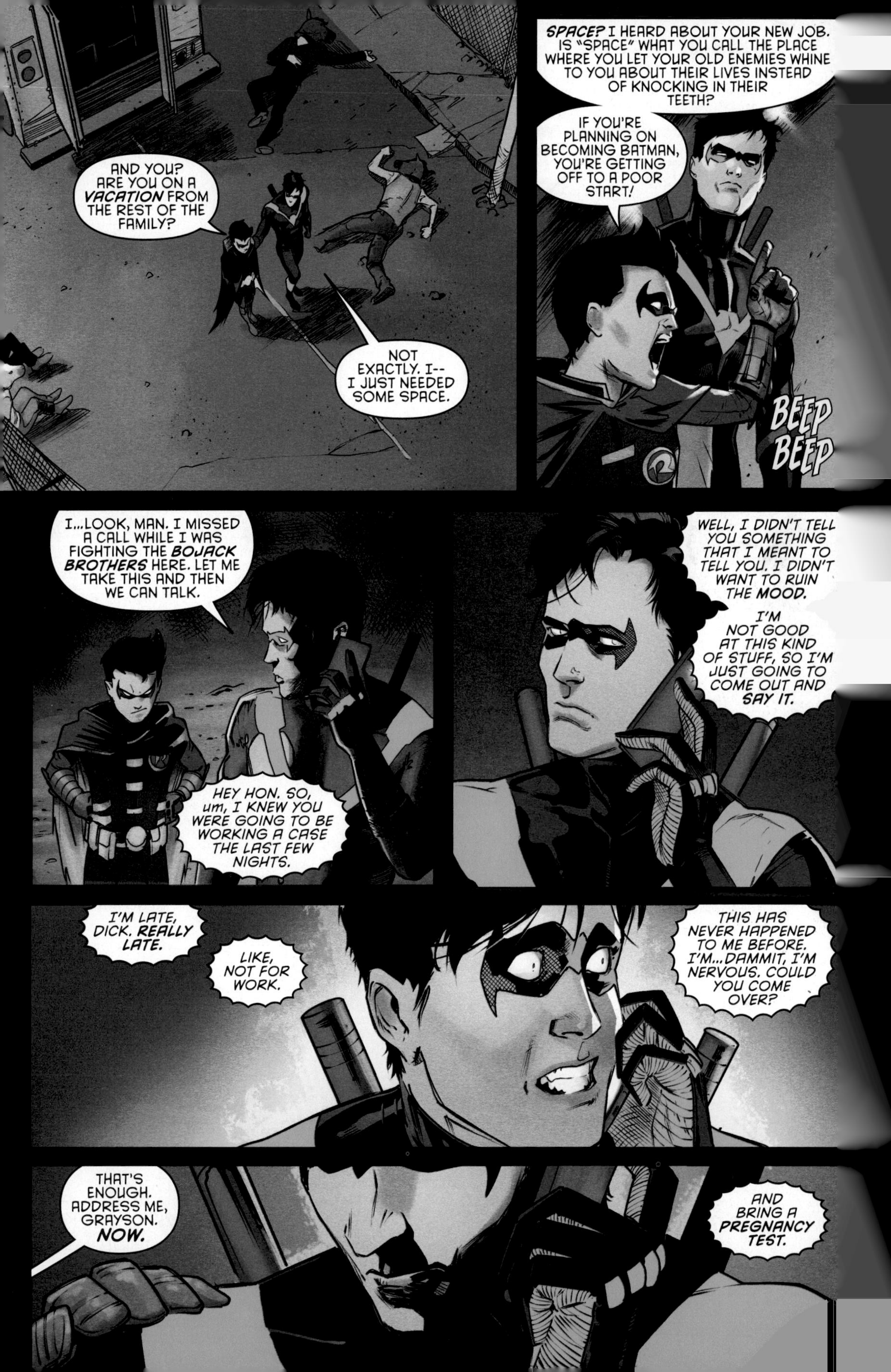
AND YOU? ARE YOU ON A VACATION FROM THE REST OF THE FAMILY?
NOT EXACTLY. I-- I JUST NEEDED SOME SPACE.
SPACE? I HEARD ABOUT YOUR NEW JOB. IS "SPACE" WHAT YOU CALL THE PLACE WHERE YOU LET YOUR OLD ENEMIES WHINE TO YOU ABOUT THEIR LIVES INSTEAD OF KNOCKING IN THEIR TEETH?
IF YOU'RE PLANNING ON BECOMING BATMAN, YOU'RE GETTING OFF TO A POOR START!
BEEP BEEP
I...LOOK, MAN. I MISSED A CALL WHILE I WAS FIGHTING THE BOJACK BROTHERS HERE. LET ME TAKE THIS AND THEN WE CAN TALK.
HEY HON. SO, um, I KNEW YOU WERE GOING TO BE WORKING A CASE THE LAST FEW NIGHTS.
WELL, I DIDN'T TELL YOU SOMETHING THAT I MEANT TO TELL YOU. I DIDN'T WANT TO RUIN THE MOOD.
I'M NOT GOOD AT THIS KIND OF STUFF, SO I'M JUST GOING TO COME OUT AND SAY IT.
I'M LATE, DICK. REALLY LATE.
LIKE, NOT FOR WORK.
THIS HAS NEVER HAPPENED TO ME BEFORE. I'M...DAMMIT, I'M NERVOUS. COULD YOU COME OVER?
THAT'S ENOUGH. ADDRESS ME, GRAYSON. NOW.
AND BRING A PREGNANCY TEST.

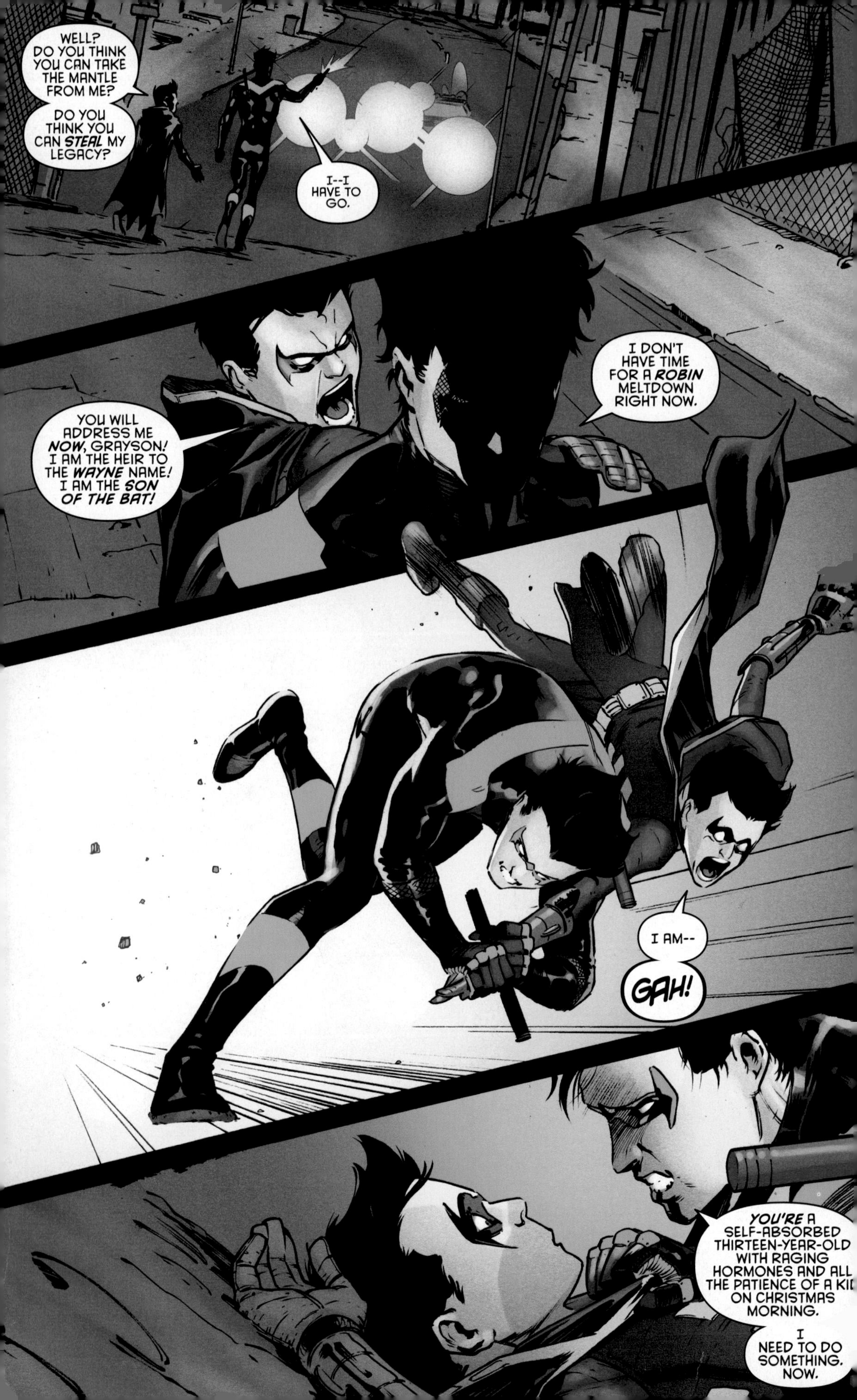
WELL? DO YOU THINK YOU CAN TAKE THE MANTLE FROM ME?
DO YOU THINK YOU CAN STEAL MY LEGACY?
I--I HAVE TO GO.
I DON'T HAVE TIME FOR A ROBIN MELTDOWN RIGHT NOW.
YOU WILL ADDRESS ME NOW, GRAYSON! I AM THE HEIR TO THE WAYNE NAME! I AM THE SON OF THE BAT!
I AM--
GAH!
YOU'RE A SELF-ABSORBED THIRTEEN-YEAR-OLD WITH RAGING HORMONES AND ALL THE PATIENCE OF A KID ON CHRISTMAS MORNING.
I NEED TO DO SOMETHING. NOW.

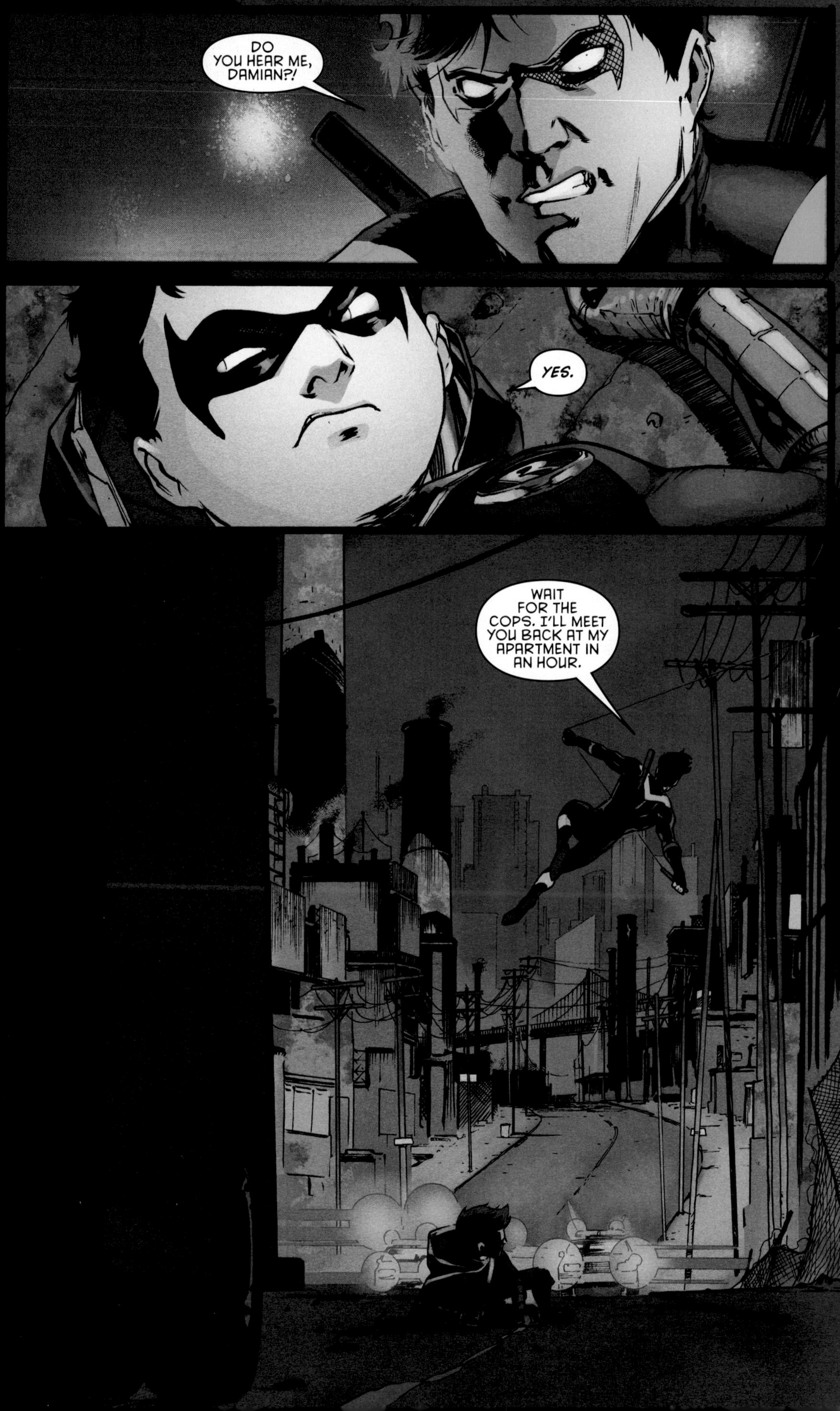
DO YOU HEAR ME, DAMIAN?!
YES.
WAIT FOR THE COPS. I'LL MEET YOU BACK AT MY APARTMENT IN AN HOUR.

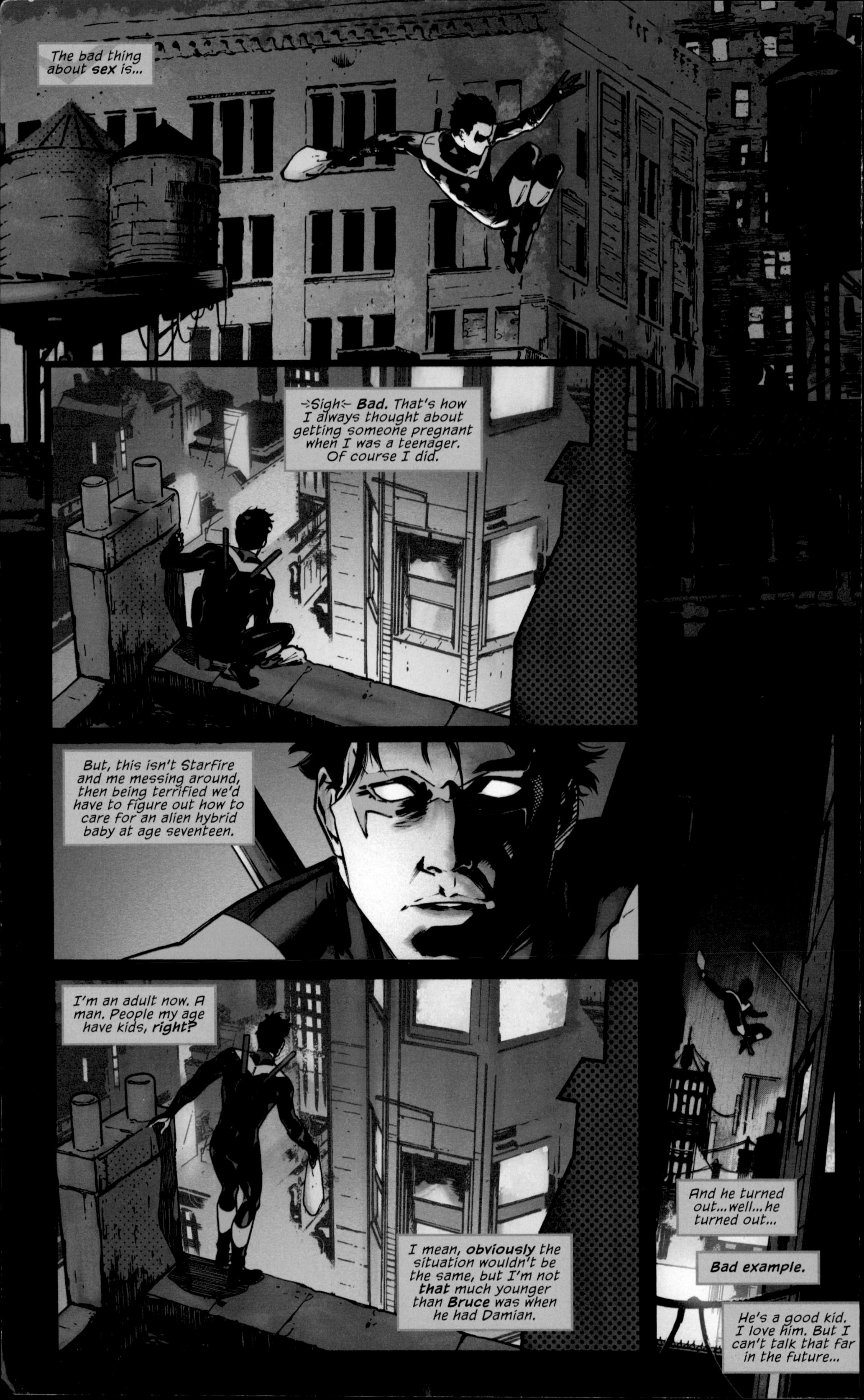
The bad thing about **sex** is...
>Sigh< **Bad.** That's how I always thought about getting someone pregnant when I was a teenager. Of course I did.
But, this isn't Starfire and me messing around, then being terrified we'd have to figure out how to care for an alien hybrid baby at age seventeen.
I'm an adult now. A man. People my age have kids, **right?**
I mean, **obviously** the situation wouldn't be the same, but I'm not **that** much younger than **Bruce** was when he had Damian.
And he turned out...well...he turned out...
Bad example.
He's a good kid. I love him. But I can't talk that far in the future...

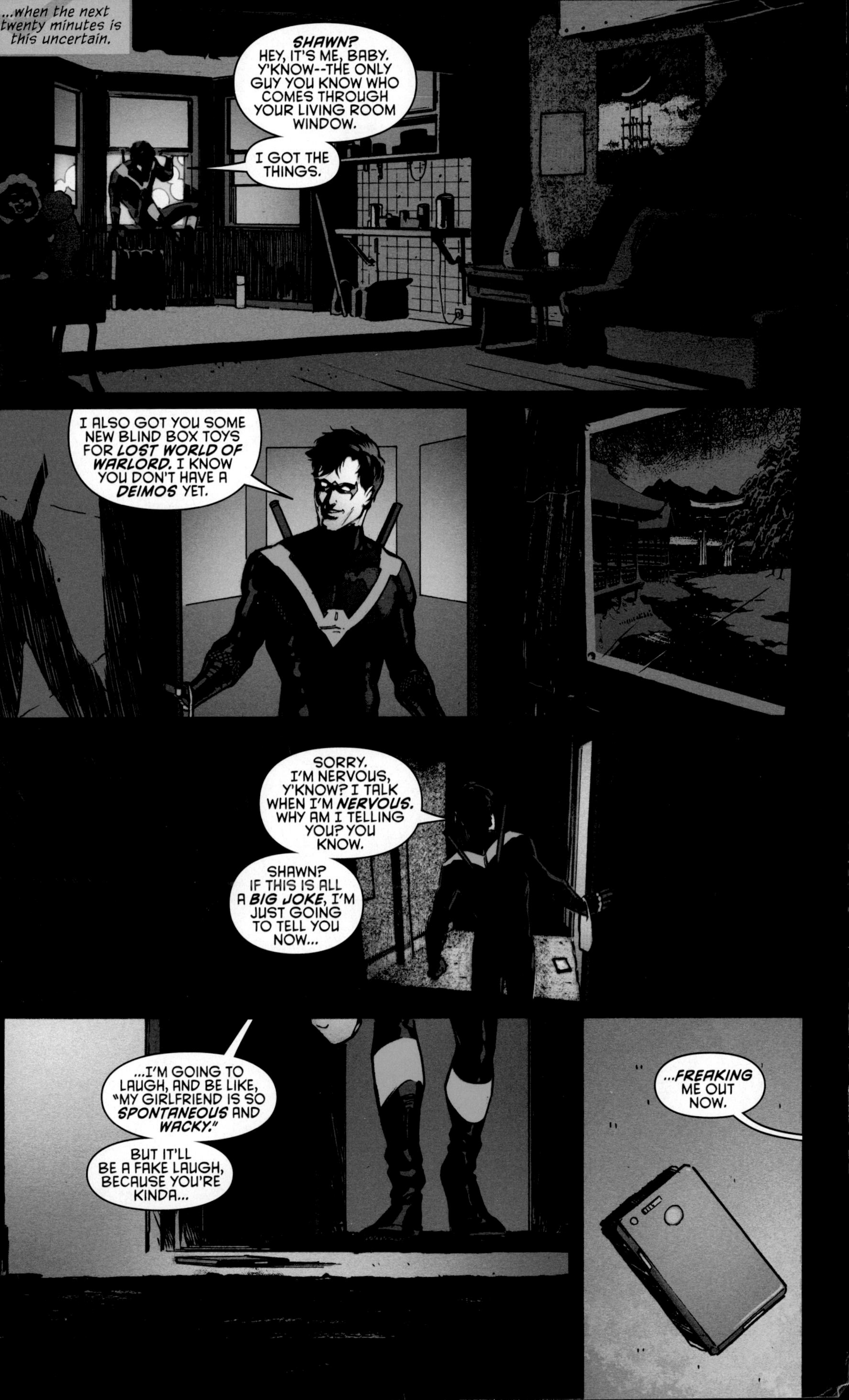
...when the next twenty minutes is this uncertain.
SHAWN? HEY, IT'S ME, BABY. Y'KNOW--THE ONLY GUY YOU KNOW WHO COMES THROUGH YOUR LIVING ROOM WINDOW.
I GOT THE THINGS.
I ALSO GOT YOU SOME NEW BLIND BOX TOYS FOR LOST WORLD OF WARLORD. I KNOW YOU DON'T HAVE A DEIMOS YET.
SORRY. I'M NERVOUS, Y'KNOW? I TALK WHEN I'M NERVOUS. WHY AM I TELLING YOU? YOU KNOW.
SHAWN? IF THIS IS ALL A BIG JOKE, I'M JUST GOING TO TELL YOU NOW...
...I'M GOING TO LAUGH, AND BE LIKE, "MY GIRLFRIEND IS SO SPONTANEOUS AND WACKY."
BUT IT'LL BE A FAKE LAUGH, BECAUSE YOU'RE KINDA...
...FREAKING ME OUT NOW.

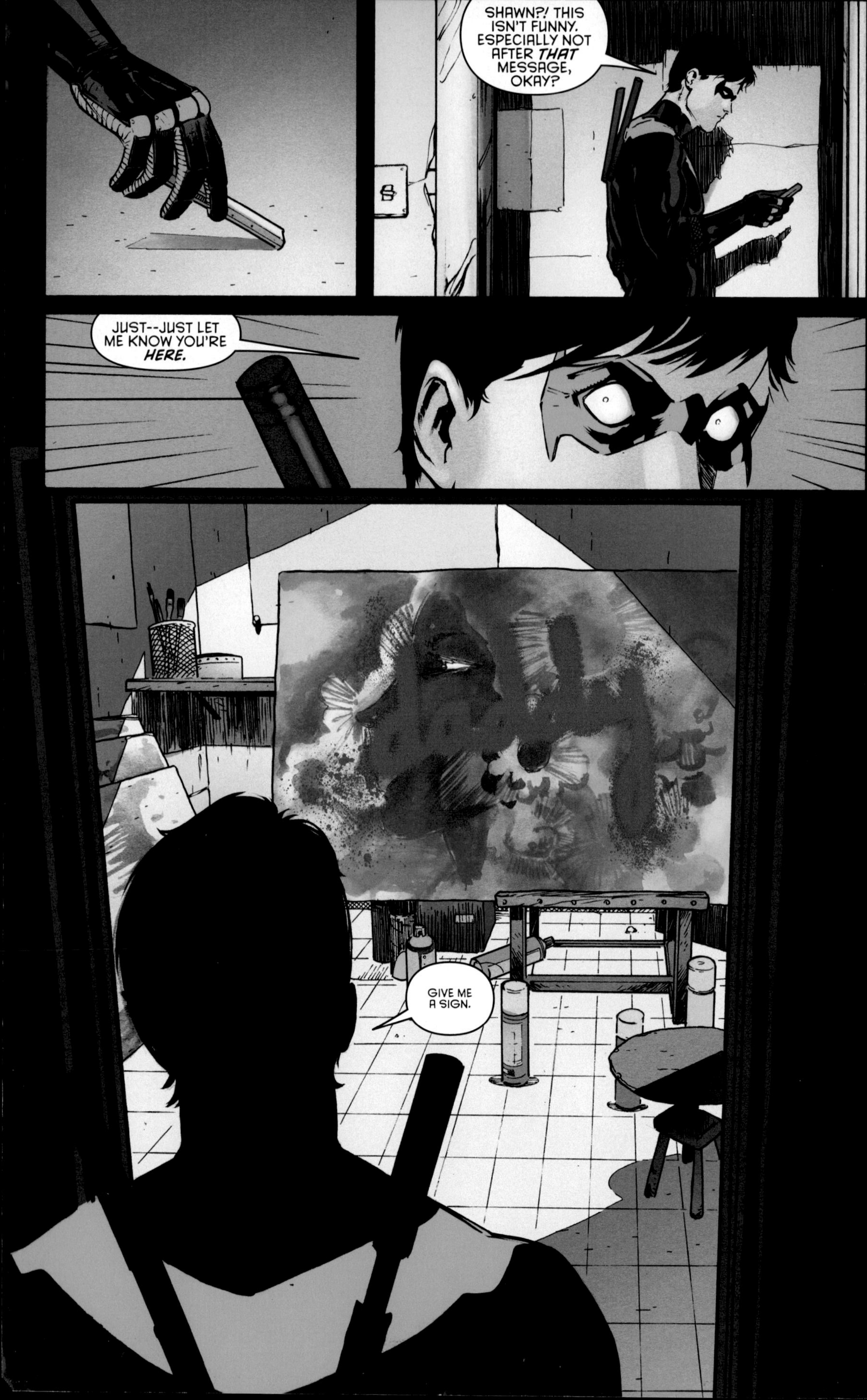
SHAWN?! THIS ISN'T FUNNY. ESPECIALLY NOT AFTER *THAT* MESSAGE, OKAY?
JUST--JUST LET ME KNOW YOU'RE *HERE.*
GIVE ME A SIGN.

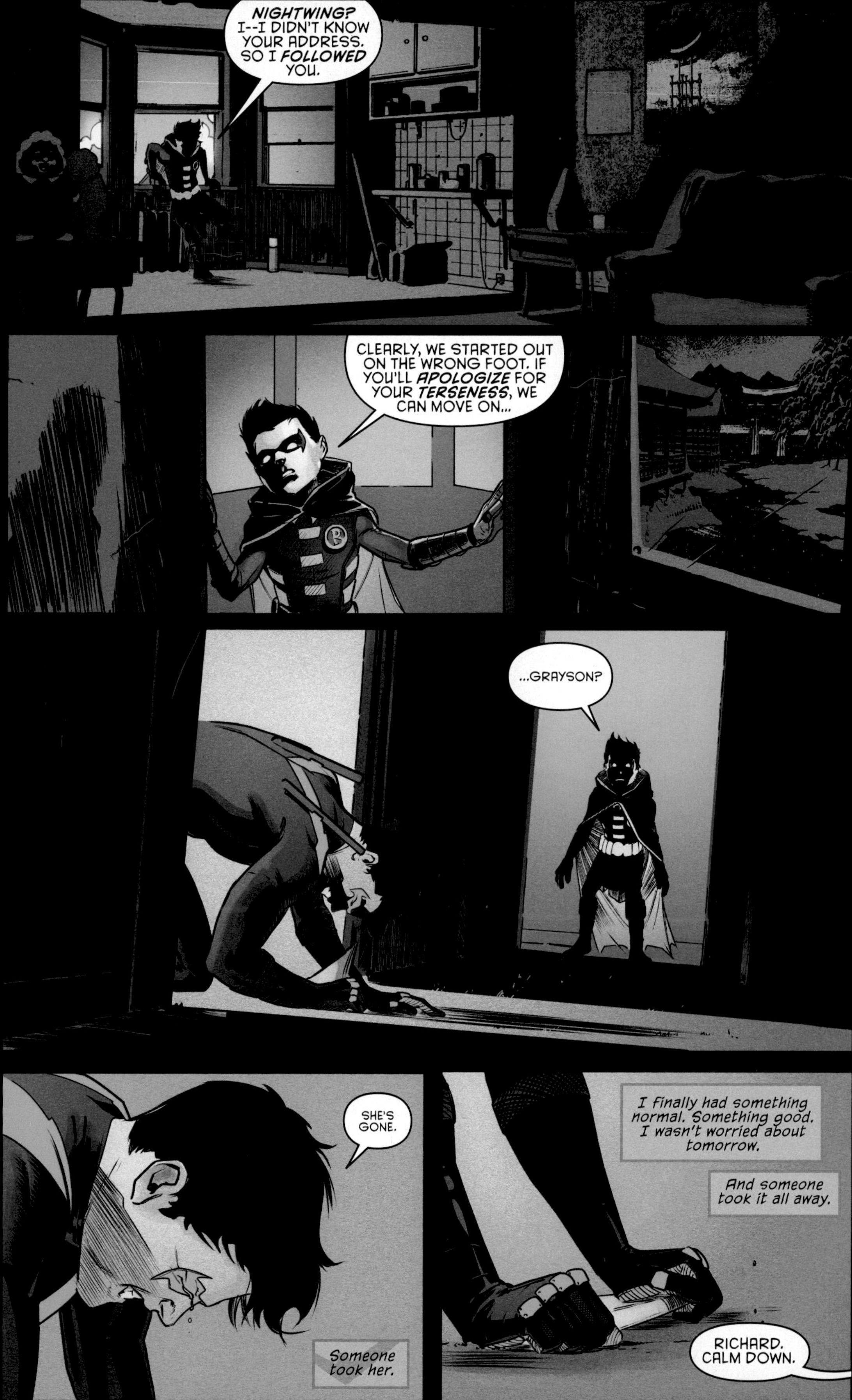
NIGHTWING? I--I DIDN'T KNOW YOUR ADDRESS. SO I FOLLOWED YOU.
CLEARLY, WE STARTED OUT ON THE WRONG FOOT. IF YOU'LL APOLOGIZE FOR YOUR TERSENESS, WE CAN MOVE ON...
...GRAYSON?
SHE'S GONE.
Someone took her.
I finally had something normal. Something good. I wasn't worried about tomorrow.
And someone took it all away.
RICHARD. CALM DOWN.

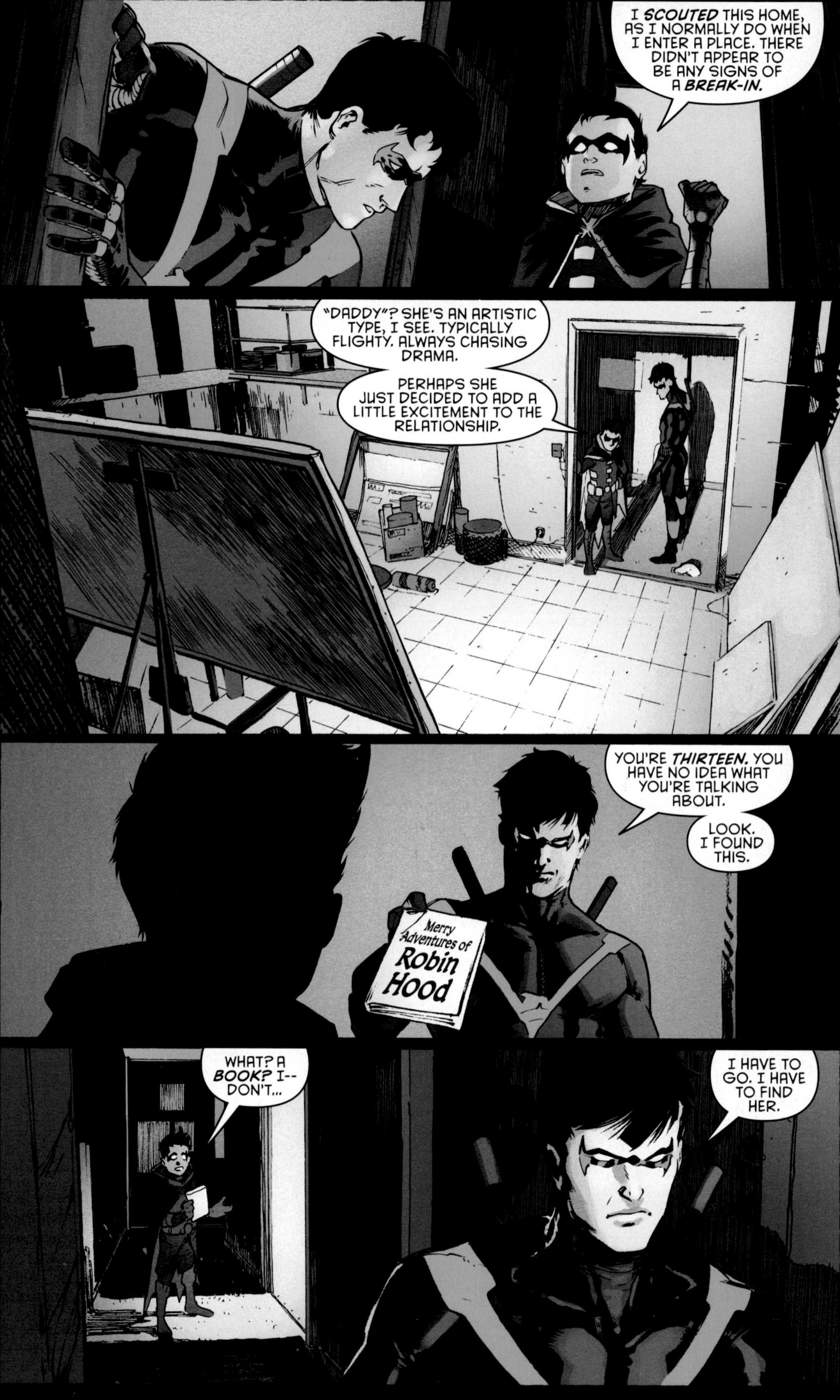
I SCOUTED THIS HOME, AS I NORMALLY DO WHEN I ENTER A PLACE. THERE DIDN'T APPEAR TO BE ANY SIGNS OF A BREAK-IN.
"DADDY"? SHE'S AN ARTISTIC TYPE, I SEE. TYPICALLY FLIGHTY. ALWAYS CHASING DRAMA.
PERHAPS SHE JUST DECIDED TO ADD A LITTLE EXCITEMENT TO THE RELATIONSHIP.
YOU'RE THIRTEEN. YOU HAVE NO IDEA WHAT YOU'RE TALKING ABOUT.
LOOK. I FOUND THIS.
Merry Adventures of Robin Hood
WHAT? A BOOK? I-- DON'T...
I HAVE TO GO. I HAVE TO FIND HER.

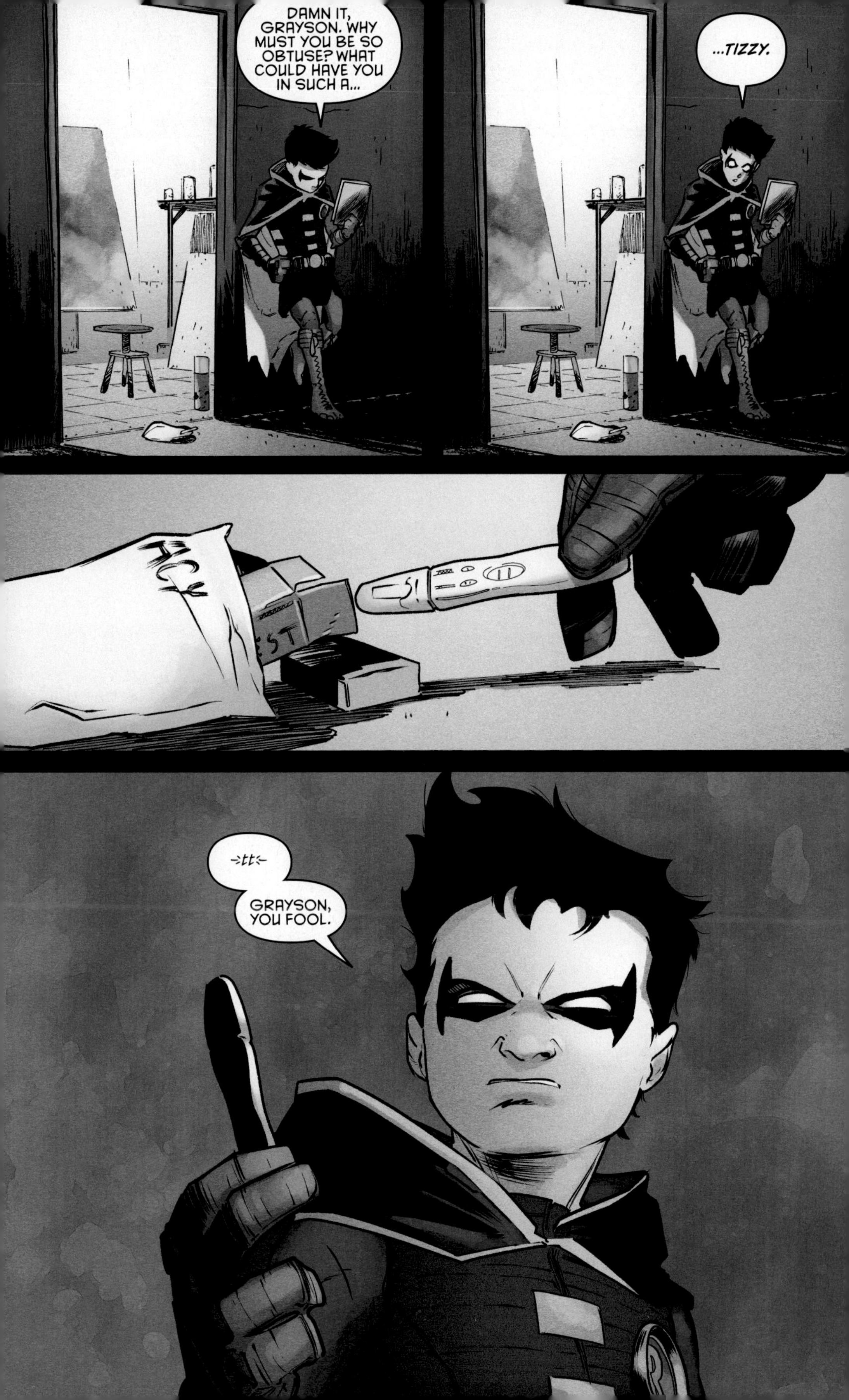
DAMN IT, GRAYSON. WHY MUST YOU BE SO OBTUSE? WHAT COULD HAVE YOU IN SUCH A...
...TIZZY.
-tt-
GRAYSON, YOU FOOL.

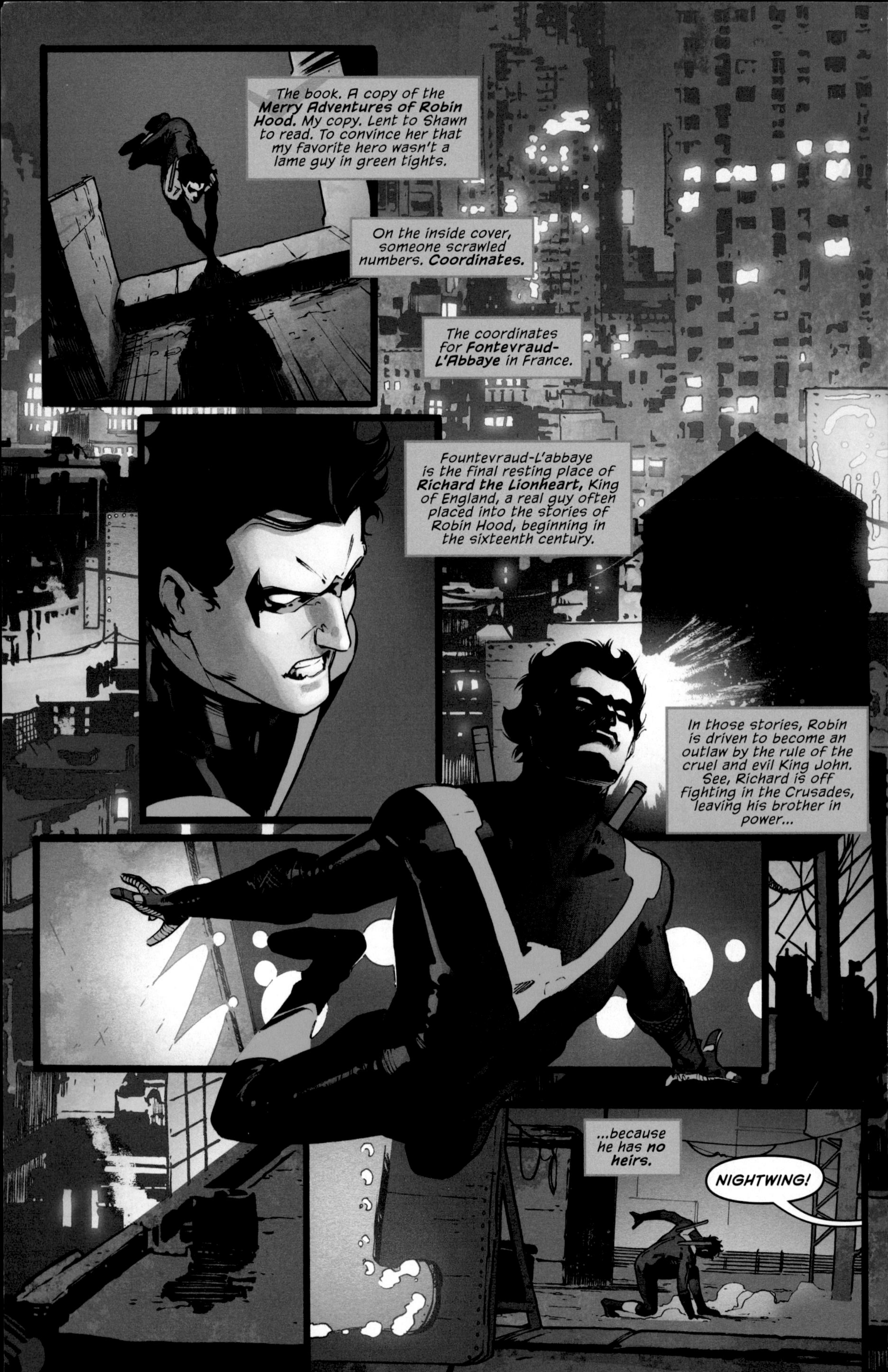
The book. A copy of the Merry Adventures of Robin Hood. My copy. Lent to Shawn to read. To convince her that my favorite hero wasn't a lame guy in green tights.
On the inside cover, someone scrawled numbers. Coordinates.
The coordinates for Fontevraud-L'Abbaye in France.
Fountevraud-L'abbaye is the final resting place of Richard the Lionheart, King of England, a real guy often placed into the stories of Robin Hood, beginning in the sixteenth century.
In those stories, Robin is driven to become an outlaw by the rule of the cruel and evil King John. See, Richard is off fighting in the Crusades, leaving his brother in power...
...because he has no heirs.
NIGHTWING!

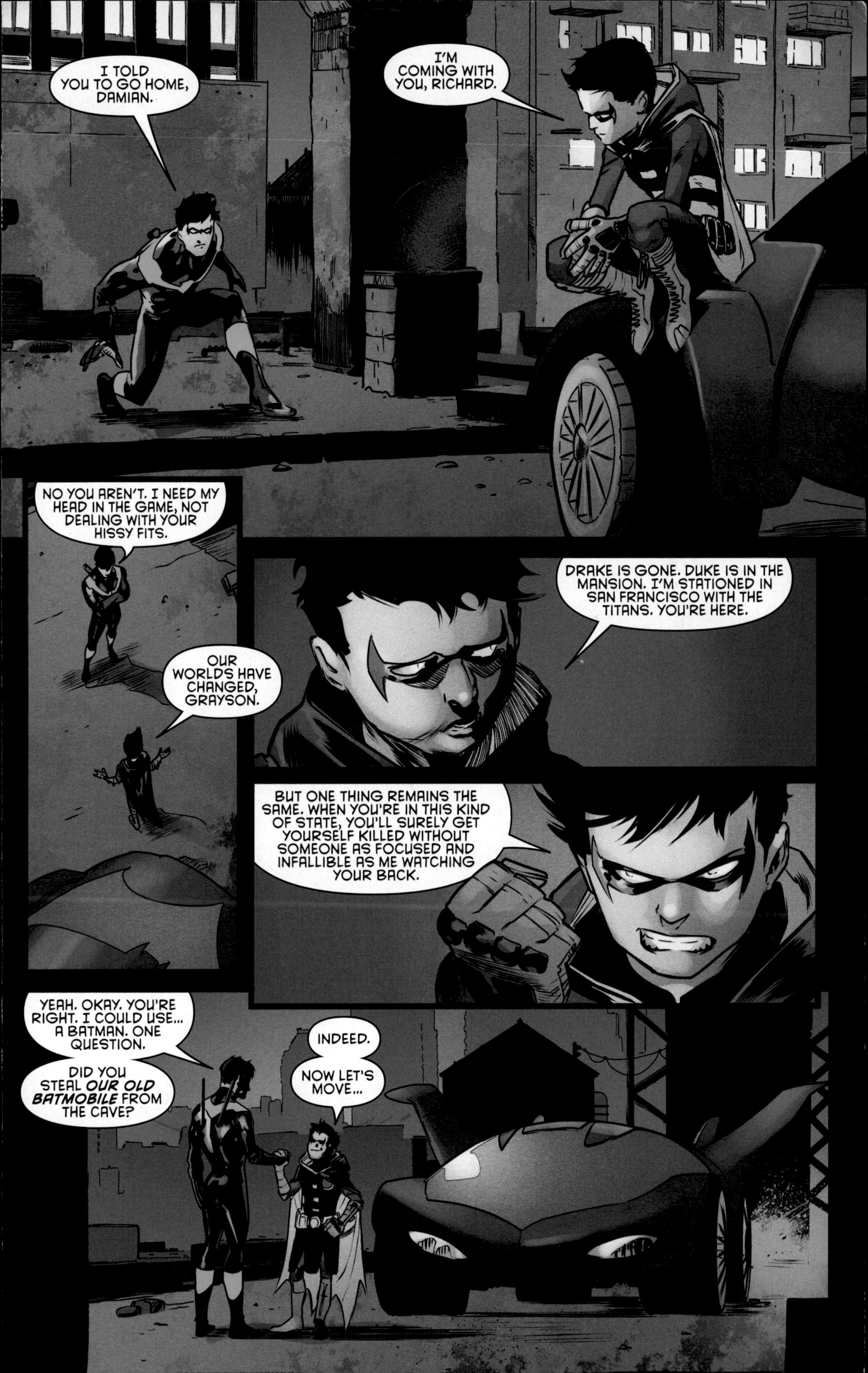
I TOLD YOU TO GO HOME, DAMIAN.
I'M COMING WITH YOU, RICHARD.
NO YOU AREN'T. I NEED MY HEAD IN THE GAME, NOT DEALING WITH YOUR HISSY FITS.
OUR WORLDS HAVE CHANGED, GRAYSON.
DRAKE IS GONE. DUKE IS IN THE MANSION. I'M STATIONED IN SAN FRANCISCO WITH THE TITANS. YOU'RE HERE.
BUT ONE THING REMAINS THE SAME. WHEN YOU'RE IN THIS KIND OF STATE, YOU'LL SURELY GET YOURSELF KILLED WITHOUT SOMEONE AS FOCUSED AND INFALLIBLE AS ME WATCHING YOUR BACK.
YEAH. OKAY. YOU'RE RIGHT. I COULD USE... A BATMAN. ONE QUESTION.
DID YOU STEAL ***OUR OLD BATMOBILE*** FROM THE CAVE?
INDEED.
NOW LET'S MOVE...

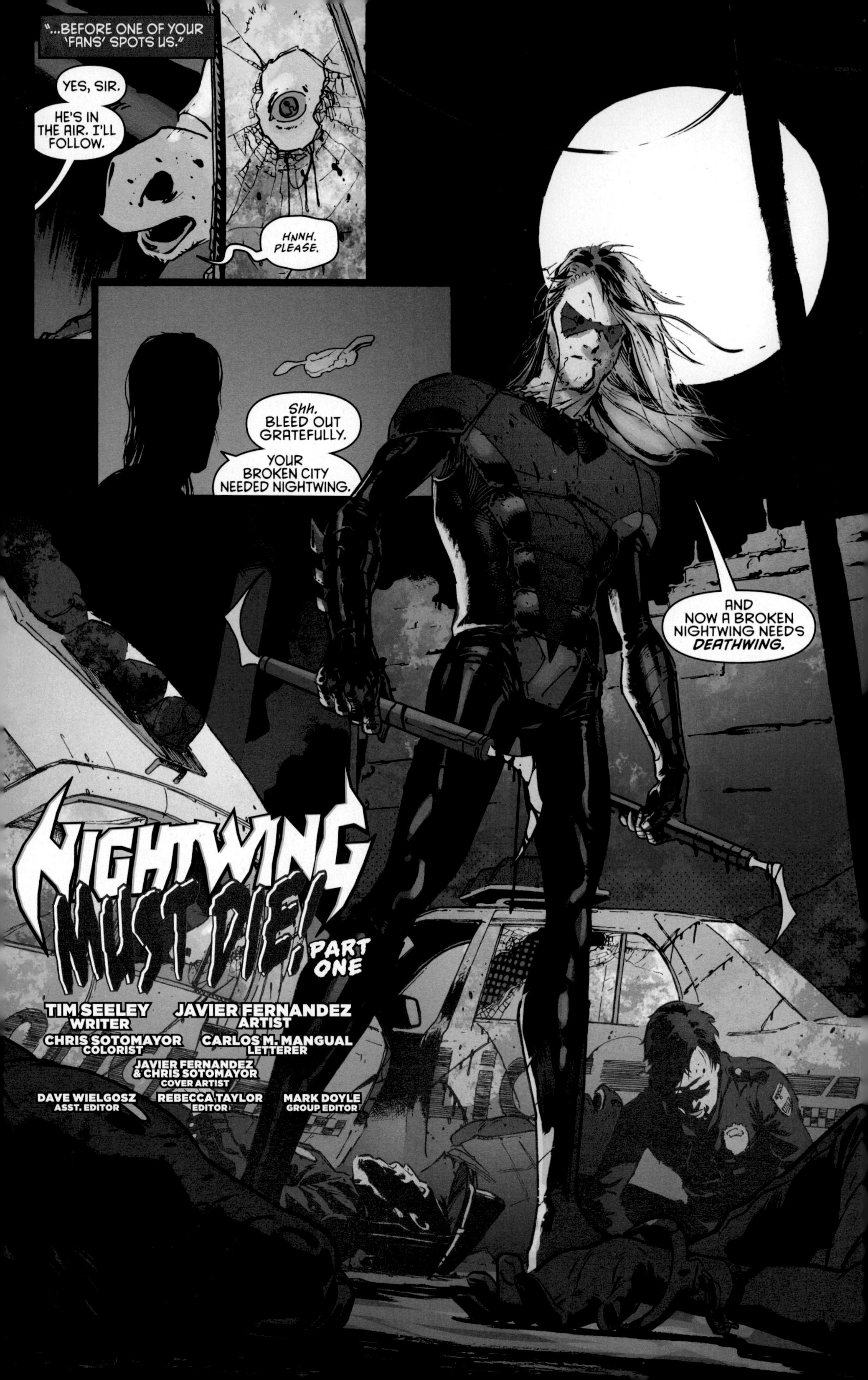

"...BEFORE ONE OF YOUR 'FANS' SPOTS US."
YES, SIR.
HE'S IN THE AIR. I'LL FOLLOW.
HNNH. PLEASE.
Shh. BLEED OUT GRATEFULLY.
YOUR BROKEN CITY NEEDED NIGHTWING.
AND NOW A BROKEN NIGHTWING NEEDS DEATHWING.
NIGHTWING MUST DIE! PART ONE
TIM SEELEY WRITER
JAVIER FERNANDEZ ARTIST
CHRIS SOTOMAYOR COLORIST
CARLOS M. MANGUAL LETTERER
JAVIER FERNANDEZ & CHRIS SOTOMAYOR COVER ARTIST
DAVE WIELGOSZ ASST. EDITOR
REBECCA TAYLOR EDITOR
MARK DOYLE GROUP EDITOR

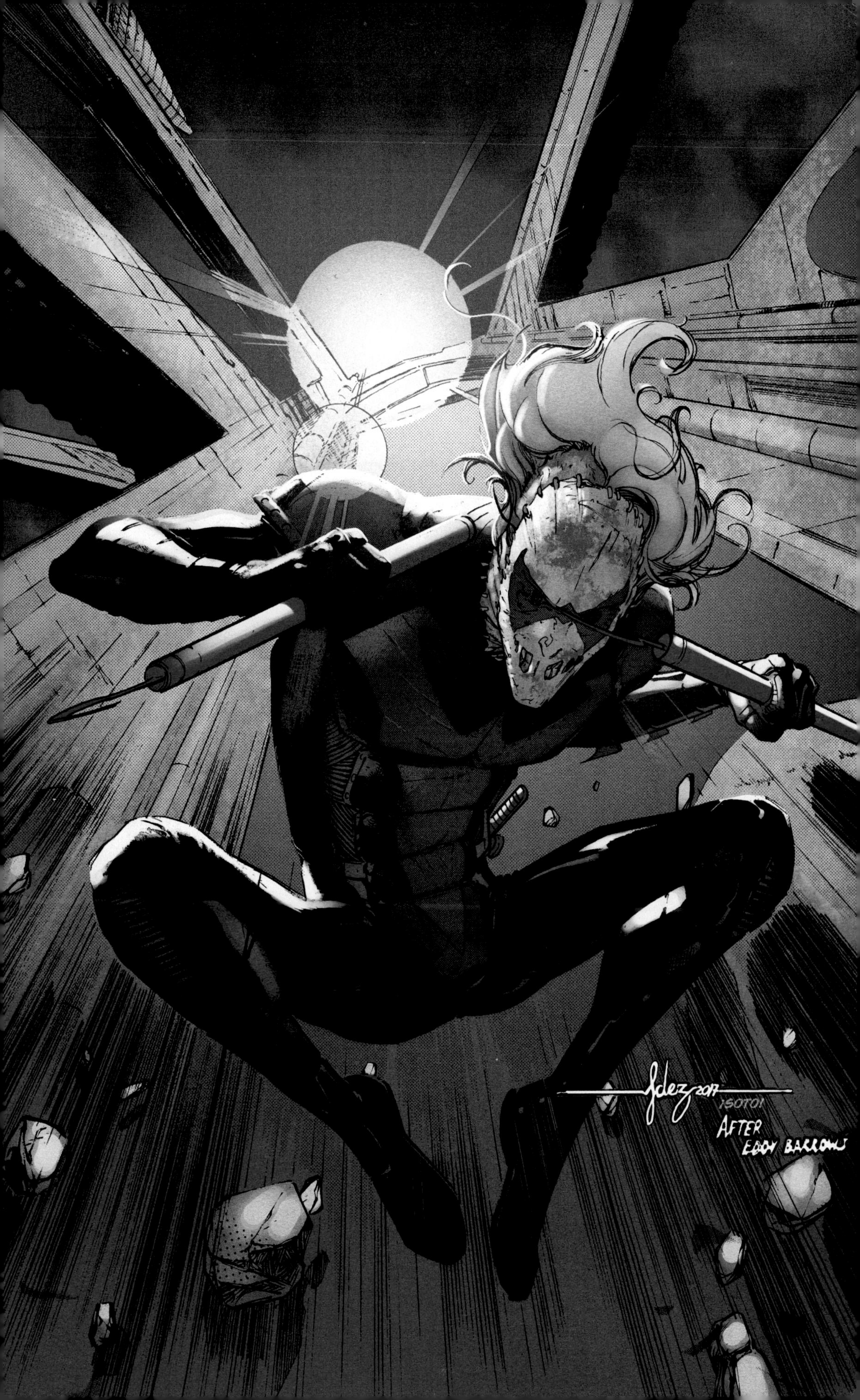
AFTER EDDY BARROWS

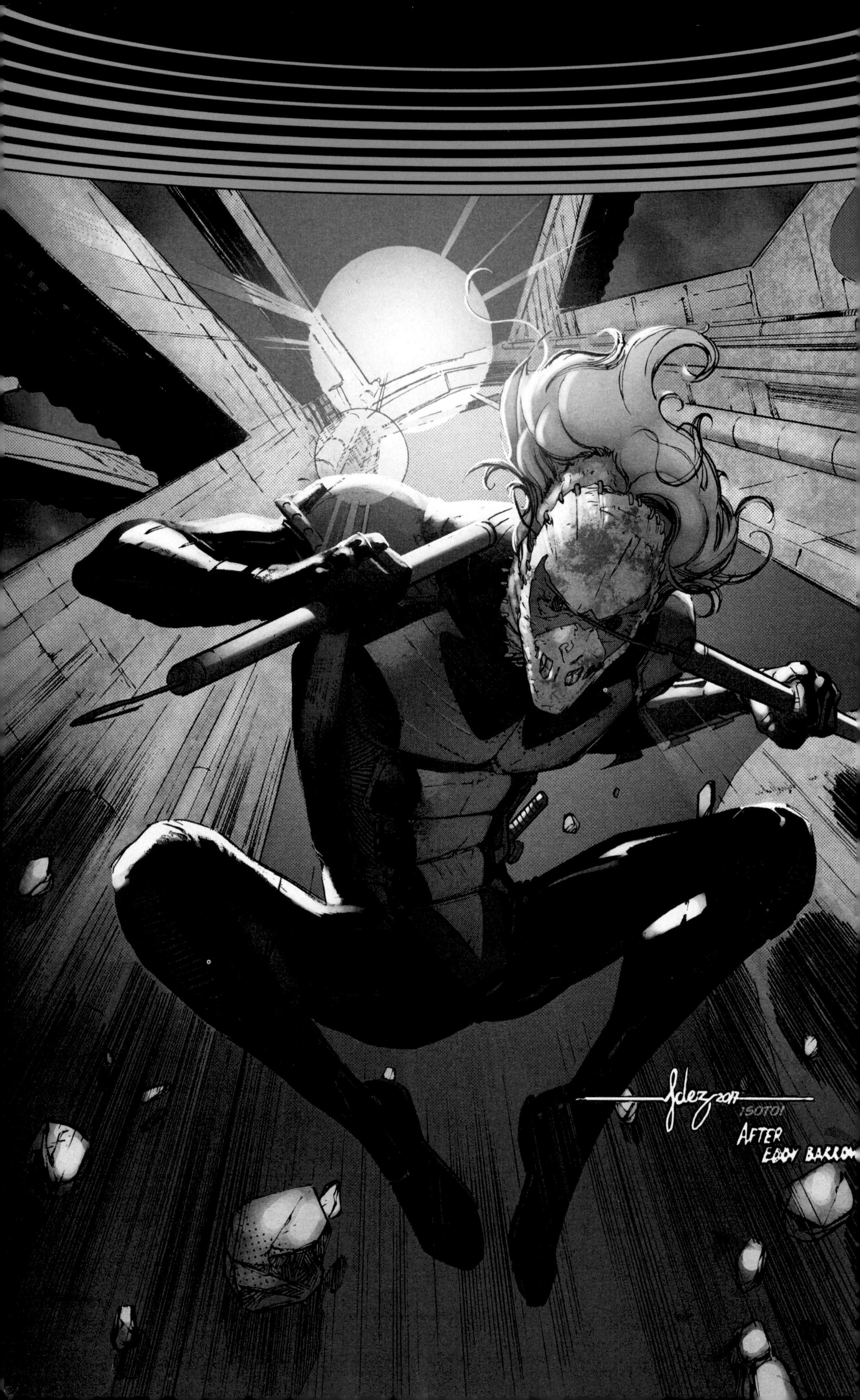
Fdez 2017
¡SOTO!
AFTER
EDDY BARROW

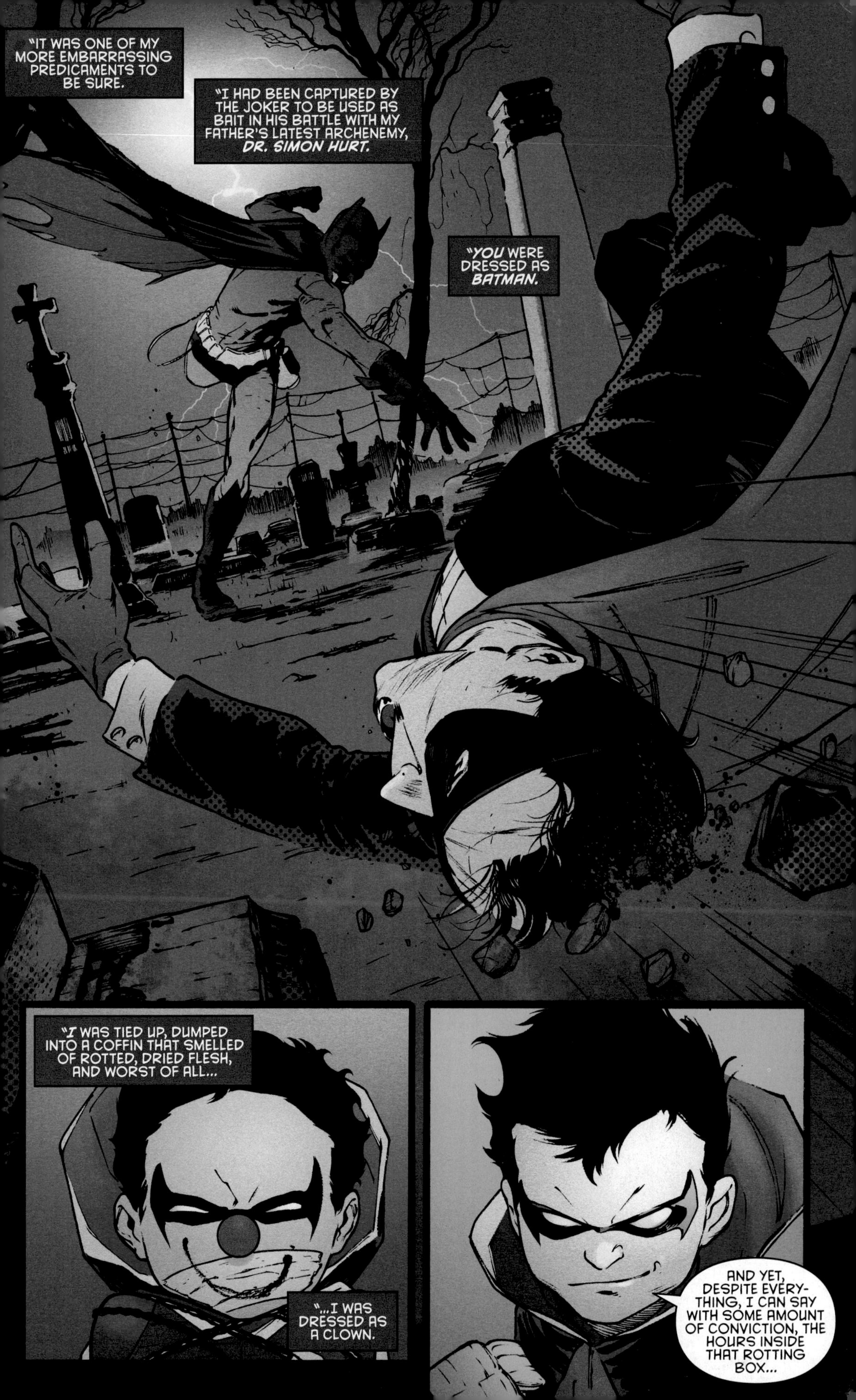
"IT WAS ONE OF MY MORE EMBARRASSING PREDICAMENTS TO BE SURE.
"I HAD BEEN CAPTURED BY THE JOKER TO BE USED AS BAIT IN HIS BATTLE WITH MY FATHER'S LATEST ARCHENEMY, DR. SIMON HURT.
"YOU WERE DRESSED AS BATMAN.
"I WAS TIED UP, DUMPED INTO A COFFIN THAT SMELLED OF ROTTED, DRIED FLESH, AND WORST OF ALL...
"...I WAS DRESSED AS A CLOWN.
AND YET, DESPITE EVERY-THING, I CAN SAY WITH SOME AMOUNT OF CONVICTION, THE HOURS INSIDE THAT ROTTING BOX...

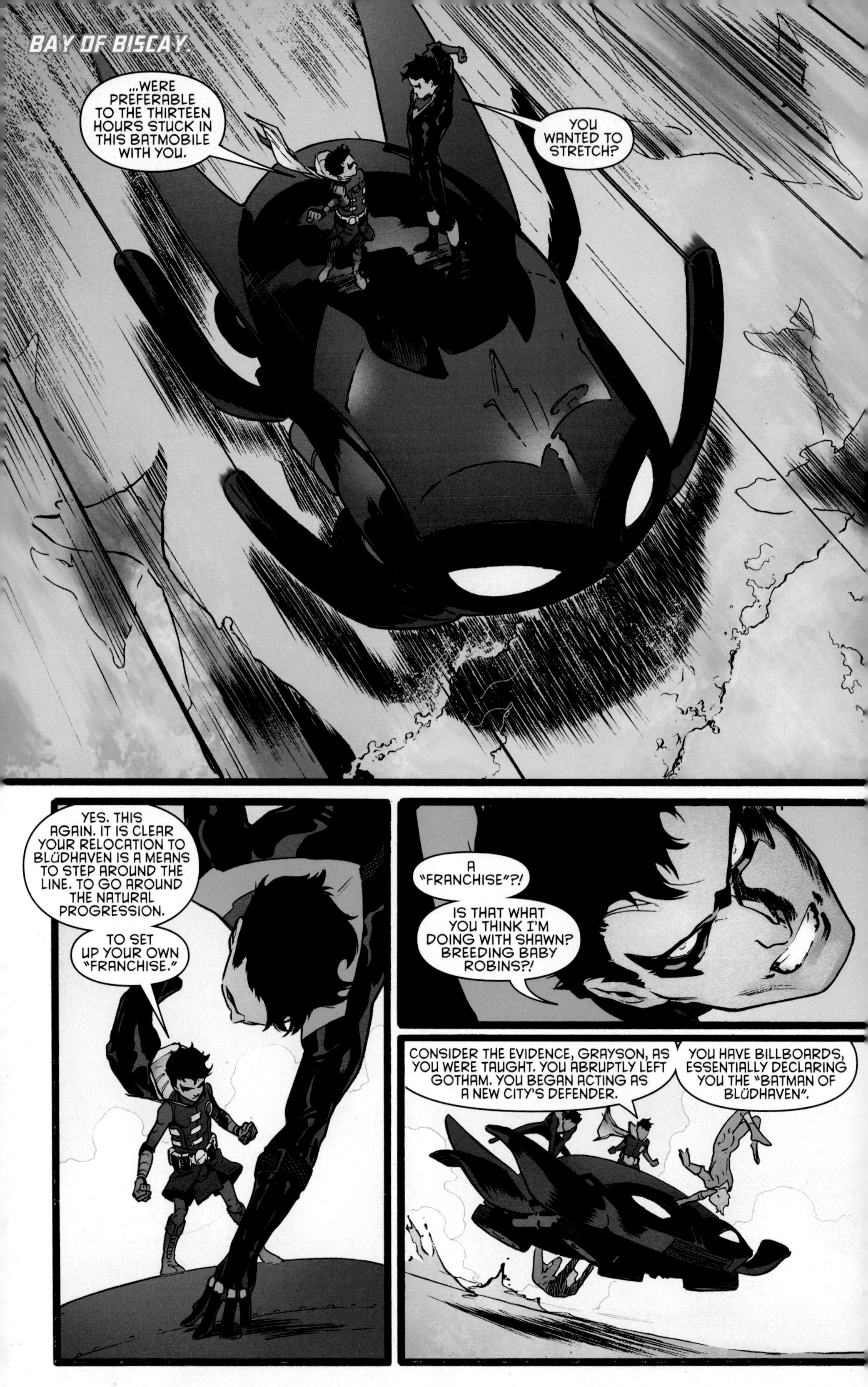
BAY OF BISCAY.
...WERE PREFERABLE TO THE THIRTEEN HOURS STUCK IN THIS BATMOBILE WITH YOU.
YOU WANTED TO STRETCH?
YES. THIS AGAIN. IT IS CLEAR YOUR RELOCATION TO BLÜDHAVEN IS A MEANS TO STEP AROUND THE LINE. TO GO AROUND THE NATURAL PROGRESSION.
TO SET UP YOUR OWN "FRANCHISE."
A "FRANCHISE"?!
IS THAT WHAT YOU THINK I'M DOING WITH SHAWN? BREEDING BABY ROBINS?!
CONSIDER THE EVIDENCE, GRAYSON, AS YOU WERE TAUGHT. YOU ABRUPTLY LEFT GOTHAM. YOU BEGAN ACTING AS A NEW CITY'S DEFENDER.
YOU HAVE BILLBOARDS, ESSENTIALLY DECLARING YOU THE "BATMAN OF BLÜDHAVEN".

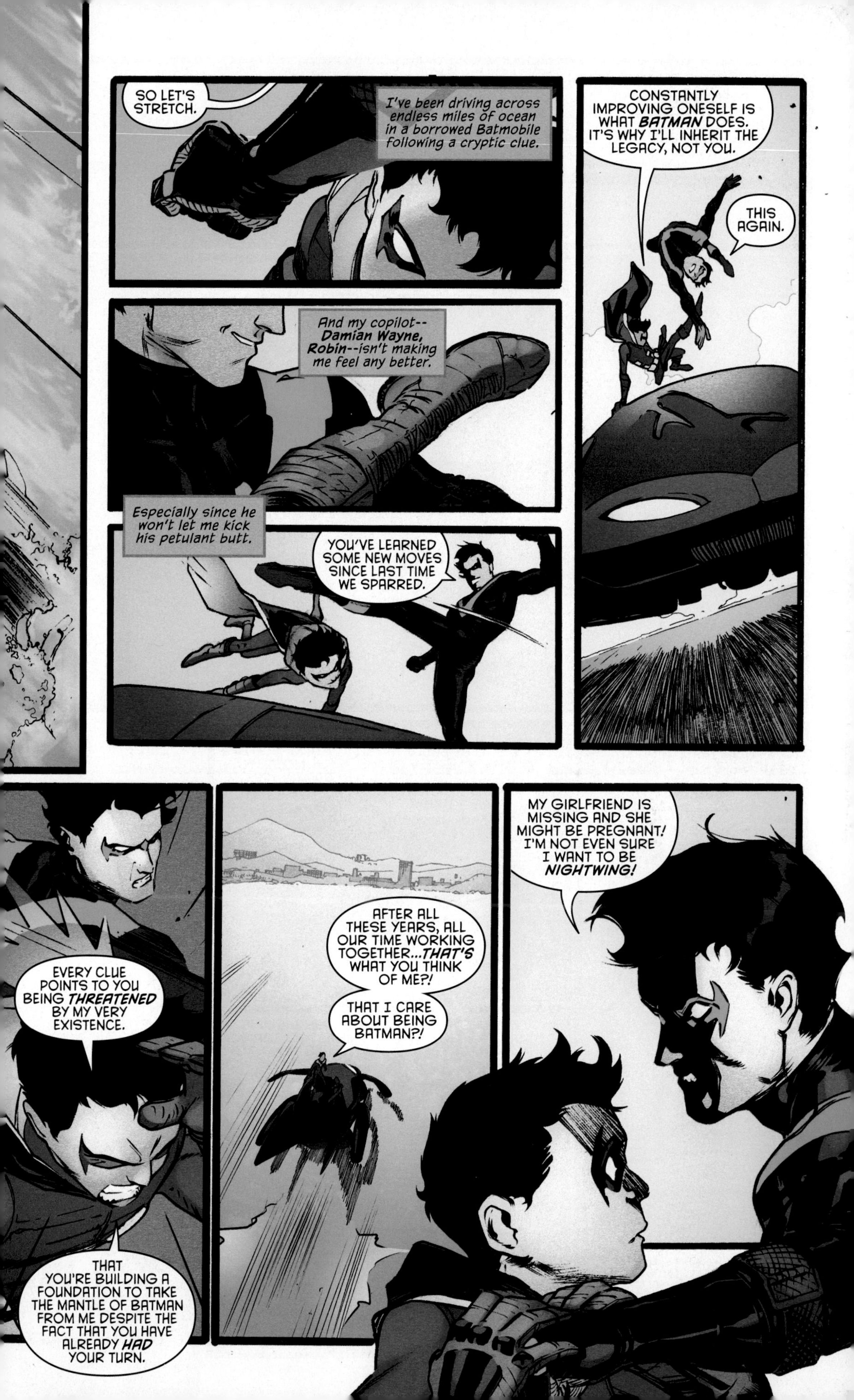
SO LET'S STRETCH.
I've been driving across endless miles of ocean in a borrowed Batmobile following a cryptic clue.
And my copilot--Damian Wayne, Robin--isn't making me feel any better.
Especially since he won't let me kick his petulant butt.
YOU'VE LEARNED SOME NEW MOVES SINCE LAST TIME WE SPARRED.
CONSTANTLY IMPROVING ONESELF IS WHAT BATMAN DOES. IT'S WHY I'LL INHERIT THE LEGACY, NOT YOU.
THIS AGAIN.
EVERY CLUE POINTS TO YOU BEING THREATENED BY MY VERY EXISTENCE.
THAT YOU'RE BUILDING A FOUNDATION TO TAKE THE MANTLE OF BATMAN FROM ME DESPITE THE FACT THAT YOU HAVE ALREADY HAD YOUR TURN.
AFTER ALL THESE YEARS, ALL OUR TIME WORKING TOGETHER...THAT'S WHAT YOU THINK OF ME?!
THAT I CARE ABOUT BEING BATMAN?!
MY GIRLFRIEND IS MISSING AND SHE MIGHT BE PREGNANT! I'M NOT EVEN SURE I WANT TO BE NIGHTWING!

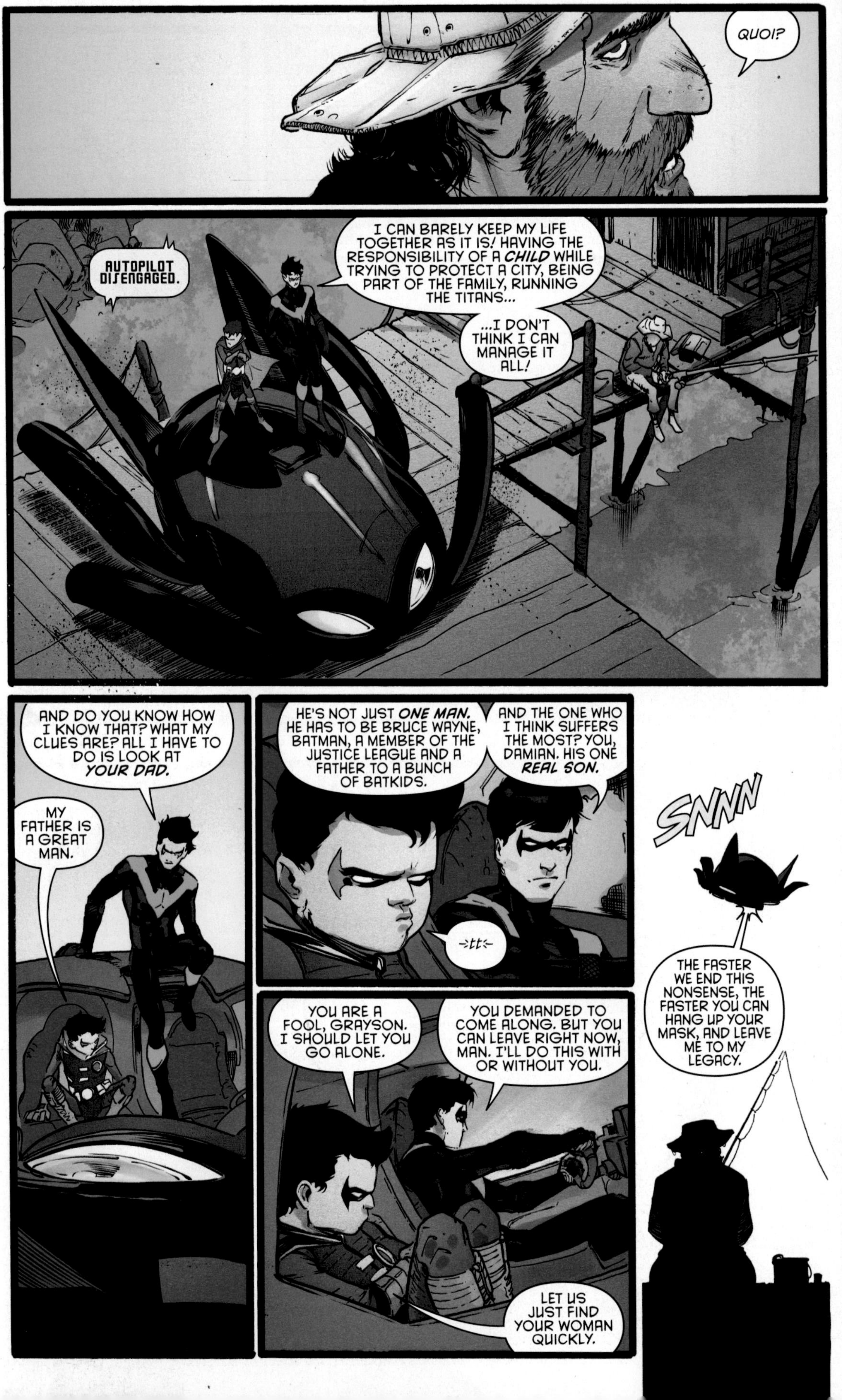
QUOI?
AUTOPILOT DISENGAGED.
I CAN BARELY KEEP MY LIFE TOGETHER AS IT IS! HAVING THE RESPONSIBILITY OF A CHILD WHILE TRYING TO PROTECT A CITY, BEING PART OF THE FAMILY, RUNNING THE TITANS...
...I DON'T THINK I CAN MANAGE IT ALL!
AND DO YOU KNOW HOW I KNOW THAT? WHAT MY CLUES ARE? ALL I HAVE TO DO IS LOOK AT YOUR DAD.
MY FATHER IS A GREAT MAN.
HE'S NOT JUST ONE MAN. HE HAS TO BE BRUCE WAYNE, BATMAN, A MEMBER OF THE JUSTICE LEAGUE AND A FATHER TO A BUNCH OF BATKIDS.
AND THE ONE WHO I THINK SUFFERS THE MOST? YOU, DAMIAN. HIS ONE REAL SON.
-tt-
YOU ARE A FOOL, GRAYSON. I SHOULD LET YOU GO ALONE.
YOU DEMANDED TO COME ALONG. BUT YOU CAN LEAVE RIGHT NOW, MAN. I'LL DO THIS WITH OR WITHOUT YOU.
LET US JUST FIND YOUR WOMAN QUICKLY.
SNNN
THE FASTER WE END THIS NONSENSE, THE FASTER YOU CAN HANG UP YOUR MASK, AND LEAVE ME TO MY LEGACY.

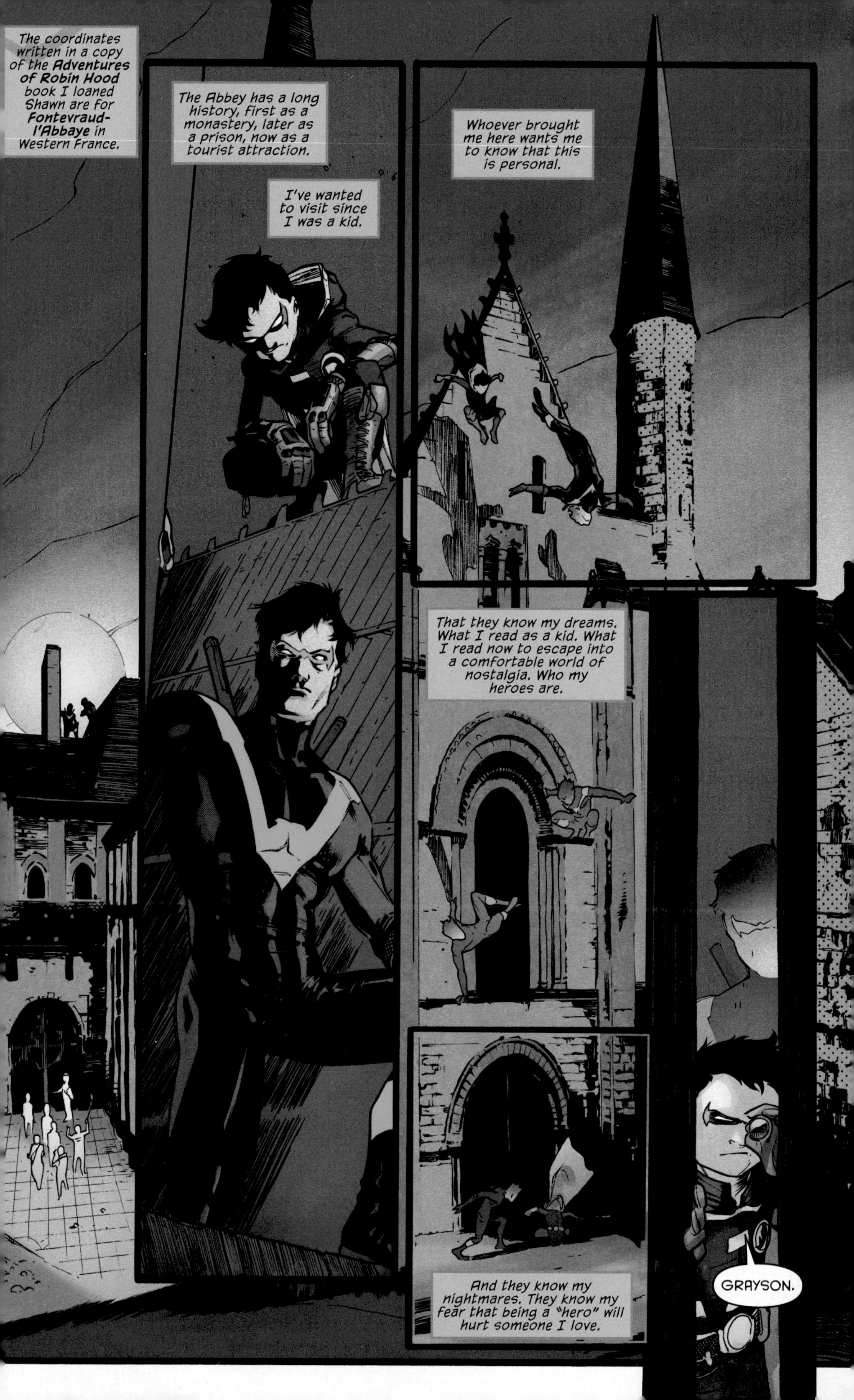
The coordinates written in a copy of the Adventures of Robin Hood book I loaned Shawn are for Fontevraud-l'Abbaye in Western France.
The Abbey has a long history, first as a monastery, later as a prison, now as a tourist attraction.
I've wanted to visit since I was a kid.
Whoever brought me here wants me to know that this is personal.
That they know my dreams. What I read as a kid. What I read now to escape into a comfortable world of nostalgia. Who my heroes are.
And they know my nightmares. They know my fear that being a "hero" will hurt someone I love.
GRAYSON.

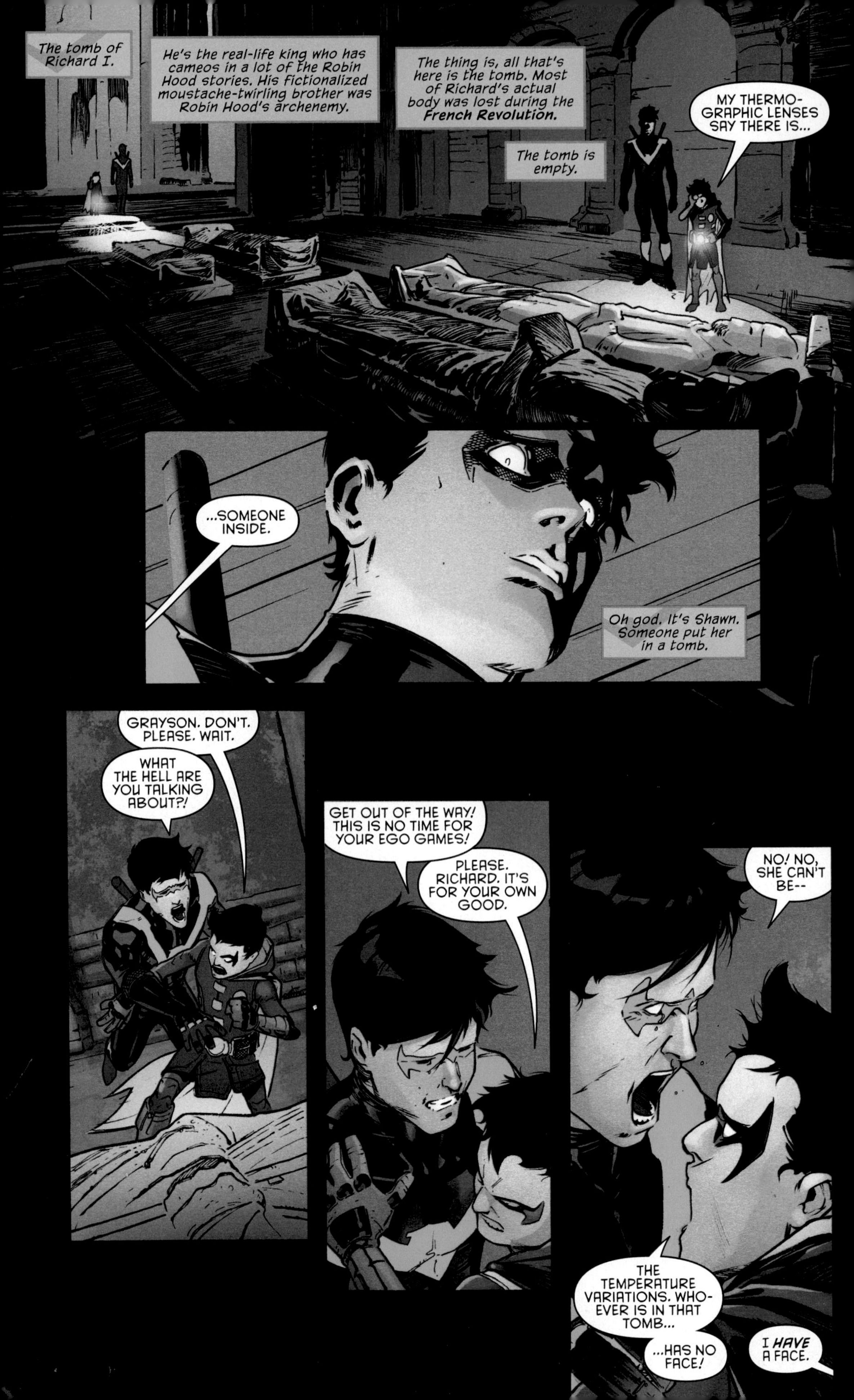
The tomb of Richard I.
He's the real-life king who has cameos in a lot of the Robin Hood stories. His fictionalized moustache-twirling brother was Robin Hood's archenemy.
The thing is, all that's here is the tomb. Most of Richard's actual body was lost during the French Revolution.
The tomb is empty.
MY THERMO-GRAPHIC LENSES SAY THERE IS...
...SOMEONE INSIDE.
Oh god. It's Shawn. Someone put her in a tomb.
GRAYSON. DON'T. PLEASE. WAIT.
WHAT THE HELL ARE YOU TALKING ABOUT?!
GET OUT OF THE WAY! THIS IS NO TIME FOR YOUR EGO GAMES!
PLEASE. RICHARD. IT'S FOR YOUR OWN GOOD.
NO! NO, SHE CAN'T BE--
THE TEMPERATURE VARIATIONS. WHO-EVER IS IN THAT TOMB...
...HAS NO FACE!
I HAVE A FACE.

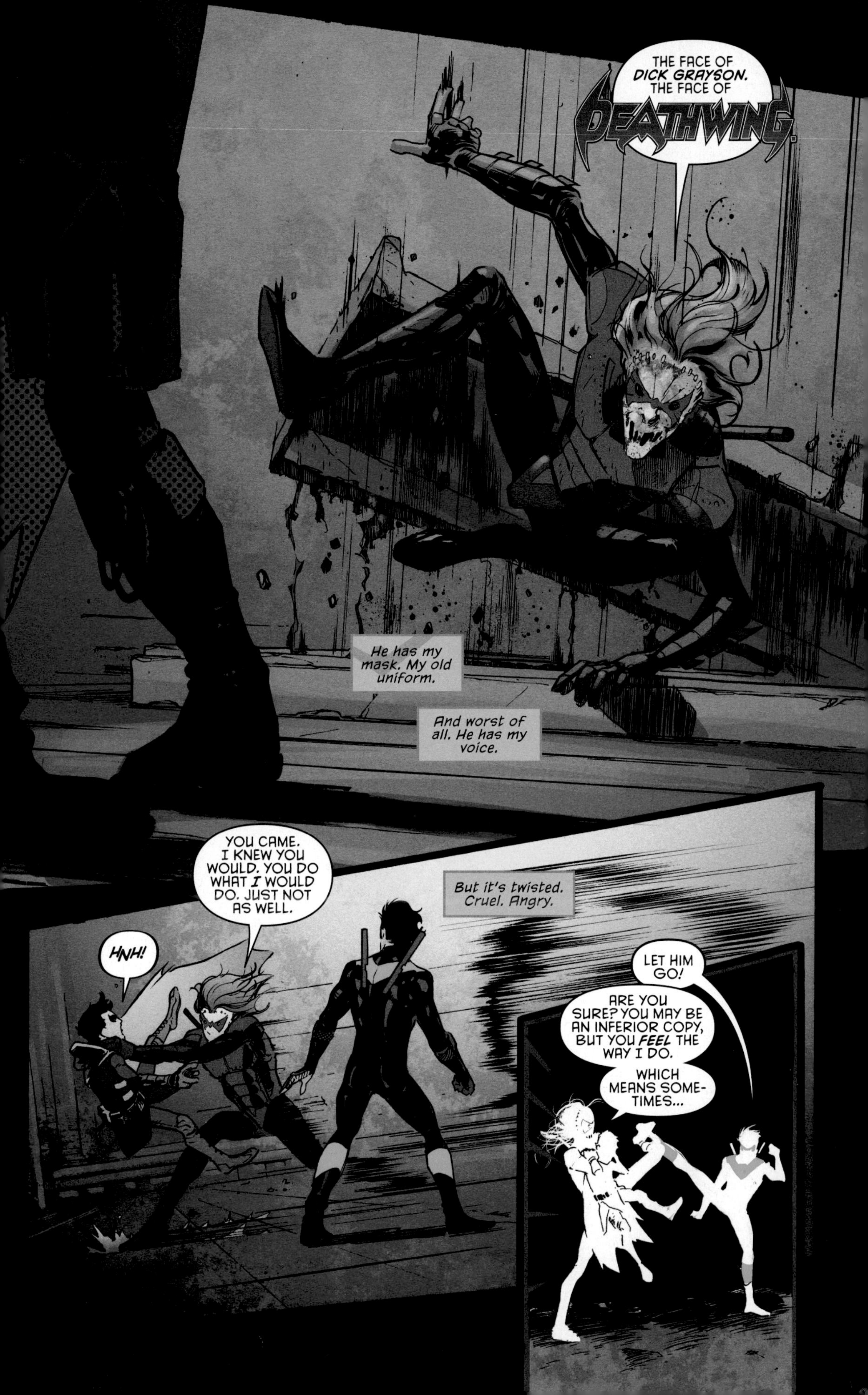
THE FACE OF DICK GRAYSON. THE FACE OF DEATHWING.
He has my mask. My old uniform.
And worst of all. He has my voice.
YOU CAME. I KNEW YOU WOULD. YOU DO WHAT I WOULD DO. JUST NOT AS WELL.
But it's twisted. Cruel. Angry.
HNH!
LET HIM GO!
ARE YOU SURE? YOU MAY BE AN INFERIOR COPY, BUT YOU FEEL THE WAY I DO.
WHICH MEANS SOME-TIMES...

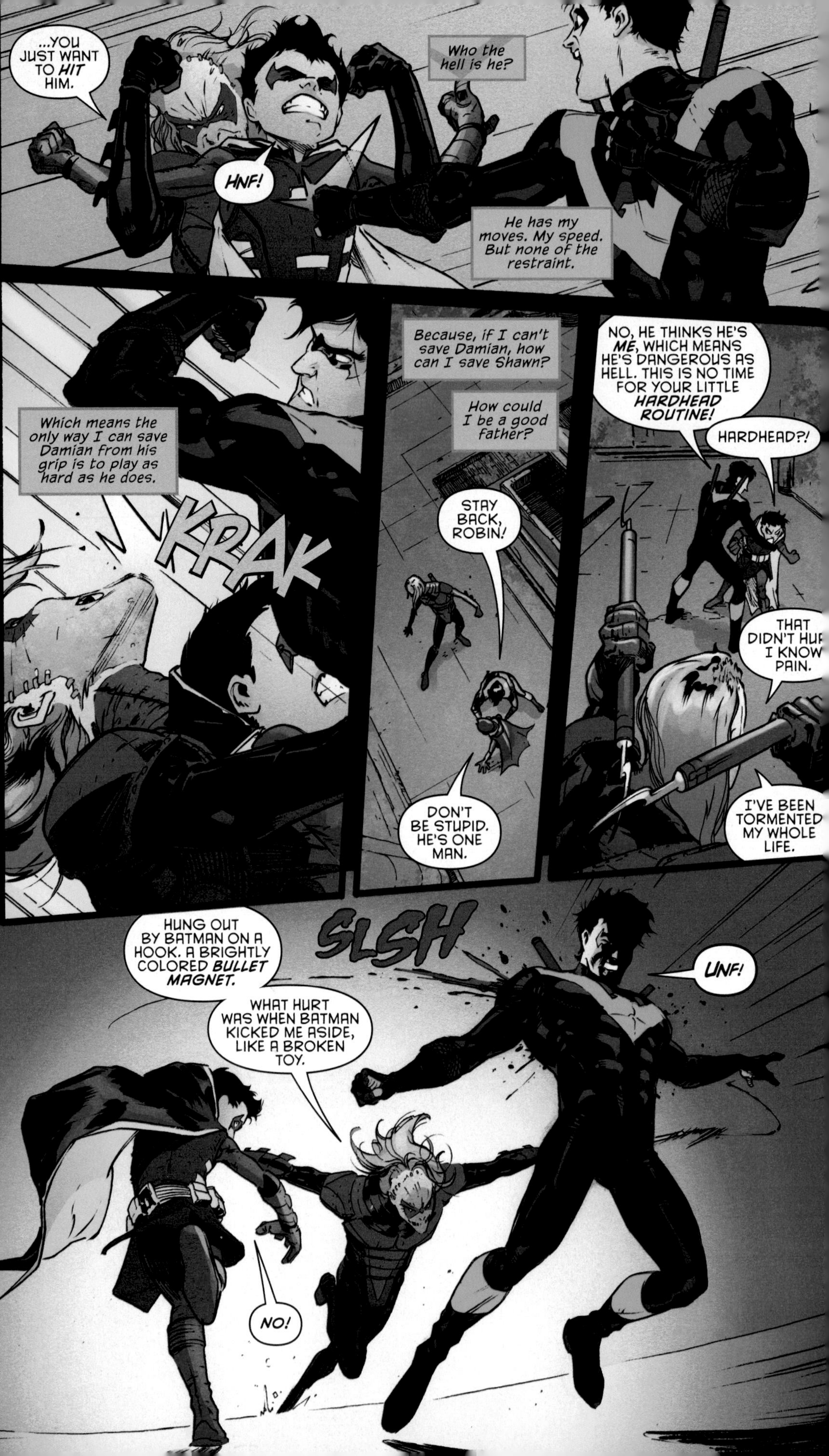
...YOU JUST WANT TO *HIT* HIM.
Who the hell is he?
HNF!
He has my moves. My speed. But none of the restraint.
Which means the only way I can save Damian from his grip is to play as hard as he does.
KRAK
Because, if I can't save Damian, how can I save Shawn?
How could I be a good father?
STAY BACK, ROBIN!
DON'T BE STUPID. HE'S ONE MAN.
NO, HE THINKS HE'S *ME*, WHICH MEANS HE'S DANGEROUS AS HELL. THIS IS NO TIME FOR YOUR LITTLE *HARDHEAD ROUTINE!*
HARDHEAD?!
THAT DIDN'T HUR I KNOW PAIN.
I'VE BEEN TORMENTED MY WHOLE LIFE.
HUNG OUT BY BATMAN ON A HOOK. A BRIGHTLY COLORED *BULLET MAGNET.*
WHAT HURT WAS WHEN BATMAN KICKED ME ASIDE, LIKE A BROKEN TOY.
SLSH
UNF!
NO!

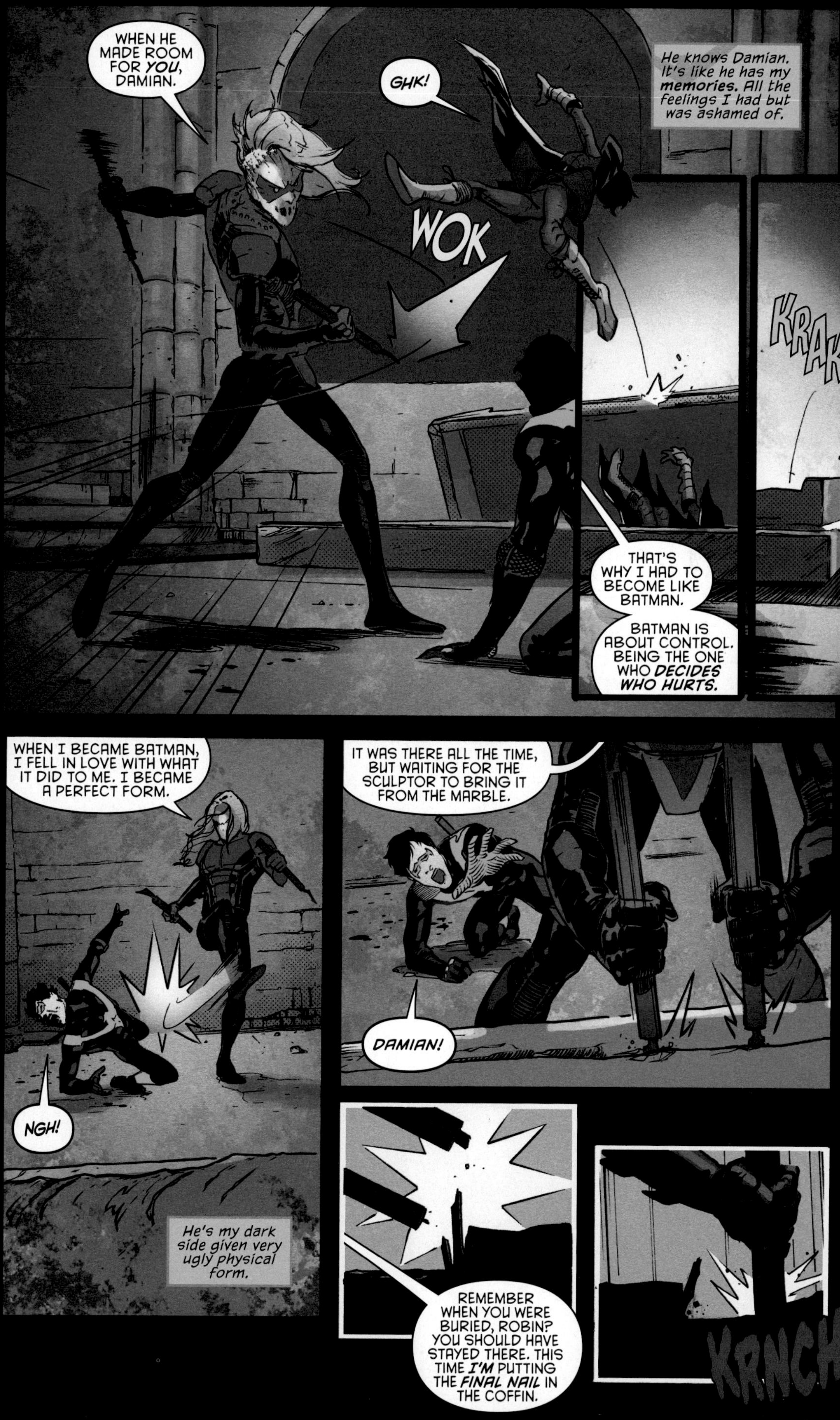
WHEN HE MADE ROOM FOR YOU, DAMIAN.
GHK!
He knows Damian. It's like he has my memories. All the feelings I had but was ashamed of.
WOK
KRAK
THAT'S WHY I HAD TO BECOME LIKE BATMAN.
BATMAN IS ABOUT CONTROL. BEING THE ONE WHO DECIDES WHO HURTS.
WHEN I BECAME BATMAN, I FELL IN LOVE WITH WHAT IT DID TO ME. I BECAME A PERFECT FORM.
NGH!
He's my dark side given very ugly physical form.
IT WAS THERE ALL THE TIME, BUT WAITING FOR THE SCULPTOR TO BRING IT FROM THE MARBLE.
DAMIAN!
REMEMBER WHEN YOU WERE BURIED, ROBIN? YOU SHOULD HAVE STAYED THERE. THIS TIME I'M PUTTING THE FINAL NAIL IN THE COFFIN.
KRNCH

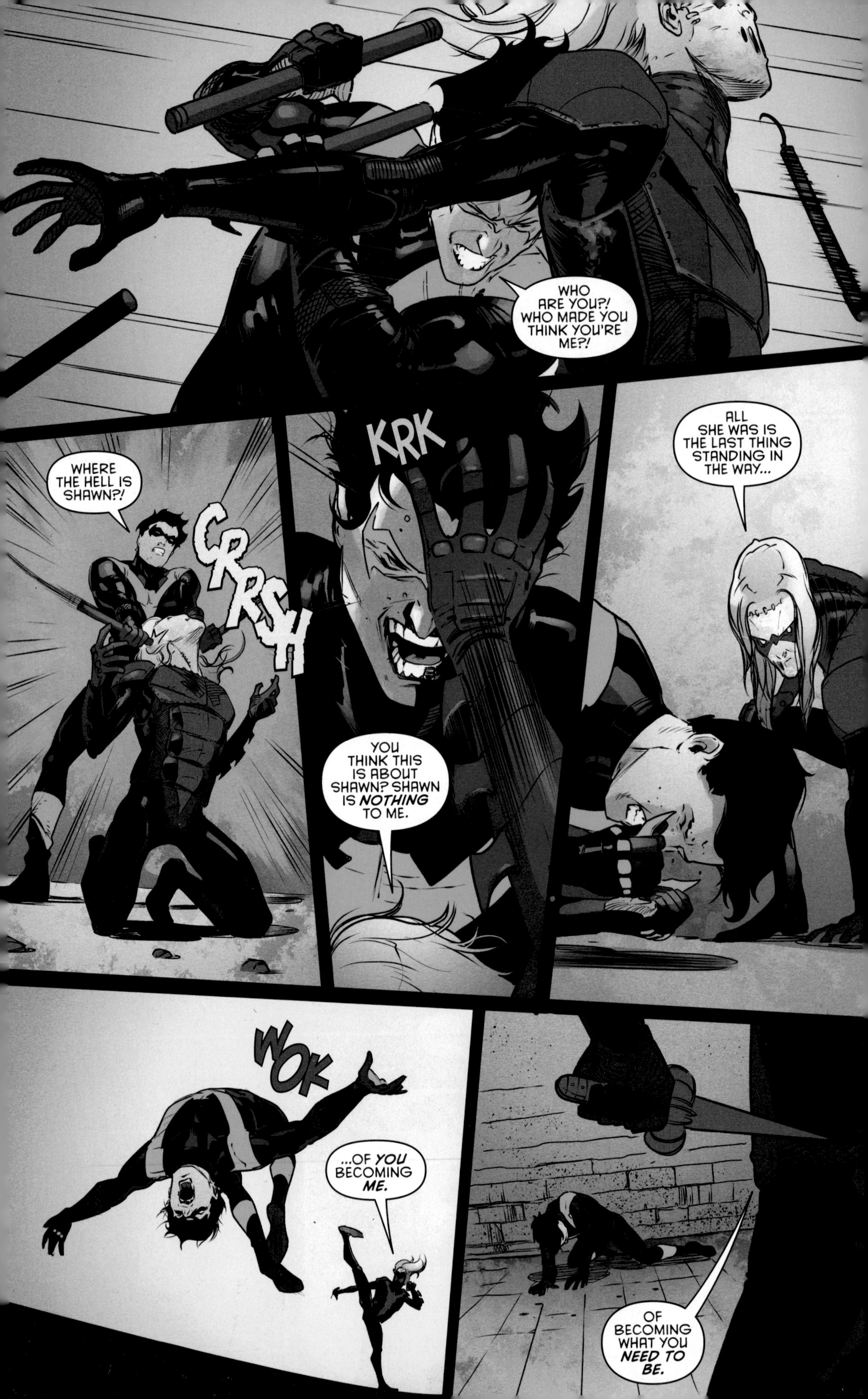
WHO ARE YOU?! WHO MADE YOU THINK YOU'RE ME?!
WHERE THE HELL IS SHAWN?!
CRSH
KRK
YOU THINK THIS IS ABOUT SHAWN? SHAWN IS *NOTHING* TO ME.
ALL SHE WAS IS THE LAST THING STANDING IN THE WAY...
WOK
...OF *YOU* BECOMING *ME.*
OF BECOMING WHAT YOU *NEED TO BE.*

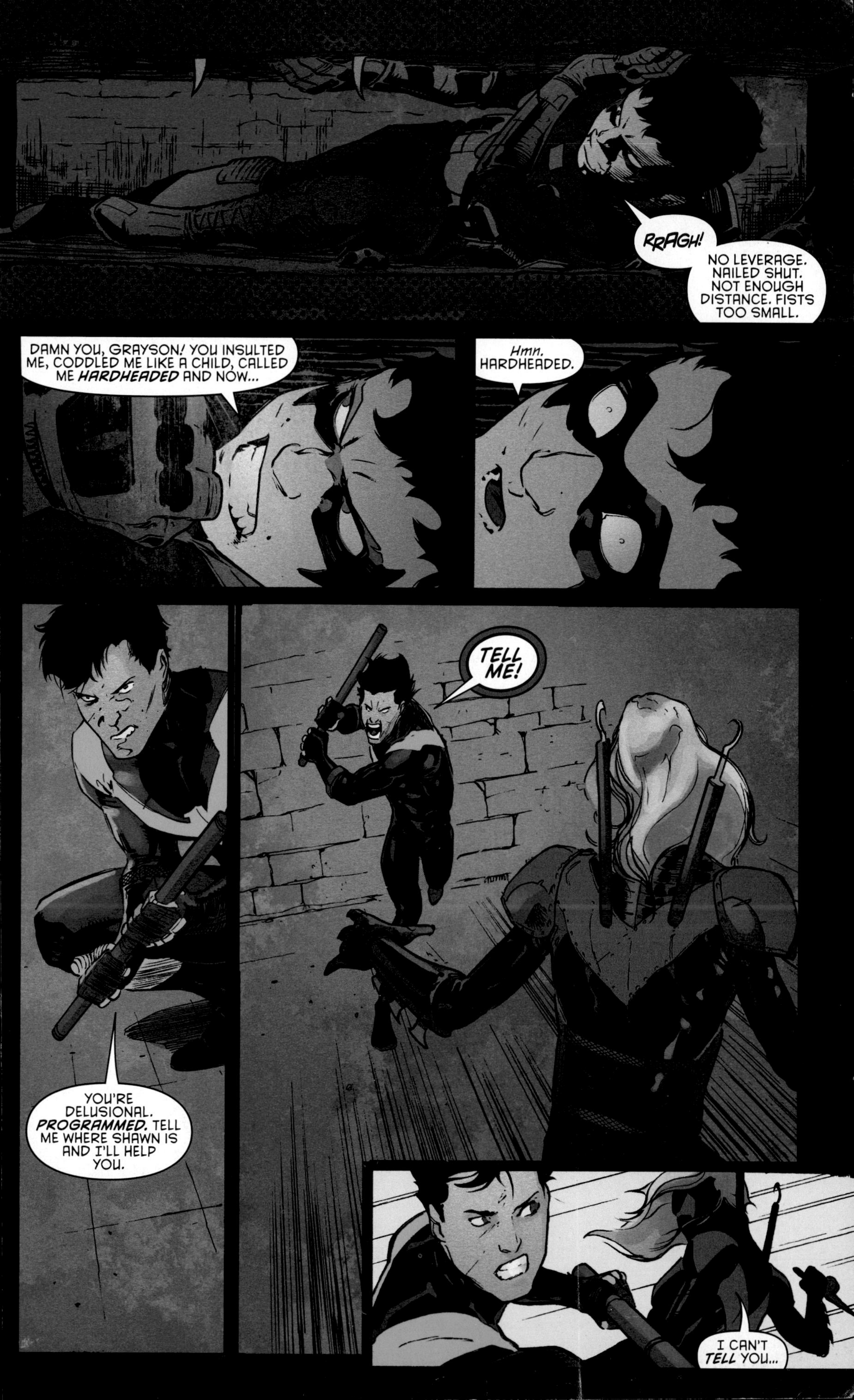
RRAGH!
NO LEVERAGE. NAILED SHUT. NOT ENOUGH DISTANCE. FISTS TOO SMALL.
DAMN YOU, GRAYSON! YOU INSULTED ME, CODDLED ME LIKE A CHILD, CALLED ME HARDHEADED AND NOW...
Hmn. HARDHEADED.
TELL ME!
YOU'RE DELUSIONAL. PROGRAMMED. TELL ME WHERE SHAWN IS AND I'LL HELP YOU.
I CAN'T TELL YOU...

...YOU NEED TO SEE WHAT WAS SHOWN TO ME. YOU NEED TO SEE WHAT'S COMING.
SLSH
The blade glints black. Like it's made out of night.
The cut doesn't hurt. Not exactly. But it feels like something is spilling out. My mind maybe.
HNGH.
GIVE IN TO THE BLOOD.
A drop of blood hangs for an eternity before my eyes.
And then it drops.
And I go with it.
All the way down.
GIVE IN...
AH.

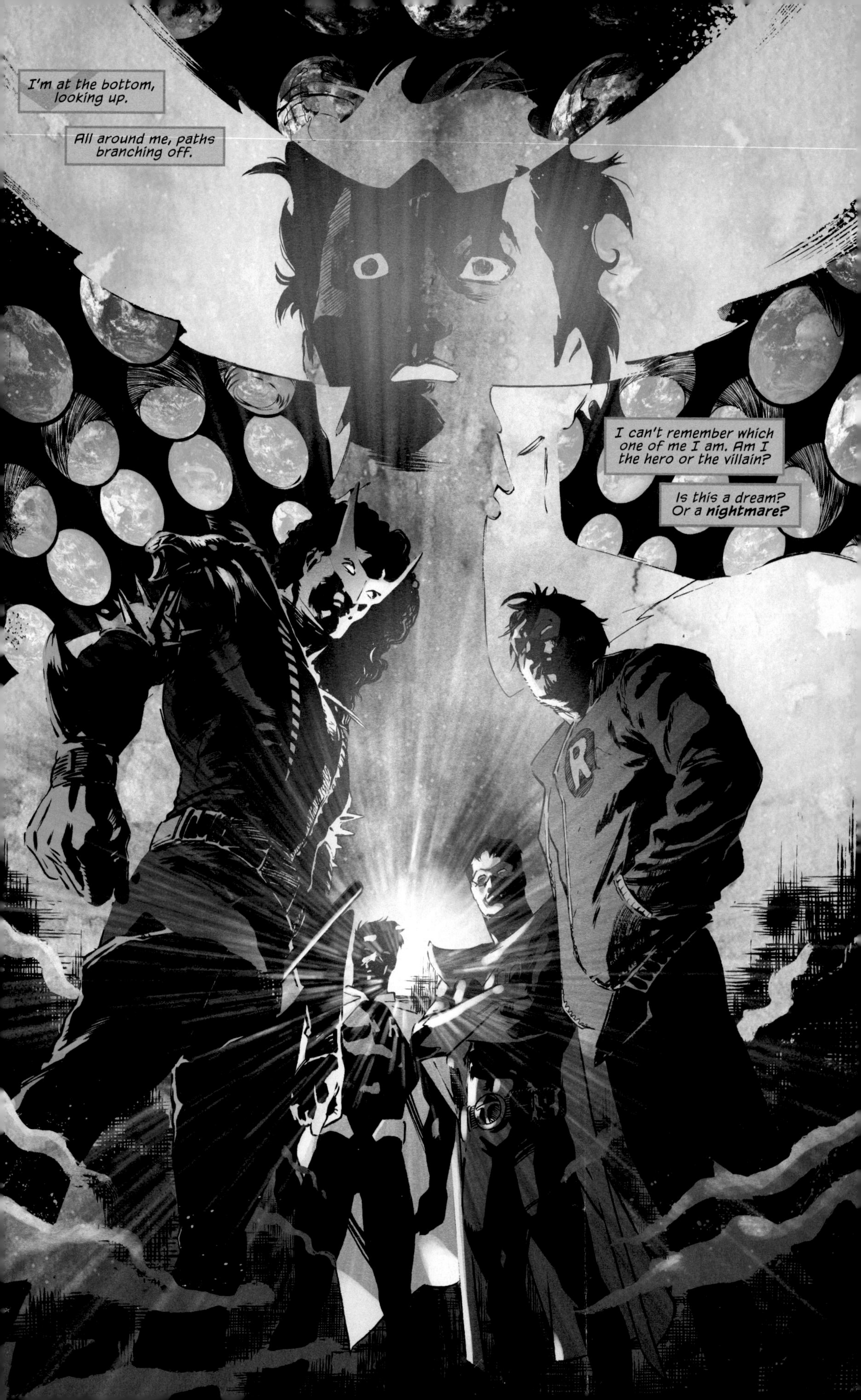
I'm at the bottom, looking up.
All around me, paths branching off.
I can't remember which one of me I am. Am I the hero or the villain?
Is this a dream? Or a nightmare?

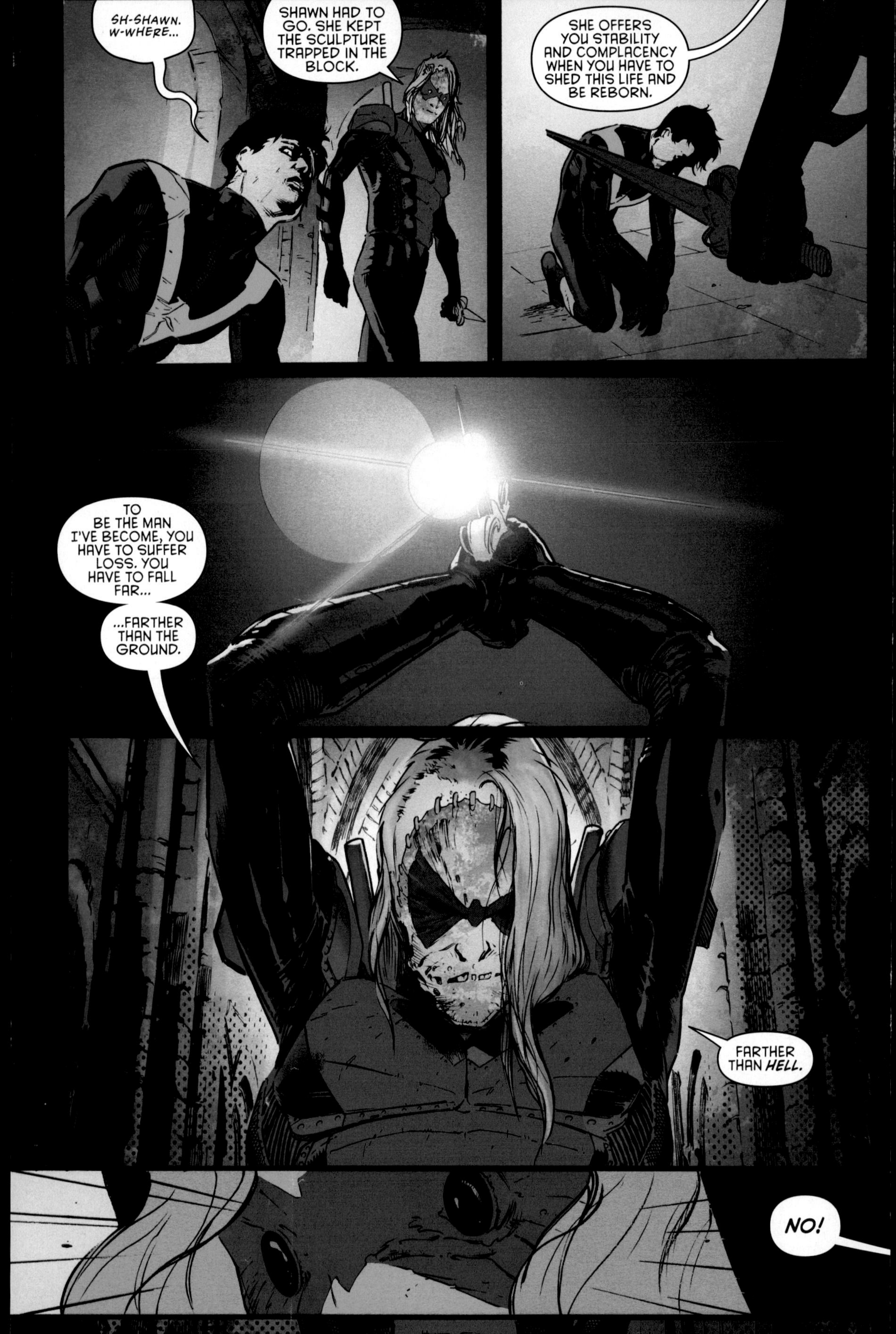
SH-SHAWN. W-WHERE...
SHAWN HAD TO GO. SHE KEPT THE SCULPTURE TRAPPED IN THE BLOCK.
SHE OFFERS YOU STABILITY AND COMPLACENCY WHEN YOU HAVE TO SHED THIS LIFE AND BE REBORN.
TO BE THE MAN I'VE BECOME, YOU HAVE TO SUFFER LOSS. YOU HAVE TO FALL FAR...
...FARTHER THAN THE GROUND.
FARTHER THAN *HELL.*
NO!

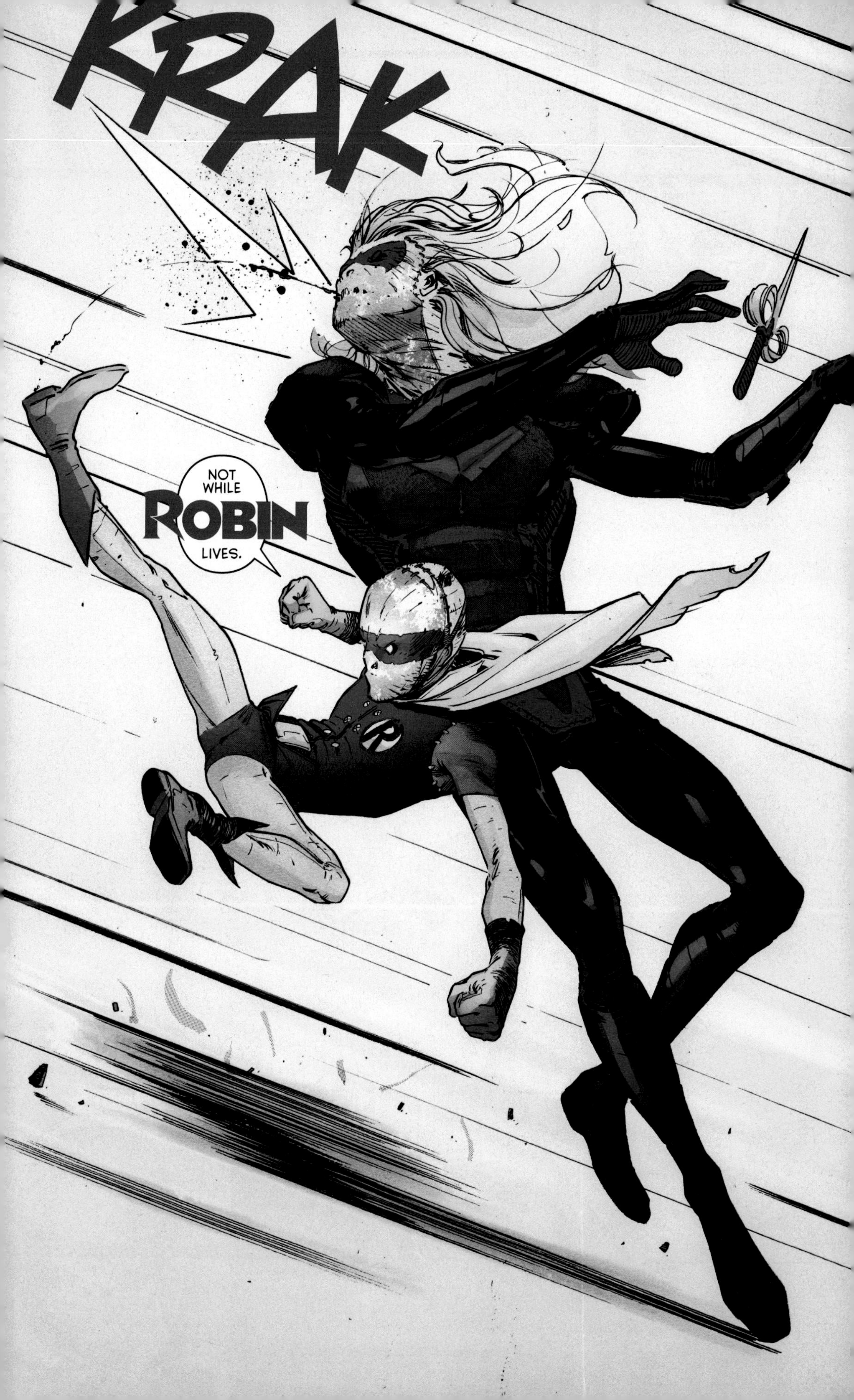
KRAK
NOT WHILE ROBIN LIVES.

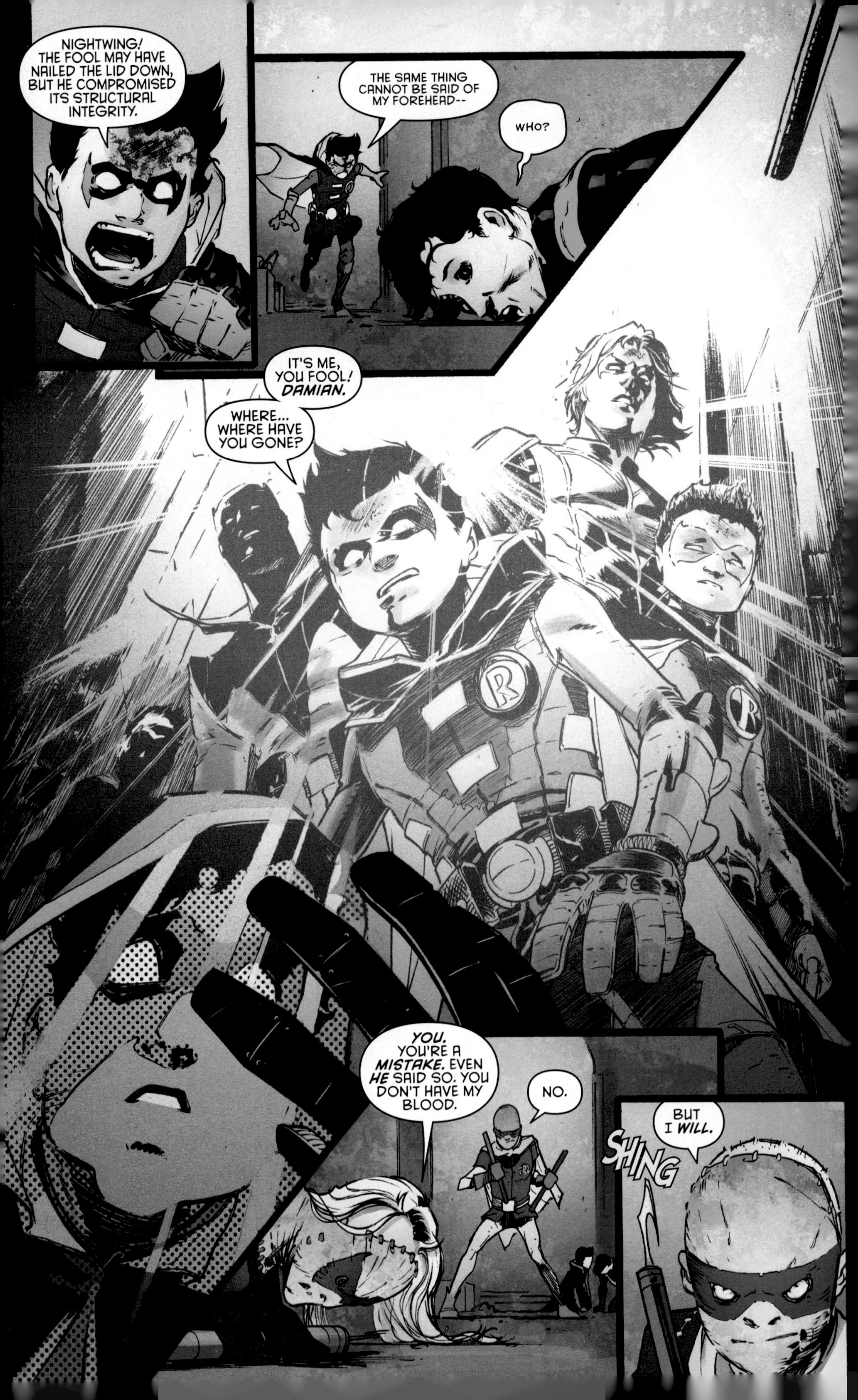
NIGHTWING! THE FOOL MAY HAVE NAILED THE LID DOWN, BUT HE COMPROMISED ITS STRUCTURAL INTEGRITY.
THE SAME THING CANNOT BE SAID OF MY FOREHEAD--
WHO?
IT'S ME, YOU FOOL! DAMIAN.
WHERE... WHERE HAVE YOU GONE?
YOU. YOU'RE A MISTAKE. EVEN HE SAID SO. YOU DON'T HAVE MY BLOOD.
NO.
BUT I WILL.
SHING

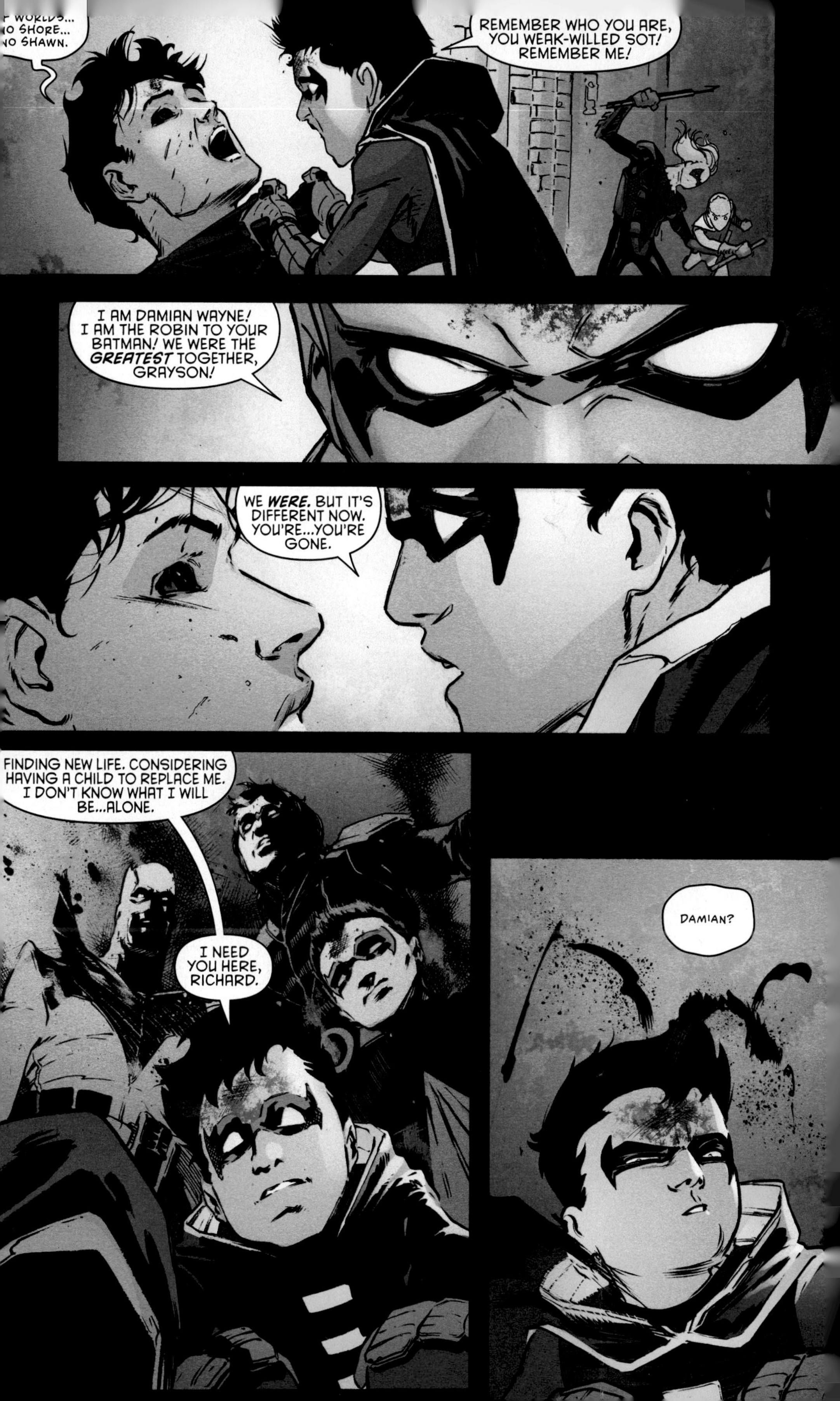
...F WORLDS... ...O SHORE... ...NO SHAWN.
REMEMBER WHO YOU ARE, YOU WEAK-WILLED SOT! REMEMBER ME!
I AM DAMIAN WAYNE! I AM THE ROBIN TO YOUR BATMAN! WE WERE THE GREATEST TOGETHER, GRAYSON!
WE WERE. BUT IT'S DIFFERENT NOW. YOU'RE...YOU'RE GONE.
FINDING NEW LIFE. CONSIDERING HAVING A CHILD TO REPLACE ME. I DON'T KNOW WHAT I WILL BE...ALONE.
I NEED YOU HERE, RICHARD.
DAMIAN?

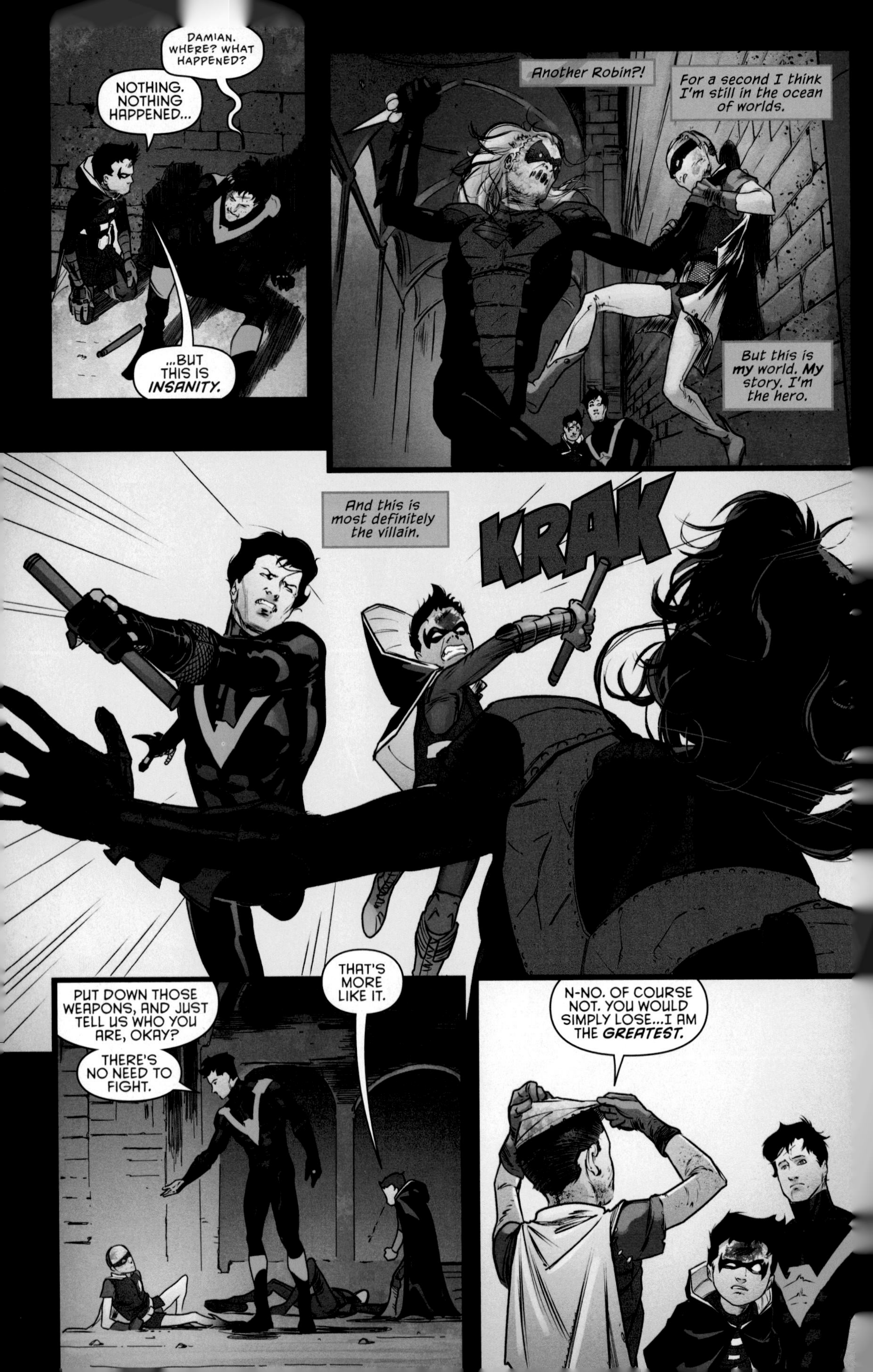
DAMIAN. WHERE? WHAT HAPPENED?
NOTHING. NOTHING HAPPENED...
...BUT THIS IS INSANITY.
Another Robin?!
For a second I think I'm still in the ocean of worlds.
But this is my world. My story. I'm the hero.
And this is most definitely the villain.
KRAK
PUT DOWN THOSE WEAPONS, AND JUST TELL US WHO YOU ARE, OKAY?
THERE'S NO NEED TO FIGHT.
THAT'S MORE LIKE IT.
N-NO. OF COURSE NOT. YOU WOULD SIMPLY LOSE...I AM THE GREATEST.

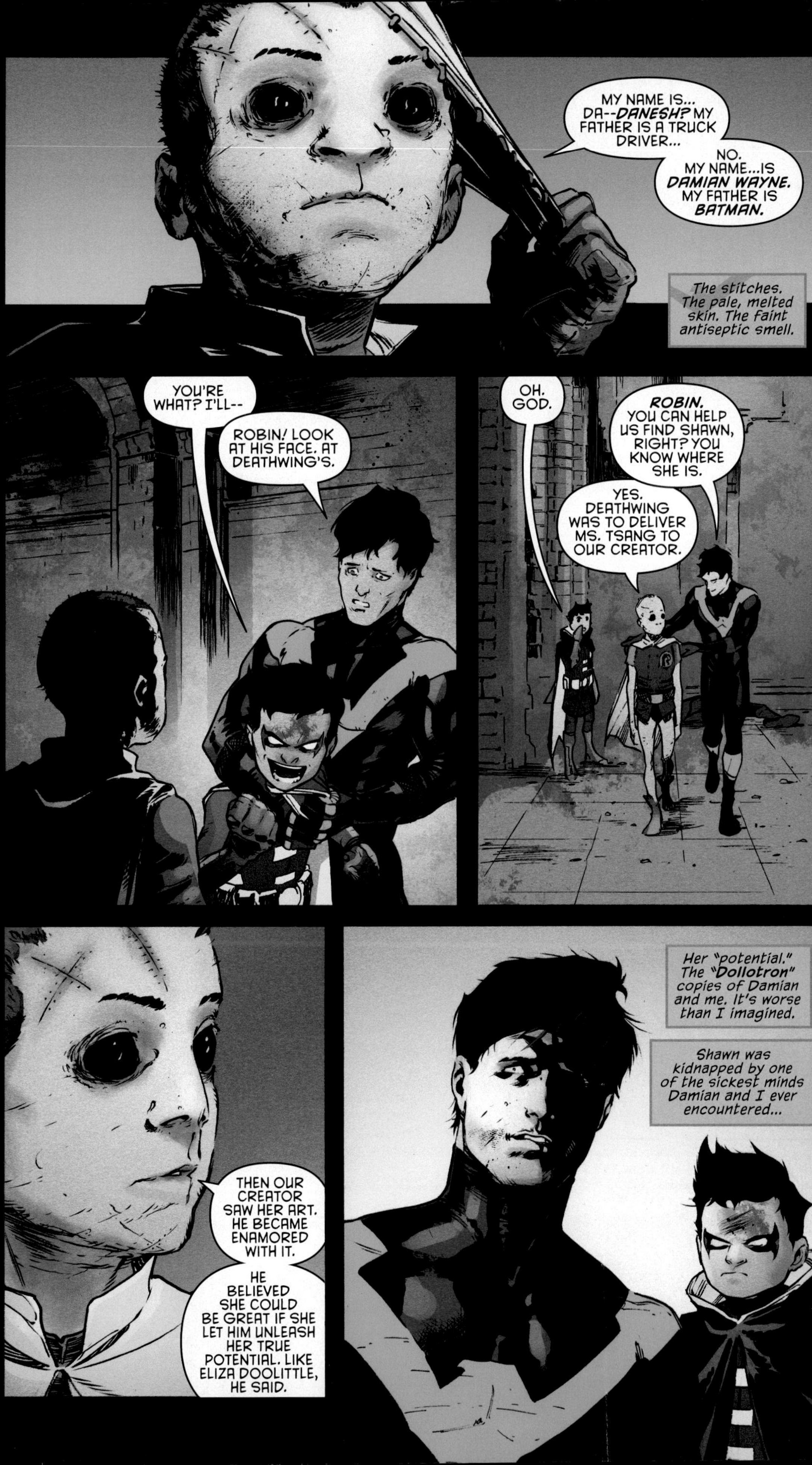

MY NAME IS... DA--DANESH? MY FATHER IS A TRUCK DRIVER...
NO. MY NAME...IS DAMIAN WAYNE. MY FATHER IS BATMAN.
The stitches. The pale, melted skin. The faint antiseptic smell.
YOU'RE WHAT? I'LL--
ROBIN! LOOK AT HIS FACE. AT DEATHWING'S.
OH. GOD.
ROBIN. YOU CAN HELP US FIND SHAWN, RIGHT? YOU KNOW WHERE SHE IS.
YES. DEATHWING WAS TO DELIVER MS. TSANG TO OUR CREATOR.
THEN OUR CREATOR SAW HER ART. HE BECAME ENAMORED WITH IT.
HE BELIEVED SHE COULD BE GREAT IF SHE LET HIM UNLEASH HER TRUE POTENTIAL. LIKE ELIZA DOOLITTLE, HE SAID.
Her "potential." The "Dollotron" copies of Damian and me. It's worse than I imagined.
Shawn was kidnapped by one of the sickest minds Damian and I ever encountered...

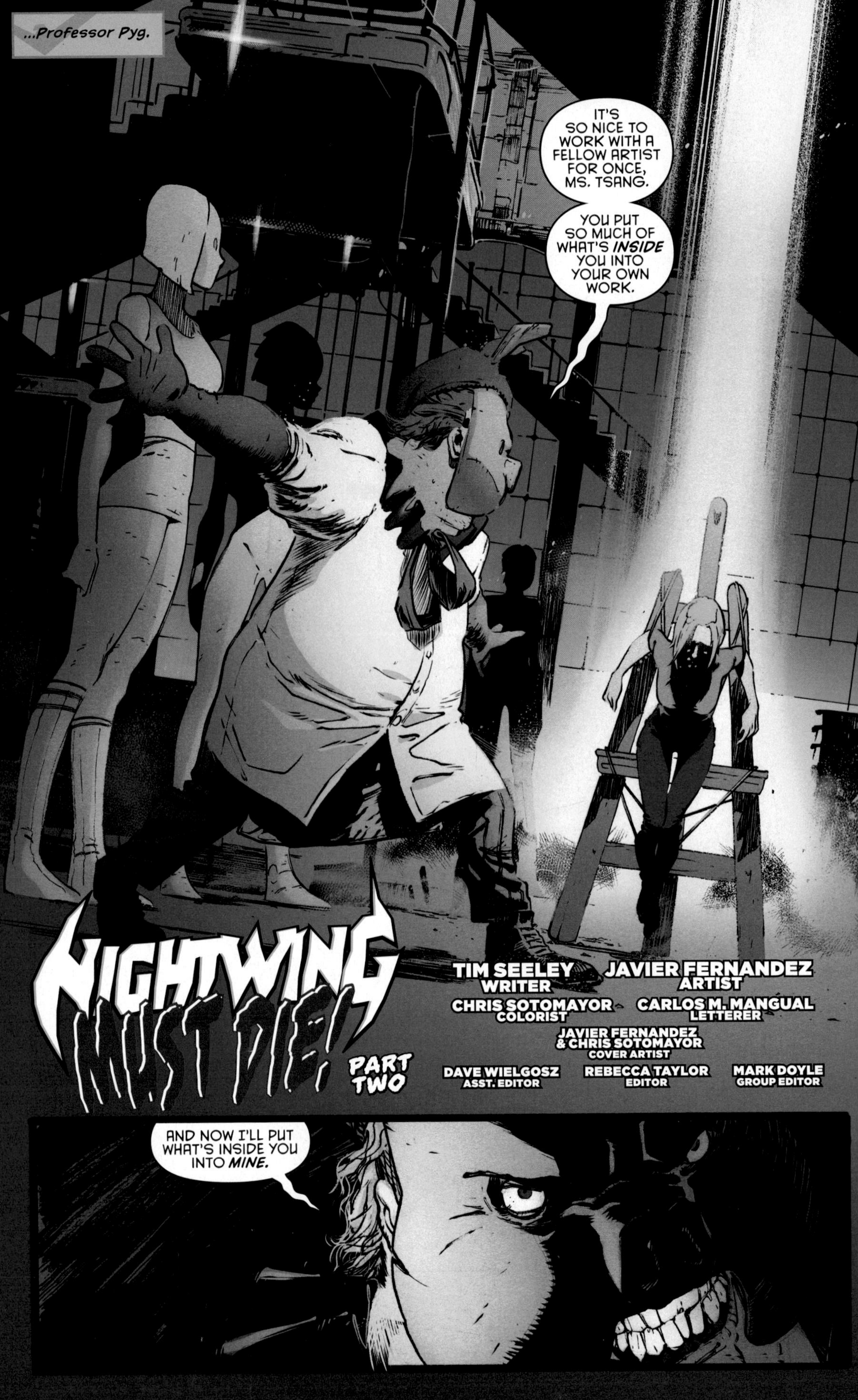

...Professor Pyg.
IT'S SO NICE TO WORK WITH A FELLOW ARTIST FOR ONCE, MS. TSANG.
YOU PUT SO MUCH OF WHAT'S *INSIDE* YOU INTO YOUR OWN WORK.
NIGHTWING MUST DIE! PART TWO
TIM SEELEY WRITER
JAVIER FERNANDEZ ARTIST
CHRIS SOTOMAYOR COLORIST
CARLOS M. MANGUAL LETTERER
JAVIER FERNANDEZ & CHRIS SOTOMAYOR COVER ARTIST
DAVE WIELGOSZ ASST. EDITOR
REBECCA TAYLOR EDITOR
MARK DOYLE GROUP EDITOR
AND NOW I'LL PUT WHAT'S INSIDE YOU INTO *MINE.*

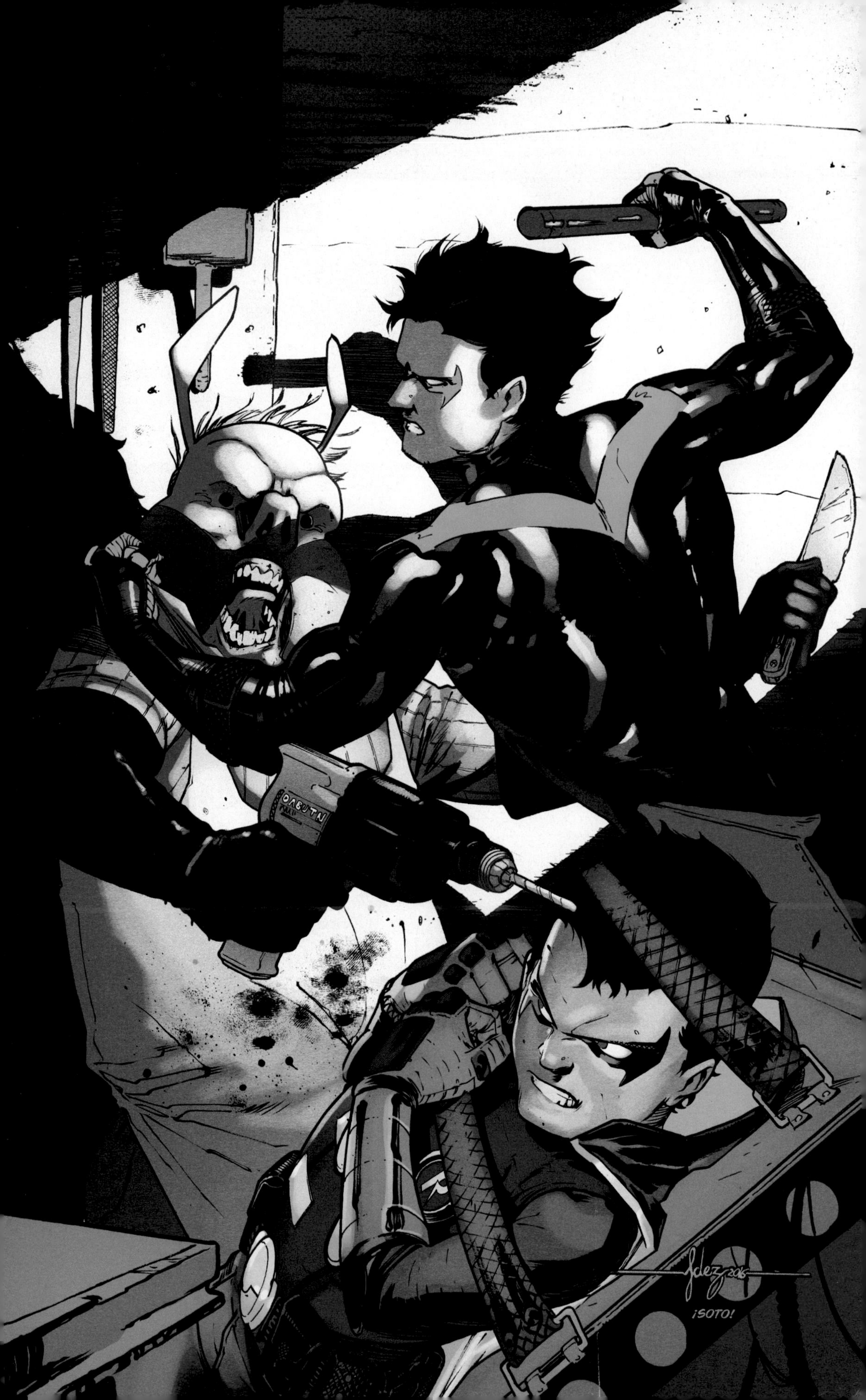
Fdez 2016
¡SOTO!

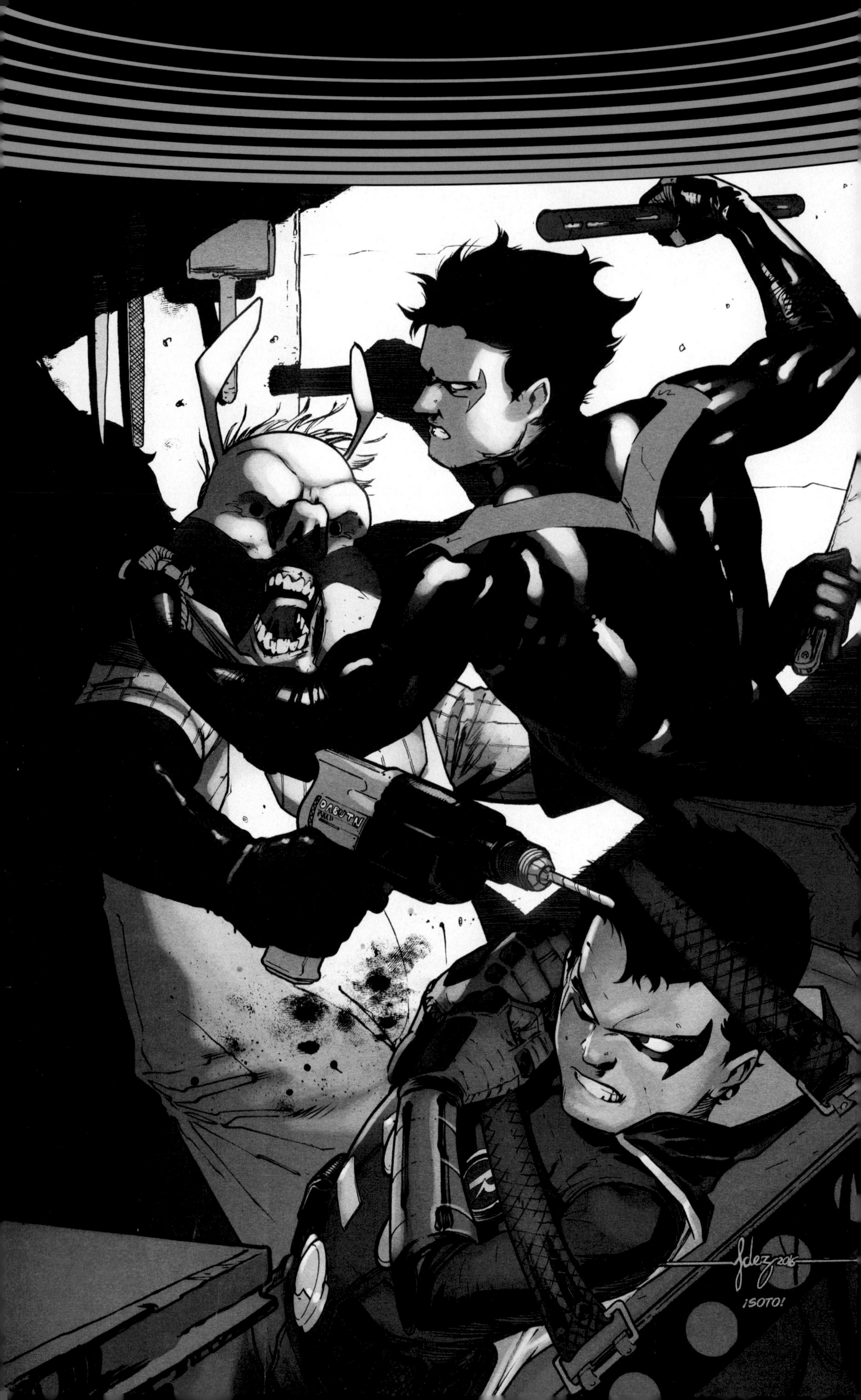
¡SOTO!

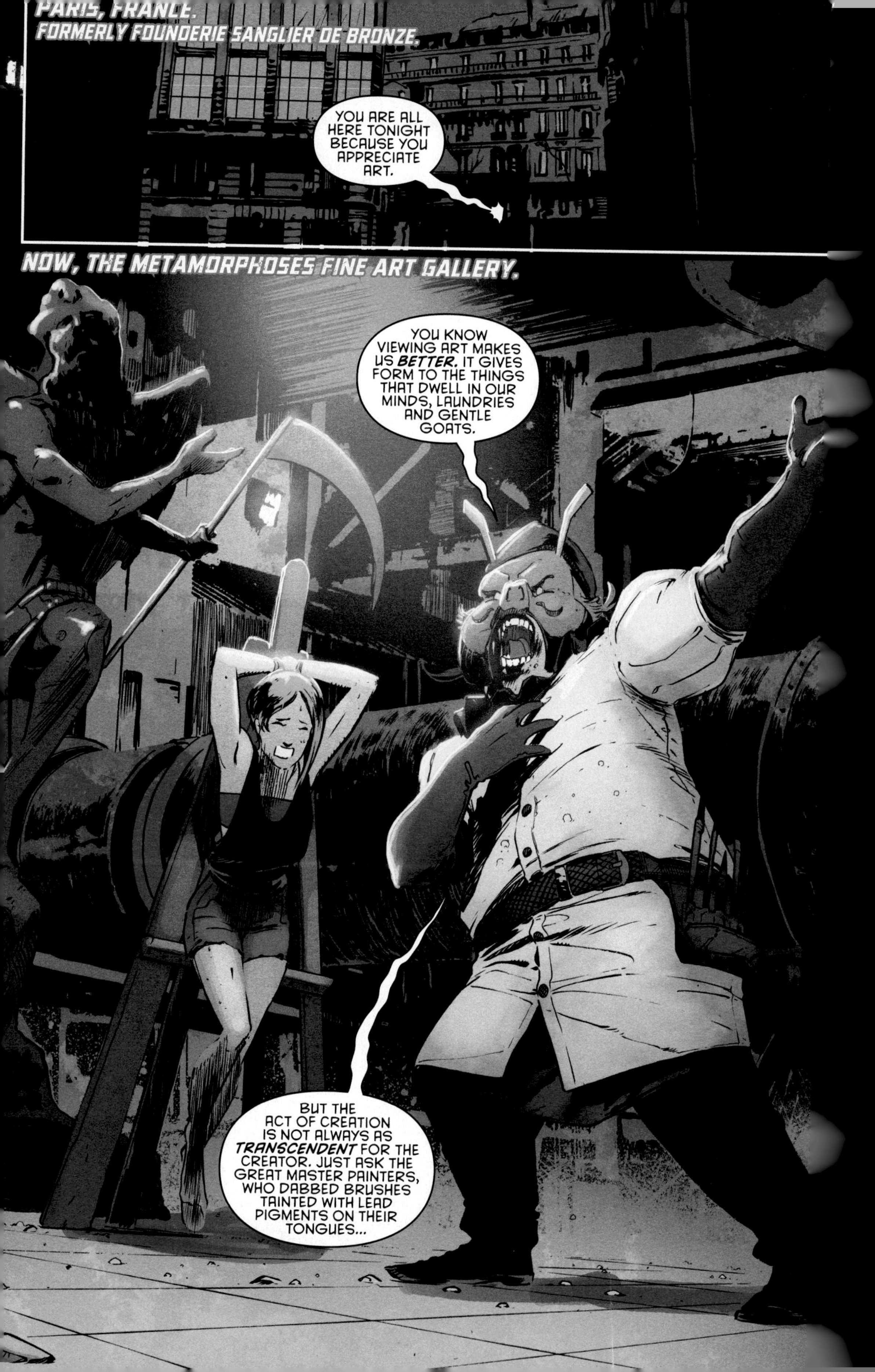
PARIS, FRANCE.
FORMERLY FOUNDERIE SANGLIER DE BRONZE.
YOU ARE ALL HERE TONIGHT BECAUSE YOU APPRECIATE ART.
NOW, THE METAMORPHOSES FINE ART GALLERY.
YOU KNOW VIEWING ART MAKES US BETTER. IT GIVES FORM TO THE THINGS THAT DWELL IN OUR MINDS, LAUNDRIES AND GENTLE GOATS.
BUT THE ACT OF CREATION IS NOT ALWAYS AS TRANSCENDENT FOR THE CREATOR. JUST ASK THE GREAT MASTER PAINTERS, WHO DABBED BRUSHES TAINTED WITH LEAD PIGMENTS ON THEIR TONGUES...

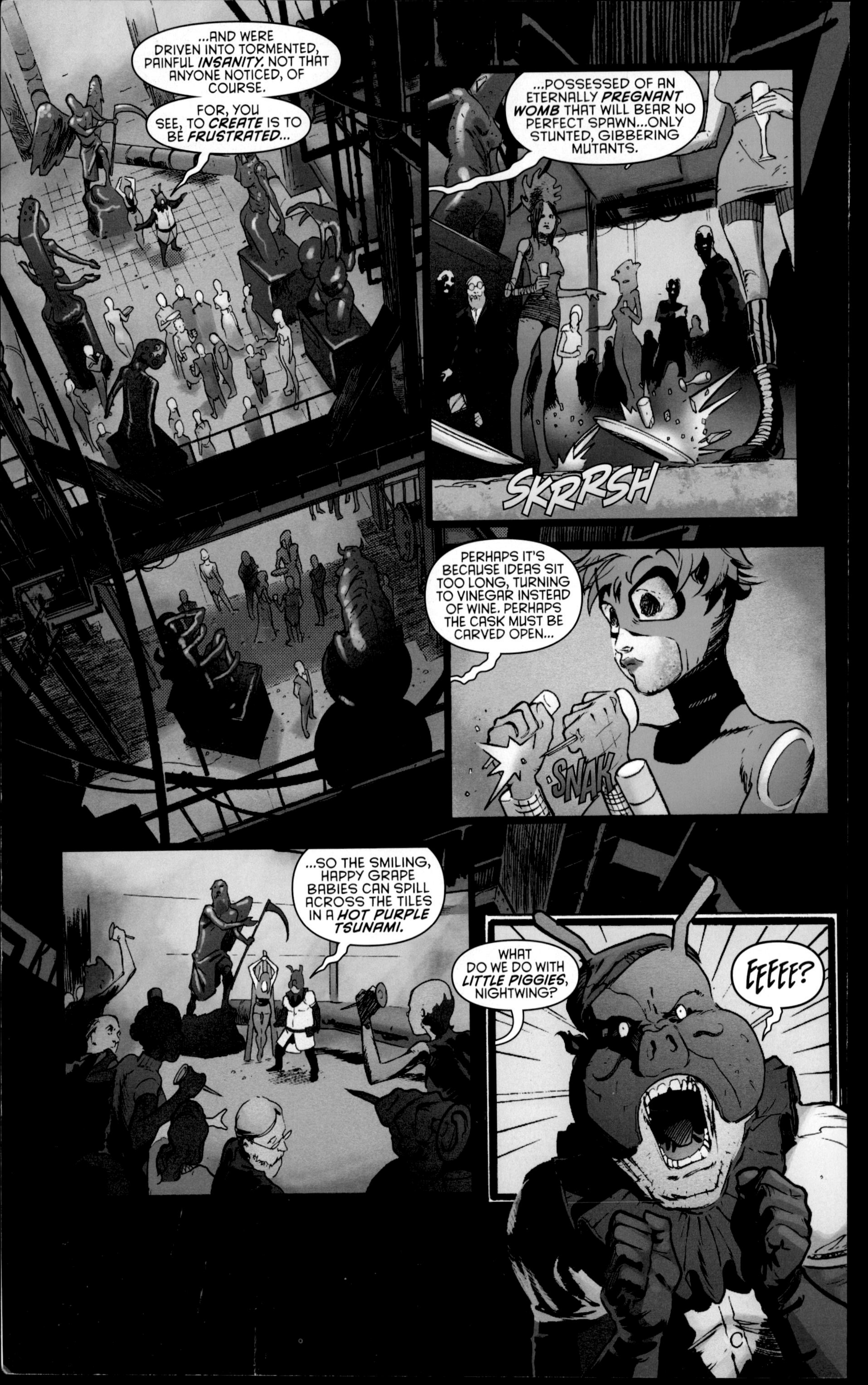
...AND WERE DRIVEN INTO TORMENTED, PAINFUL *INSANITY*. NOT THAT ANYONE NOTICED, OF COURSE.
FOR, YOU SEE, TO *CREATE* IS TO BE *FRUSTRATED*...
...POSSESSED OF AN ETERNALLY *PREGNANT WOMB* THAT WILL BEAR NO PERFECT SPAWN...ONLY STUNTED, GIBBERING MUTANTS.
SKRRSH
PERHAPS IT'S BECAUSE IDEAS SIT TOO LONG, TURNING TO VINEGAR INSTEAD OF WINE. PERHAPS THE CASK MUST BE CARVED OPEN...
SNAK
...SO THE SMILING, HAPPY GRAPE BABIES CAN SPILL ACROSS THE TILES IN A *HOT PURPLE TSUNAMI*.
WHAT DO WE DO WITH *LITTLE PIGGIES*, NIGHTWING?
EEEEE?

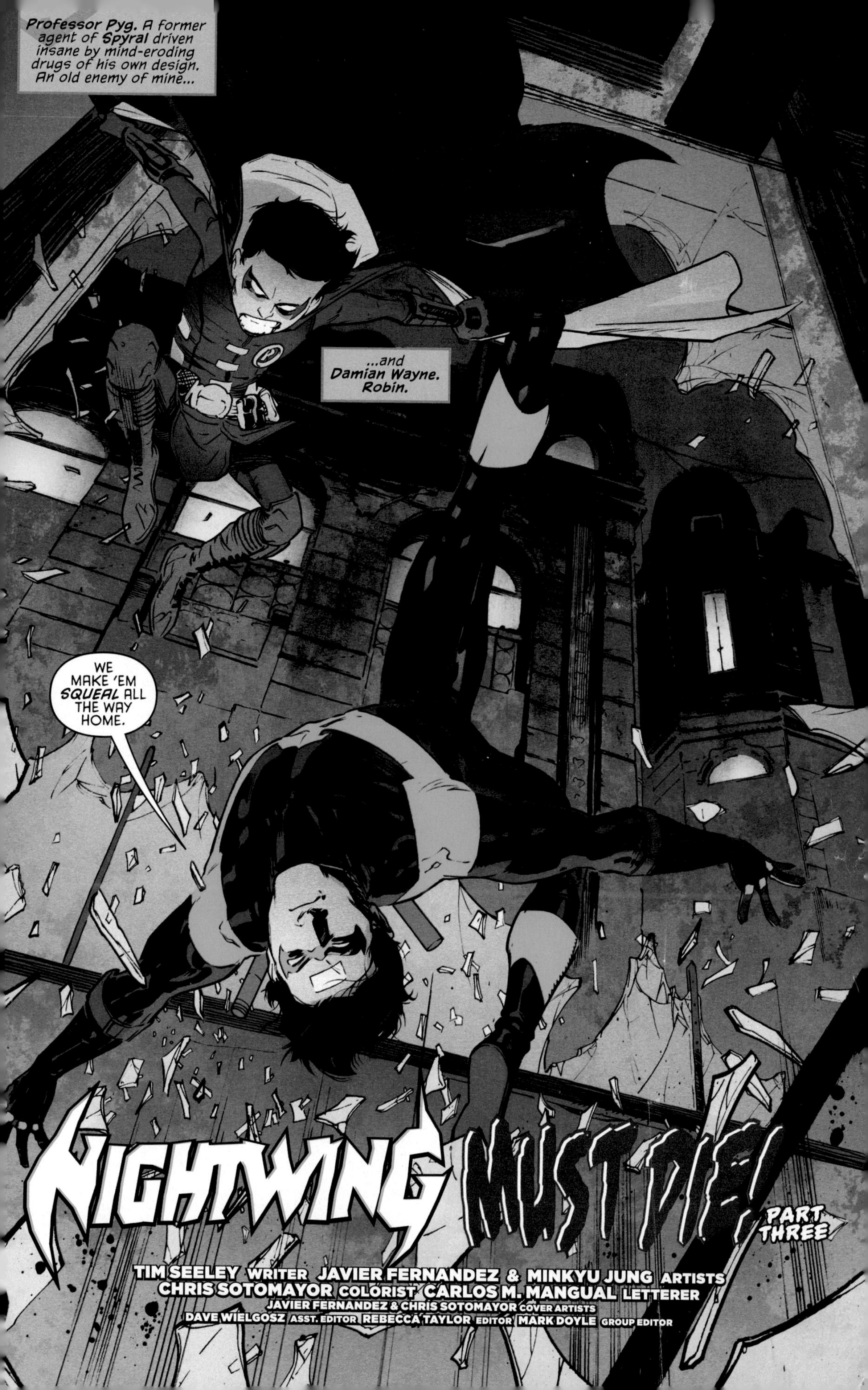

Professor Pyg. A former agent of Spyral driven insane by mind-eroding drugs of his own design. An old enemy of mine...
...and Damian Wayne. Robin.
WE MAKE 'EM SQUEAL ALL THE WAY HOME.
NIGHTWING MUST DIE! PART THREE
TIM SEELEY WRITER JAVIER FERNANDEZ & MINKYU JUNG ARTISTS
CHRIS SOTOMAYOR COLORIST CARLOS M. MANGUAL LETTERER
JAVIER FERNANDEZ & CHRIS SOTOMAYOR COVER ARTISTS
DAVE WIELGOSZ ASST. EDITOR REBECCA TAYLOR EDITOR MARK DOYLE GROUP EDITOR

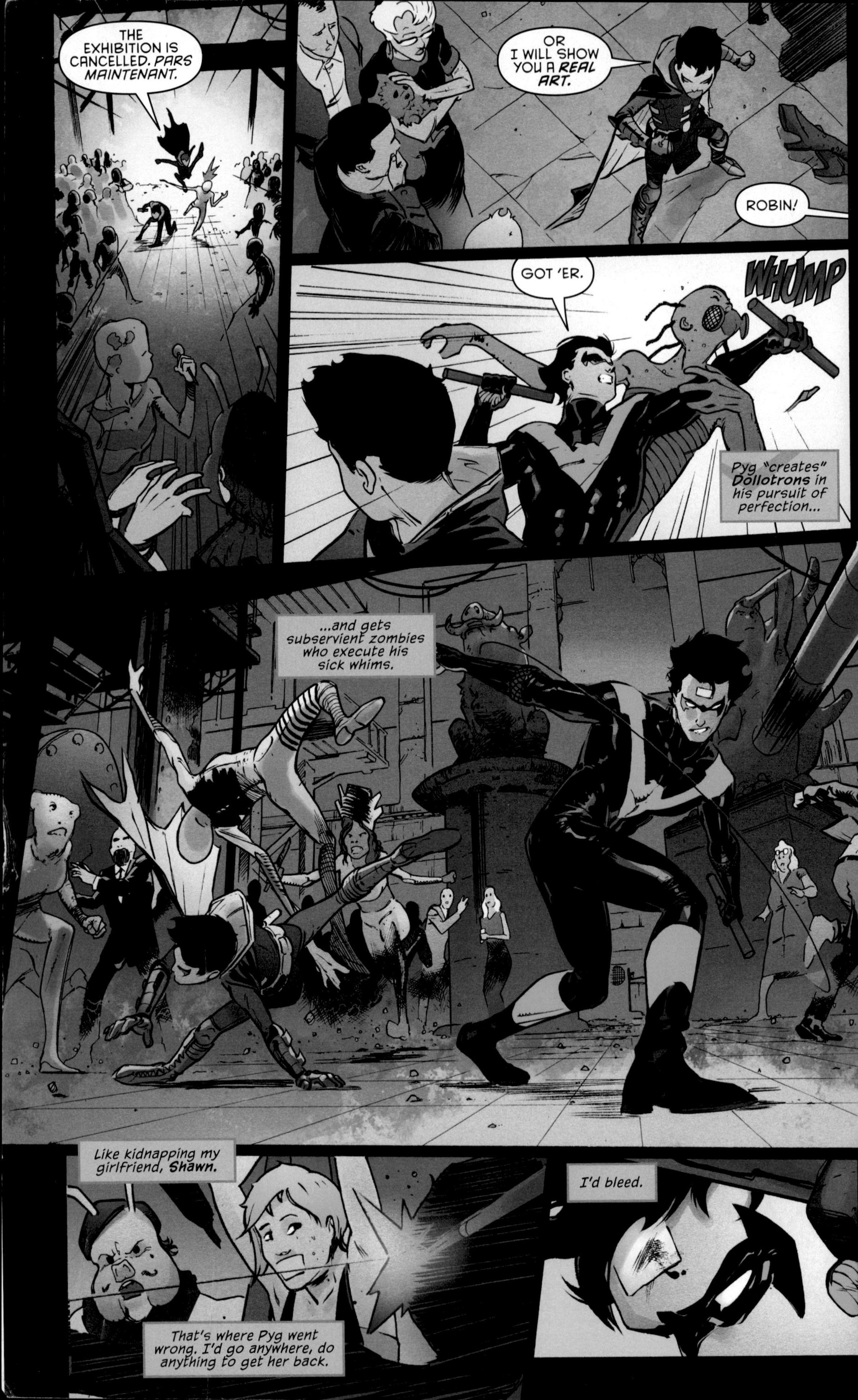
THE EXHIBITION IS CANCELLED. *PARS MAINTENANT.*
OR I WILL SHOW YOU A ***REAL ART.***
ROBIN!
GOT 'ER.
WHUMP
Pyg "creates" **Dollotrons** in his pursuit of perfection...
...and gets subservient zombies who execute his sick whims.
Like kidnapping my girlfriend, **Shawn.**
That's where Pyg went wrong. I'd go anywhere, do anything to get her back.
I'd bleed.

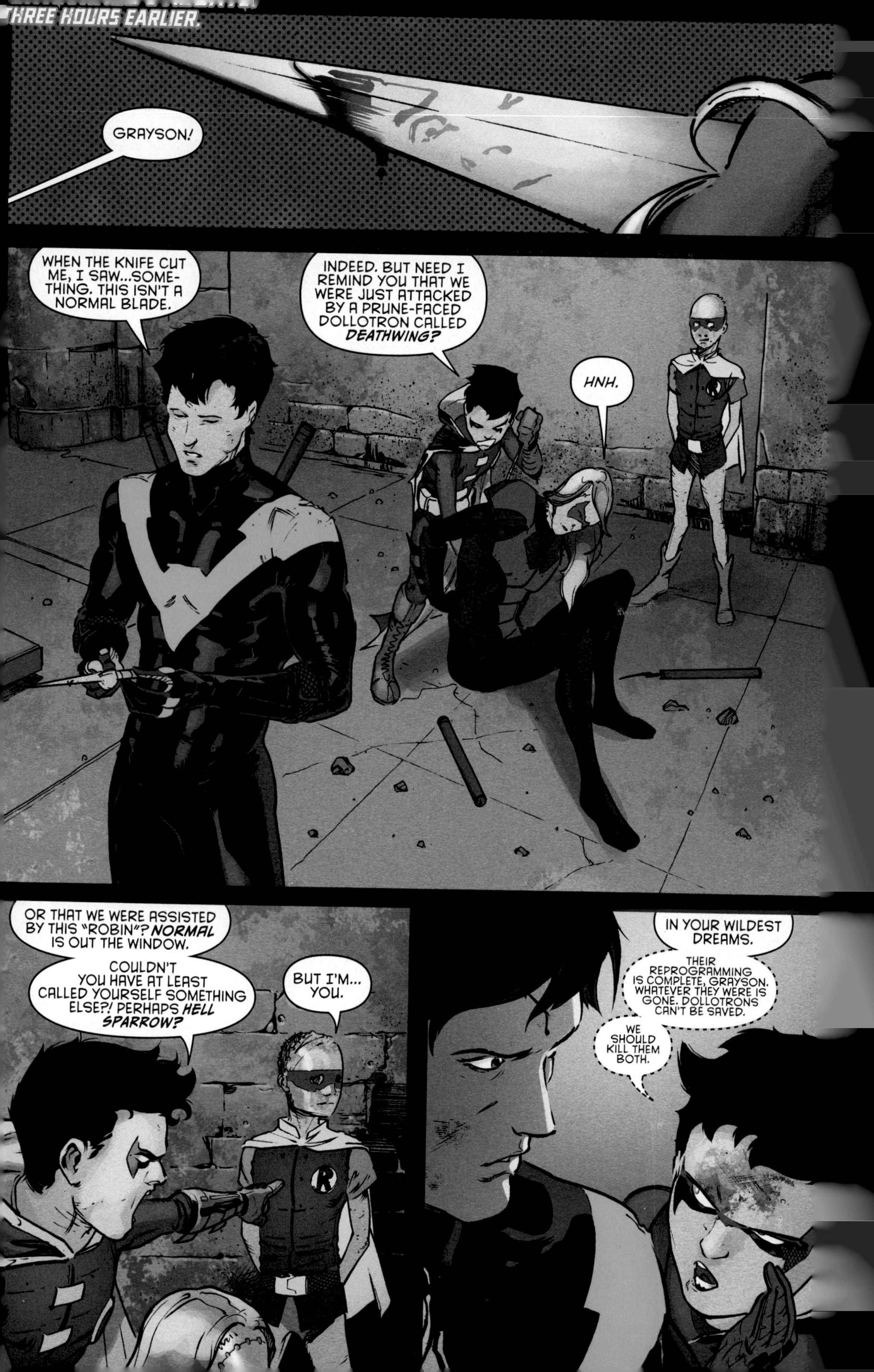
THREE HOURS EARLIER.
GRAYSON!
WHEN THE KNIFE CUT ME, I SAW...SOMETHING. THIS ISN'T A NORMAL BLADE.
INDEED. BUT NEED I REMIND YOU THAT WE WERE JUST ATTACKED BY A PRUNE-FACED DOLLOTRON CALLED DEATHWING?
HNH.
OR THAT WE WERE ASSISTED BY THIS "ROBIN"? NORMAL IS OUT THE WINDOW.
COULDN'T YOU HAVE AT LEAST CALLED YOURSELF SOMETHING ELSE?! PERHAPS HELL SPARROW?
BUT I'M... YOU.
IN YOUR WILDEST DREAMS.
THEIR REPROGRAMMING IS COMPLETE, GRAYSON. WHATEVER THEY WERE IS GONE. DOLLOTRONS CAN'T BE SAVED.
WE SHOULD KILL THEM BOTH.

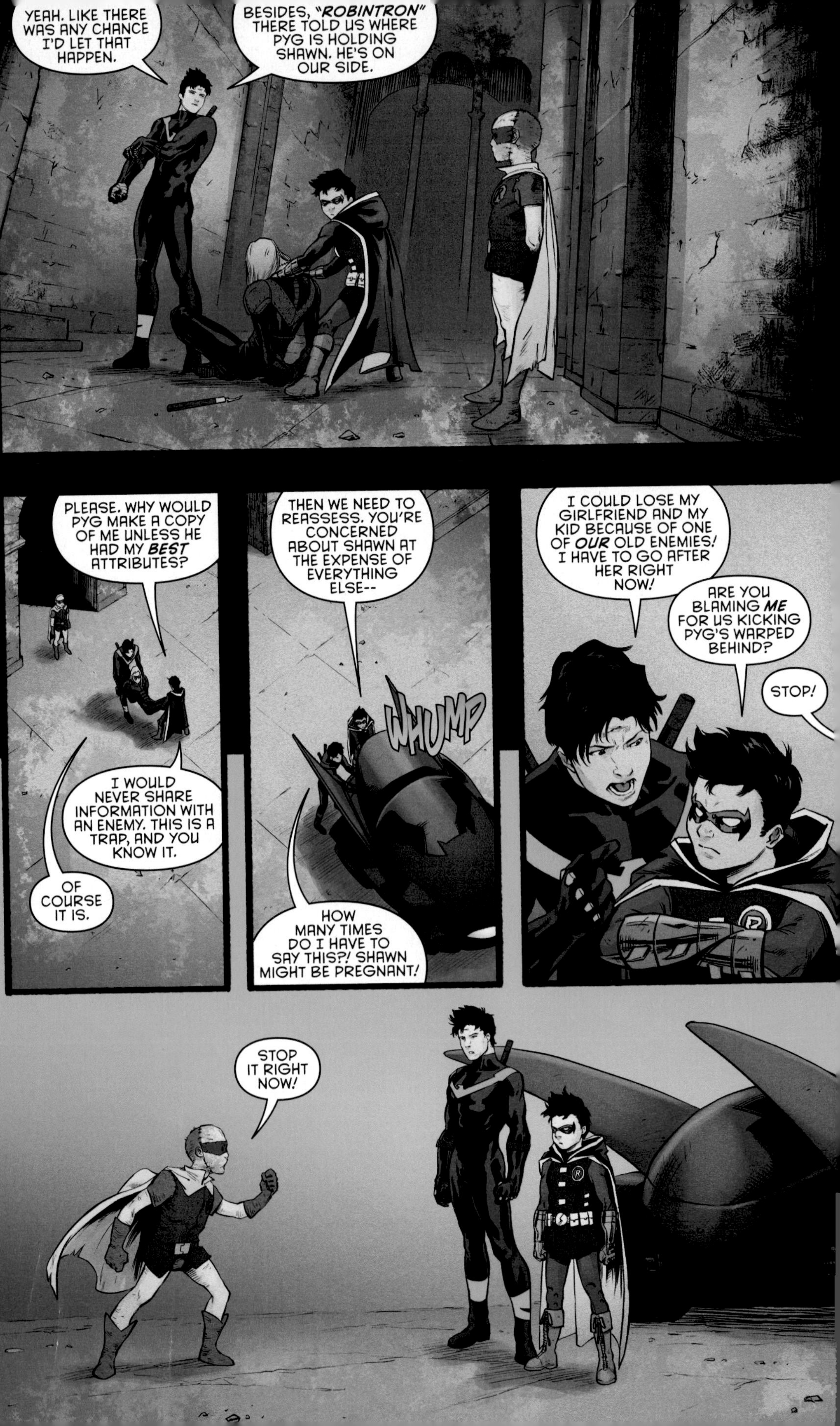

YEAH. LIKE THERE WAS ANY CHANCE I'D LET THAT HAPPEN.
BESIDES, "ROBINTRON" THERE TOLD US WHERE PYG IS HOLDING SHAWN. HE'S ON OUR SIDE.
PLEASE. WHY WOULD PYG MAKE A COPY OF ME UNLESS HE HAD MY BEST ATTRIBUTES?
I WOULD NEVER SHARE INFORMATION WITH AN ENEMY. THIS IS A TRAP, AND YOU KNOW IT.
OF COURSE IT IS.
THEN WE NEED TO REASSESS. YOU'RE CONCERNED ABOUT SHAWN AT THE EXPENSE OF EVERYTHING ELSE--
WHUMP
HOW MANY TIMES DO I HAVE TO SAY THIS?! SHAWN MIGHT BE PREGNANT!
I COULD LOSE MY GIRLFRIEND AND MY KID BECAUSE OF ONE OF OUR OLD ENEMIES! I HAVE TO GO AFTER HER RIGHT NOW!
ARE YOU BLAMING ME FOR US KICKING PYG'S WARPED BEHIND?
STOP!
STOP IT RIGHT NOW!

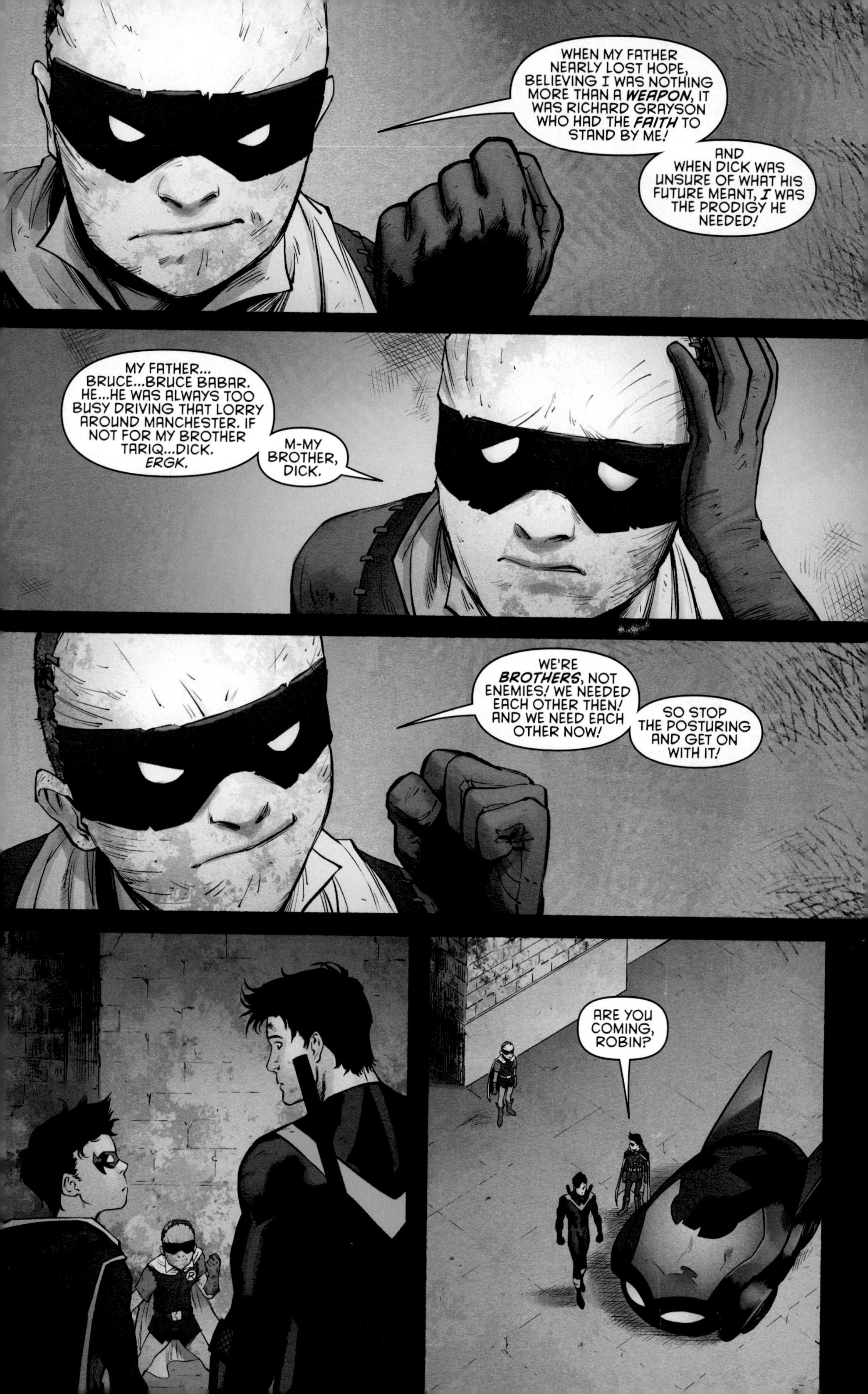
WHEN MY FATHER NEARLY LOST HOPE, BELIEVING I WAS NOTHING MORE THAN A *WEAPON*, IT WAS RICHARD GRAYSON WHO HAD THE *FAITH* TO STAND BY ME!
AND WHEN DICK WAS UNSURE OF WHAT HIS FUTURE MEANT, *I* WAS THE PRODIGY HE NEEDED!
MY FATHER... BRUCE...BRUCE BABAR. HE...HE WAS ALWAYS TOO BUSY DRIVING THAT LORRY AROUND MANCHESTER. IF NOT FOR MY BROTHER TARIQ...DICK. *ERGK.*
M-MY BROTHER, DICK.
WE'RE *BROTHERS*, NOT ENEMIES! WE NEEDED EACH OTHER THEN! AND WE NEED EACH OTHER NOW!
SO STOP THE POSTURING AND GET ON WITH IT!
ARE YOU COMING, ROBIN?

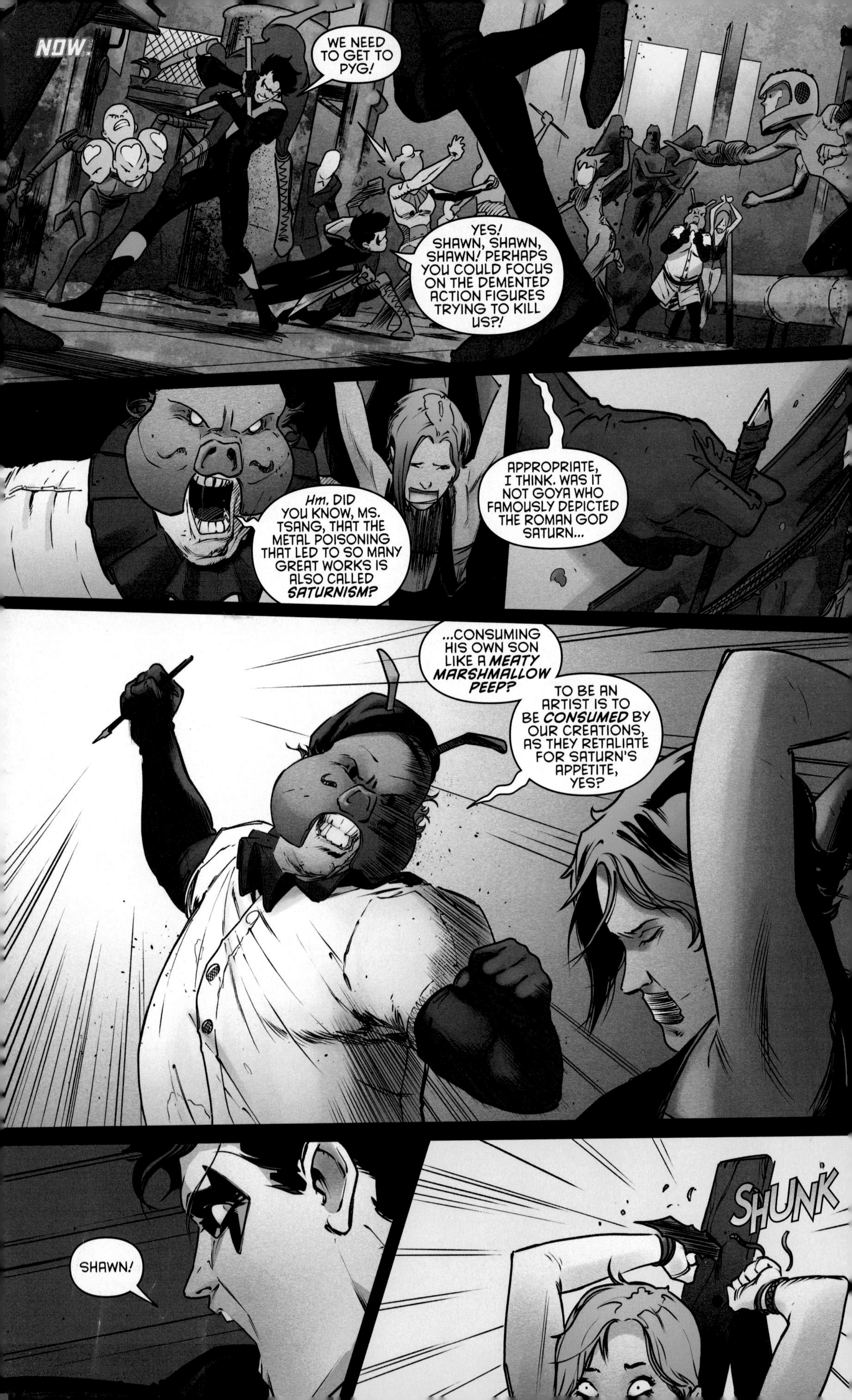
NOW.
WE NEED TO GET TO PYG!
YES! SHAWN, SHAWN, SHAWN! PERHAPS YOU COULD FOCUS ON THE DEMENTED ACTION FIGURES TRYING TO KILL US?!
Hm. DID YOU KNOW, MS. TSANG, THAT THE METAL POISONING THAT LED TO SO MANY GREAT WORKS IS ALSO CALLED SATURNISM?
APPROPRIATE, I THINK. WAS IT NOT GOYA WHO FAMOUSLY DEPICTED THE ROMAN GOD SATURN...
...CONSUMING HIS OWN SON LIKE A MEATY MARSHMALLOW PEEP?
TO BE AN ARTIST IS TO BE CONSUMED BY OUR CREATIONS, AS THEY RETALIATE FOR SATURN'S APPETITE, YES?
SHAWN!
SHUNK

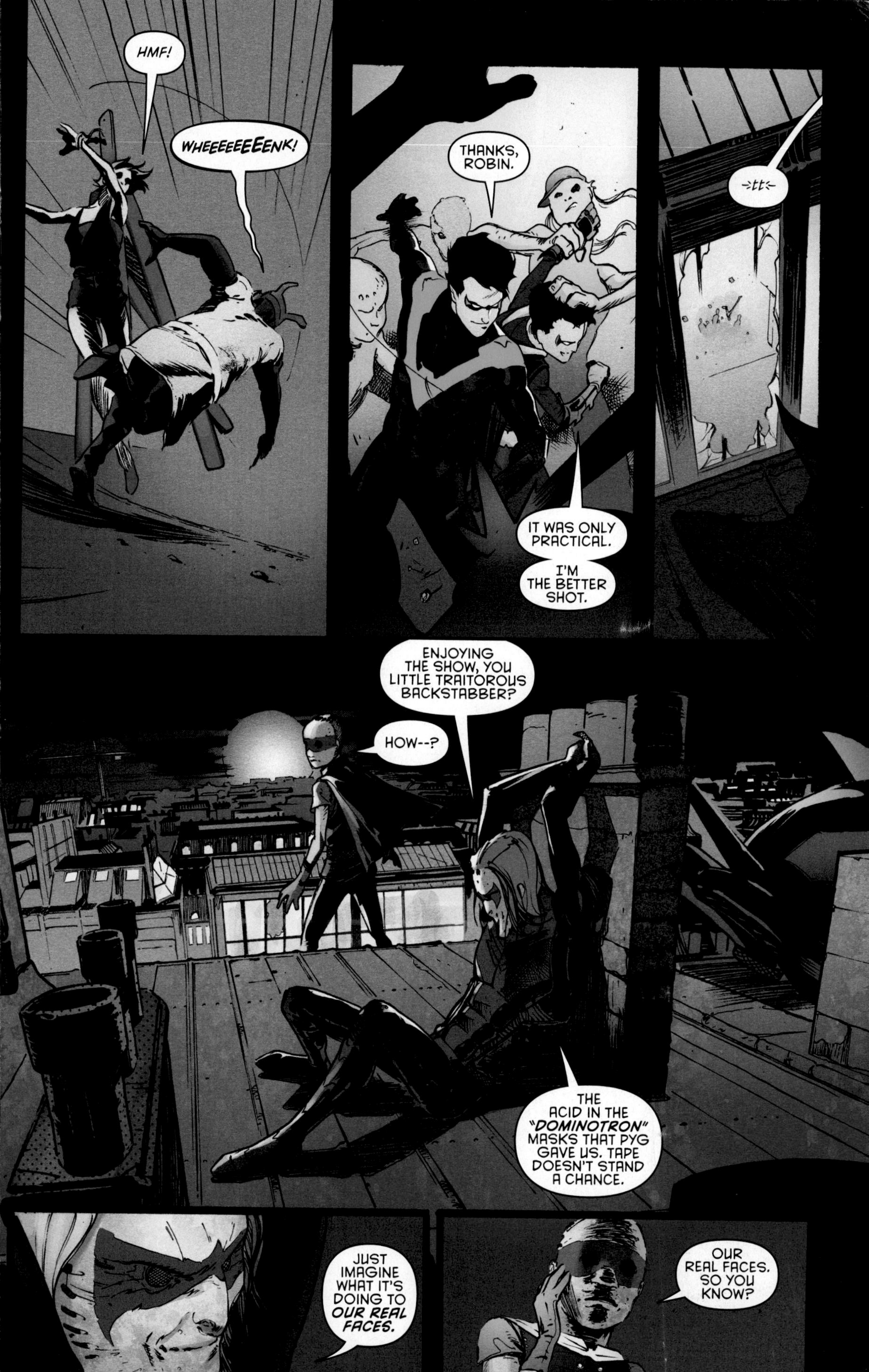
HMF!
WHEEEEEEEEENK!
THANKS, ROBIN.
IT WAS ONLY PRACTICAL.
I'M THE BETTER SHOT.
=tt=
ENJOYING THE SHOW, YOU LITTLE TRAITOROUS BACKSTABBER?
HOW--?
THE ACID IN THE "DOMINOTRON" MASKS THAT PYG GAVE US. TAPE DOESN'T STAND A CHANCE.
JUST IMAGINE WHAT IT'S DOING TO OUR REAL FACES.
OUR REAL FACES. SO YOU KNOW?

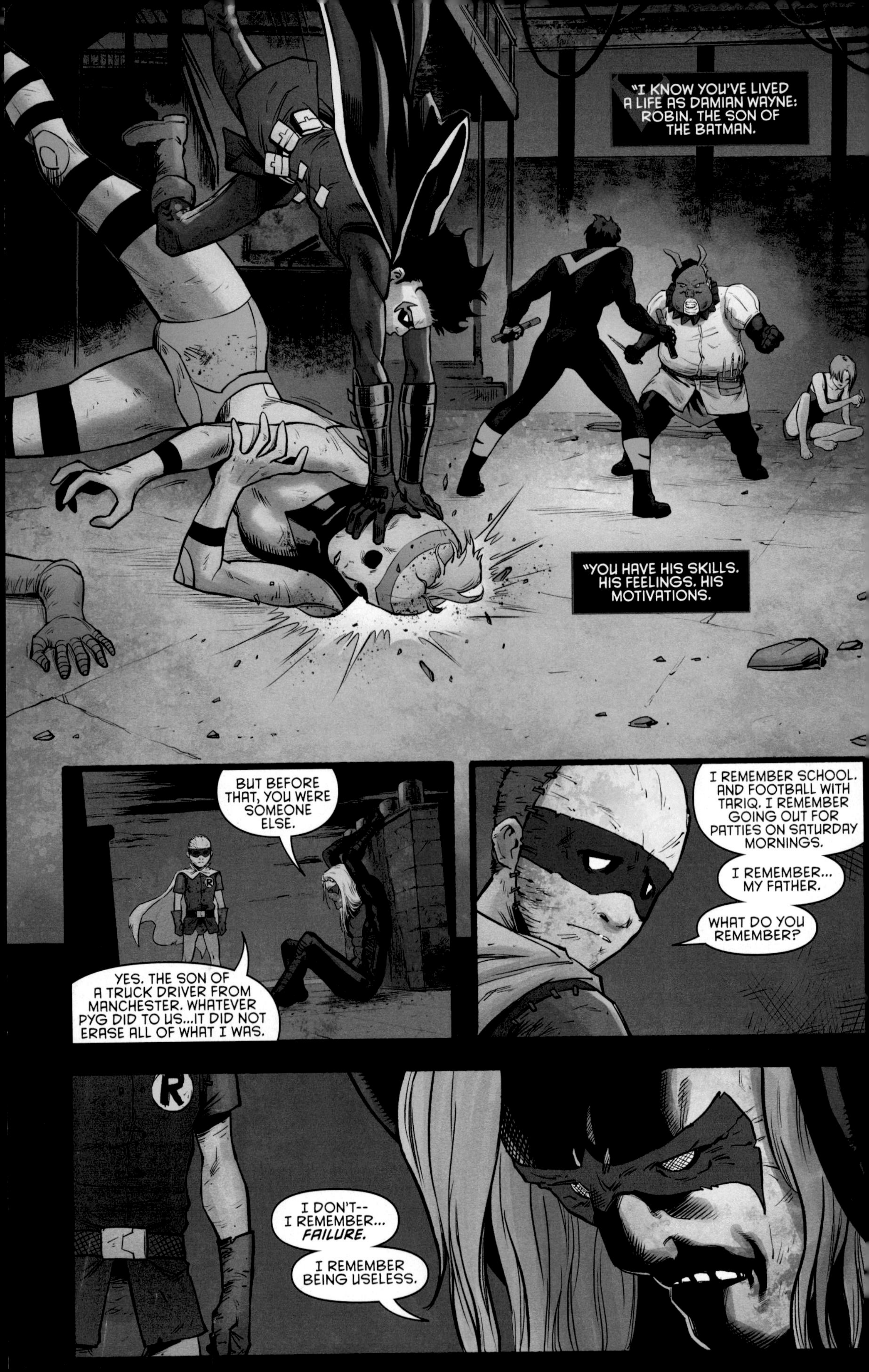

"I KNOW YOU'VE LIVED A LIFE AS DAMIAN WAYNE: ROBIN. THE SON OF THE BATMAN.
"YOU HAVE HIS SKILLS. HIS FEELINGS. HIS MOTIVATIONS.
BUT BEFORE THAT, YOU WERE SOMEONE ELSE.
YES. THE SON OF A TRUCK DRIVER FROM MANCHESTER. WHATEVER PYG DID TO US...IT DID NOT ERASE ALL OF WHAT I WAS.
I REMEMBER SCHOOL. AND FOOTBALL WITH TARIQ. I REMEMBER GOING OUT FOR PATTIES ON SATURDAY MORNINGS.
I REMEMBER... MY FATHER.
WHAT DO YOU REMEMBER?
I DON'T-- I REMEMBER... *FAILURE.*
I REMEMBER BEING USELESS.

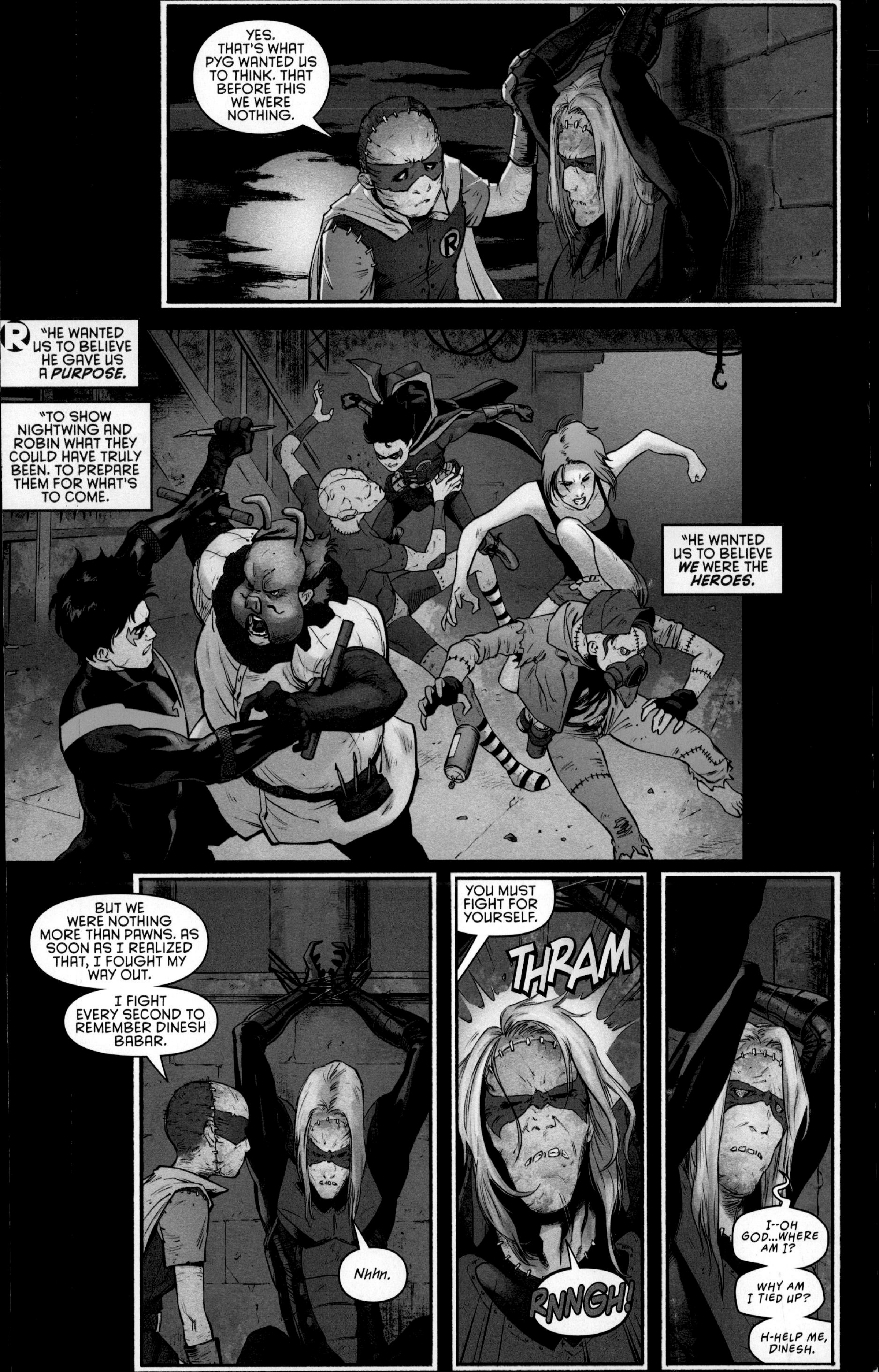
YES. THAT'S WHAT PYG WANTED US TO THINK. THAT BEFORE THIS WE WERE NOTHING.
"HE WANTED US TO BELIEVE HE GAVE US A PURPOSE.
"TO SHOW NIGHTWING AND ROBIN WHAT THEY COULD HAVE TRULY BEEN. TO PREPARE THEM FOR WHAT'S TO COME.
"HE WANTED US TO BELIEVE WE WERE THE HEROES.
BUT WE WERE NOTHING MORE THAN PAWNS. AS SOON AS I REALIZED THAT, I FOUGHT MY WAY OUT.
I FIGHT EVERY SECOND TO REMEMBER DINESH BABAR.
Nhhn.
YOU MUST FIGHT FOR YOURSELF.
THRAM
RNNGH!
I--OH GOD...WHERE AM I?
WHY AM I TIED UP?
H-HELP ME, DINESH.

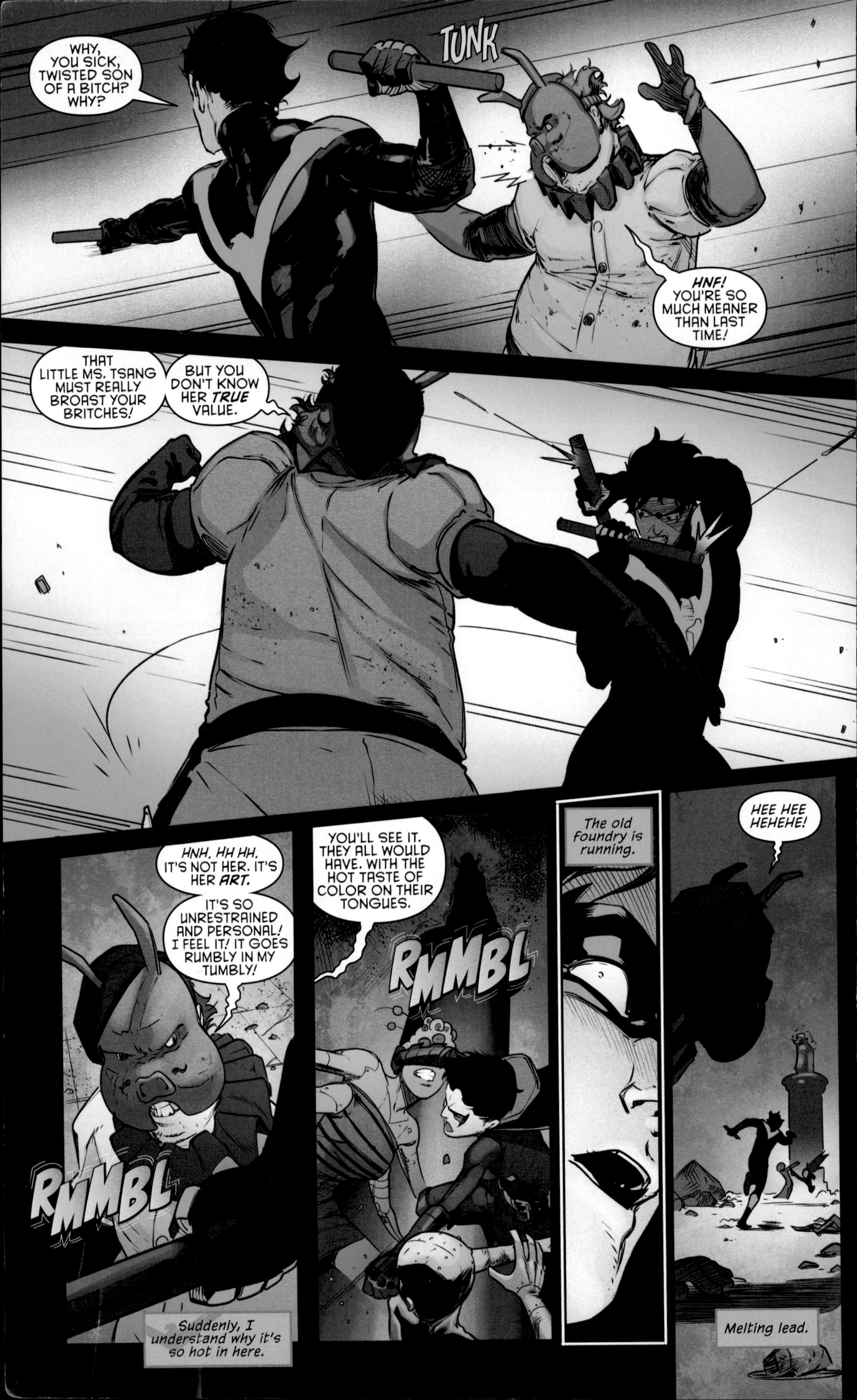
TUNK
WHY, YOU SICK, TWISTED SON OF A BITCH? WHY?
HNF! YOU'RE SO MUCH MEANER THAN LAST TIME!
THAT LITTLE MS. TSANG MUST REALLY BROAST YOUR BRITCHES!
BUT YOU DON'T KNOW HER TRUE VALUE.
HNH. HH HH. IT'S NOT HER. IT'S HER ART.
IT'S SO UNRESTRAINED AND PERSONAL! I FEEL IT! IT GOES RUMBLY IN MY TUMBLY!
RMMBL
Suddenly, I understand why it's so hot in here.
YOU'LL SEE IT. THEY ALL WOULD HAVE. WITH THE HOT TASTE OF COLOR ON THEIR TONGUES.
RMMBL
The old foundry is running.
HEE HEE HEHEHE!
Melting lead.

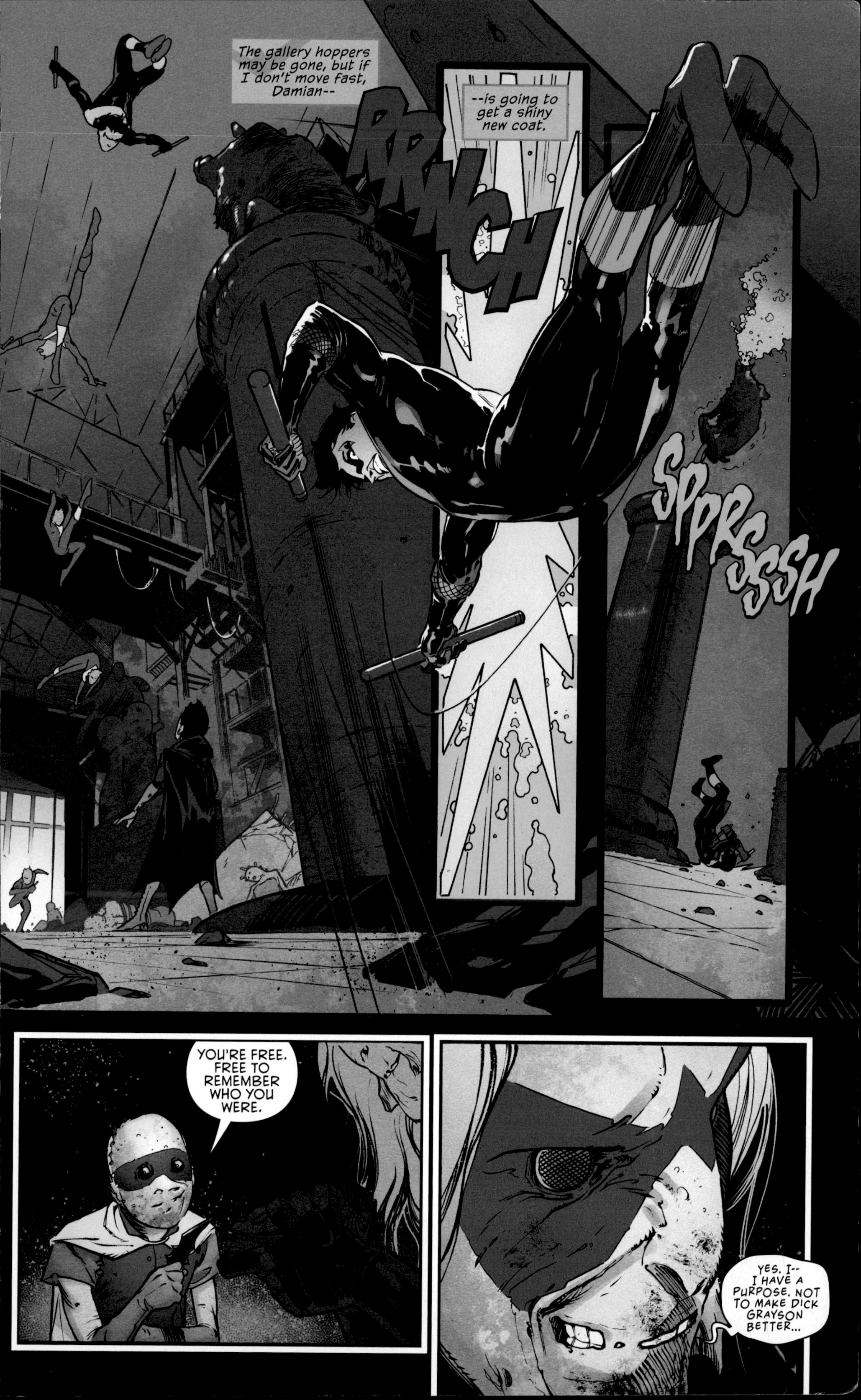
The gallery hoppers may be gone, but if I don't move fast, Damian--
RRNCH
--is going to get a shiny new coat.
SPPRSSSH
YOU'RE FREE. FREE TO REMEMBER WHO YOU WERE.
YES. I-- I HAVE A PURPOSE. NOT TO MAKE DICK GRAYSON BETTER...

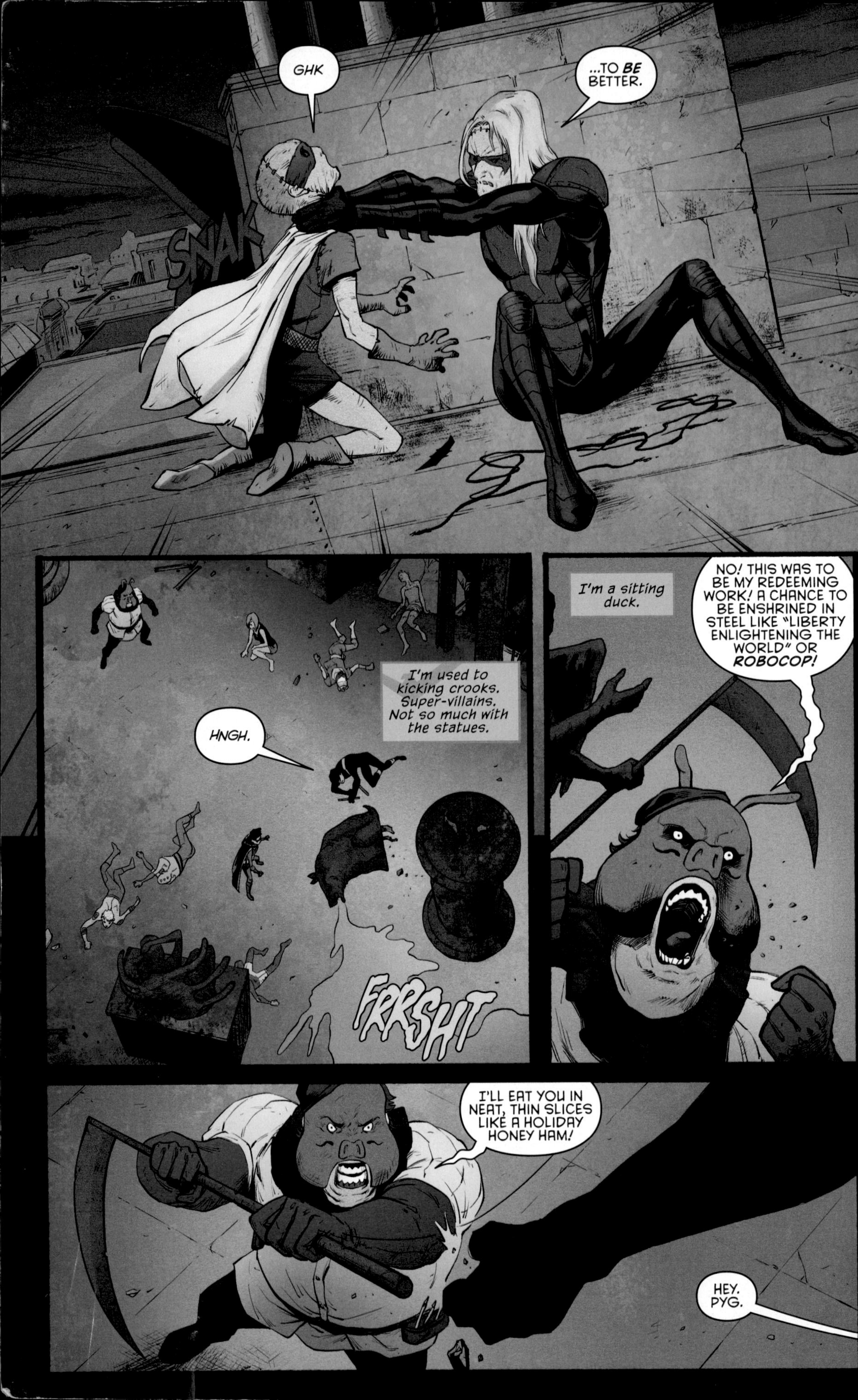
GHK
...TO *BE* BETTER.
SNAK
HNGH.
I'm used to kicking crooks. Super-villains. Not so much with the statues.
FRRSHT
I'm a sitting duck.
NO! THIS WAS TO BE MY REDEEMING WORK! A CHANCE TO BE ENSHRINED IN STEEL LIKE "LIBERTY ENLIGHTENING THE WORLD" OR *ROBOCOP!*
I'LL EAT YOU IN NEAT, THIN SLICES LIKE A HOLIDAY HONEY HAM!
HEY. PYG.

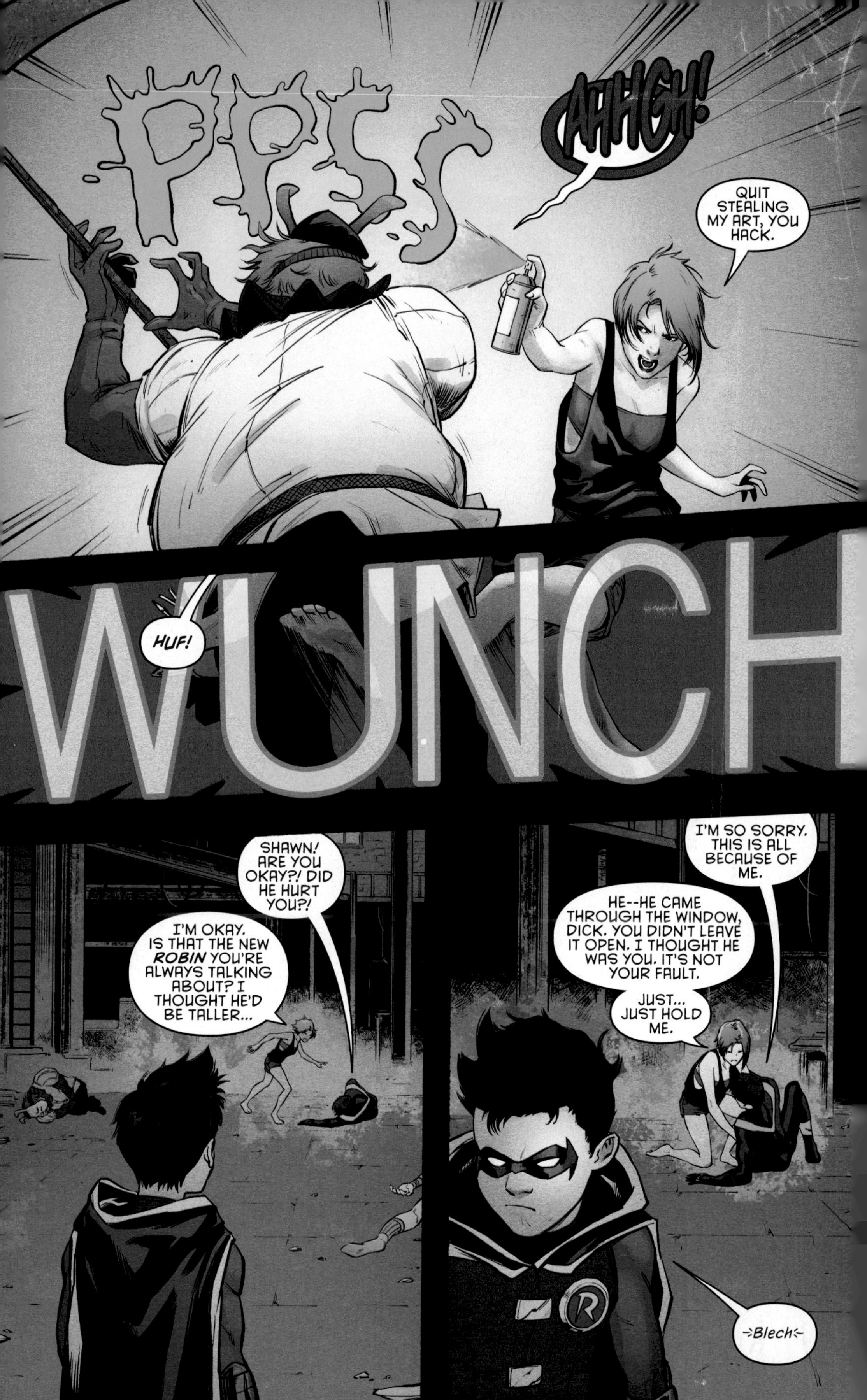
PPSS
AHHGH!
QUIT STEALING MY ART, YOU HACK.
WUNCH
HUF!
SHAWN! ARE YOU OKAY?! DID HE HURT YOU?!
I'M OKAY. IS THAT THE NEW *ROBIN* YOU'RE ALWAYS TALKING ABOUT? I THOUGHT HE'D BE TALLER...
I'M SO SORRY. THIS IS ALL BECAUSE OF ME.
HE--HE CAME THROUGH THE WINDOW, DICK. YOU DIDN'T LEAVE IT OPEN. I THOUGHT HE WAS YOU. IT'S NOT YOUR FAULT.
JUST... JUST HOLD ME.
Blech

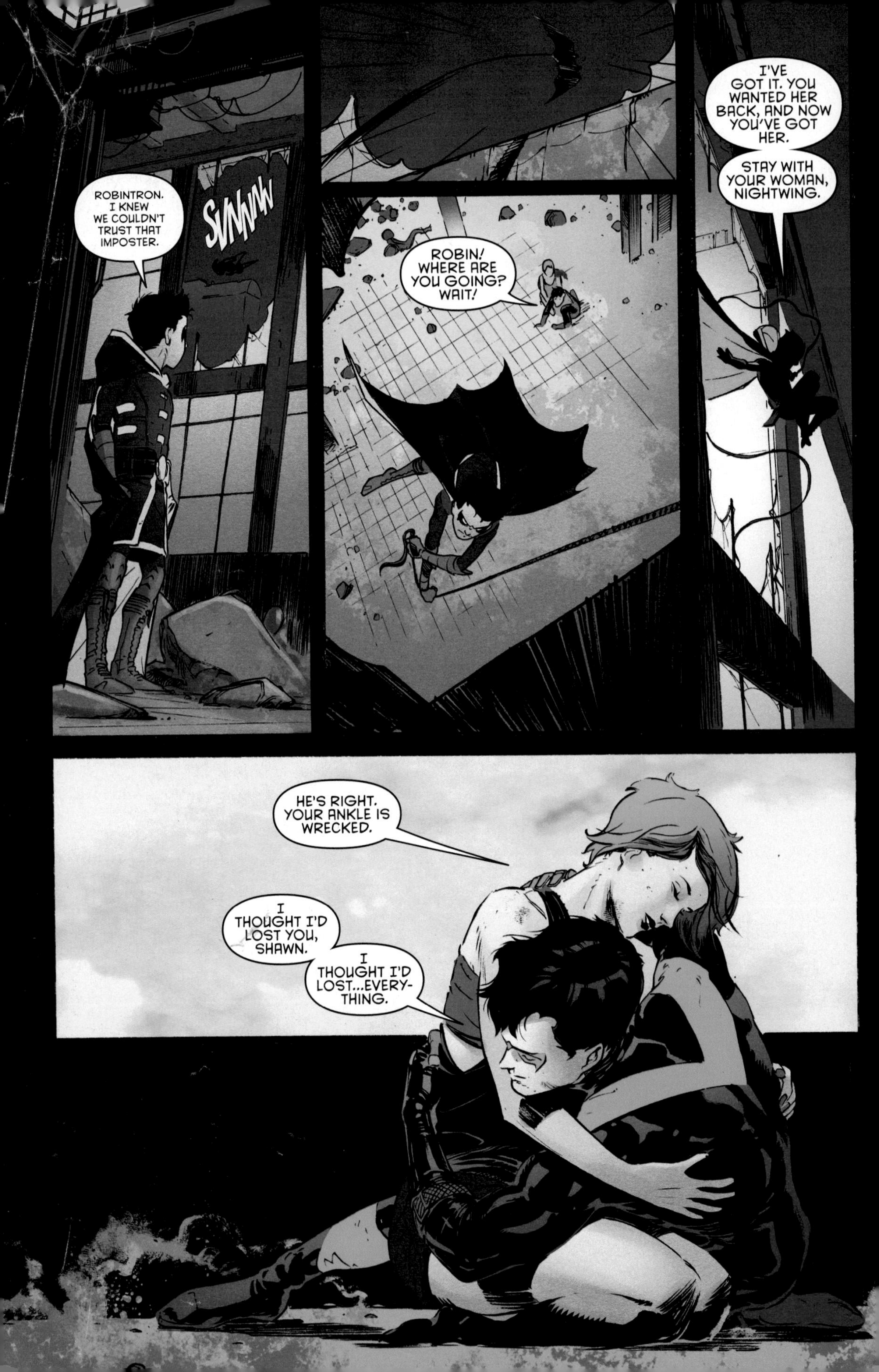
ROBINTRON. I KNEW WE COULDN'T TRUST THAT IMPOSTER.
SVNNNW
ROBIN! WHERE ARE YOU GOING? WAIT!
I'VE GOT IT. YOU WANTED HER BACK, AND NOW YOU'VE GOT HER.
STAY WITH YOUR WOMAN, NIGHTWING.
HE'S RIGHT. YOUR ANKLE IS WRECKED.
I THOUGHT I'D LOST YOU, SHAWN.
I THOUGHT I'D LOST...EVERY-THING.

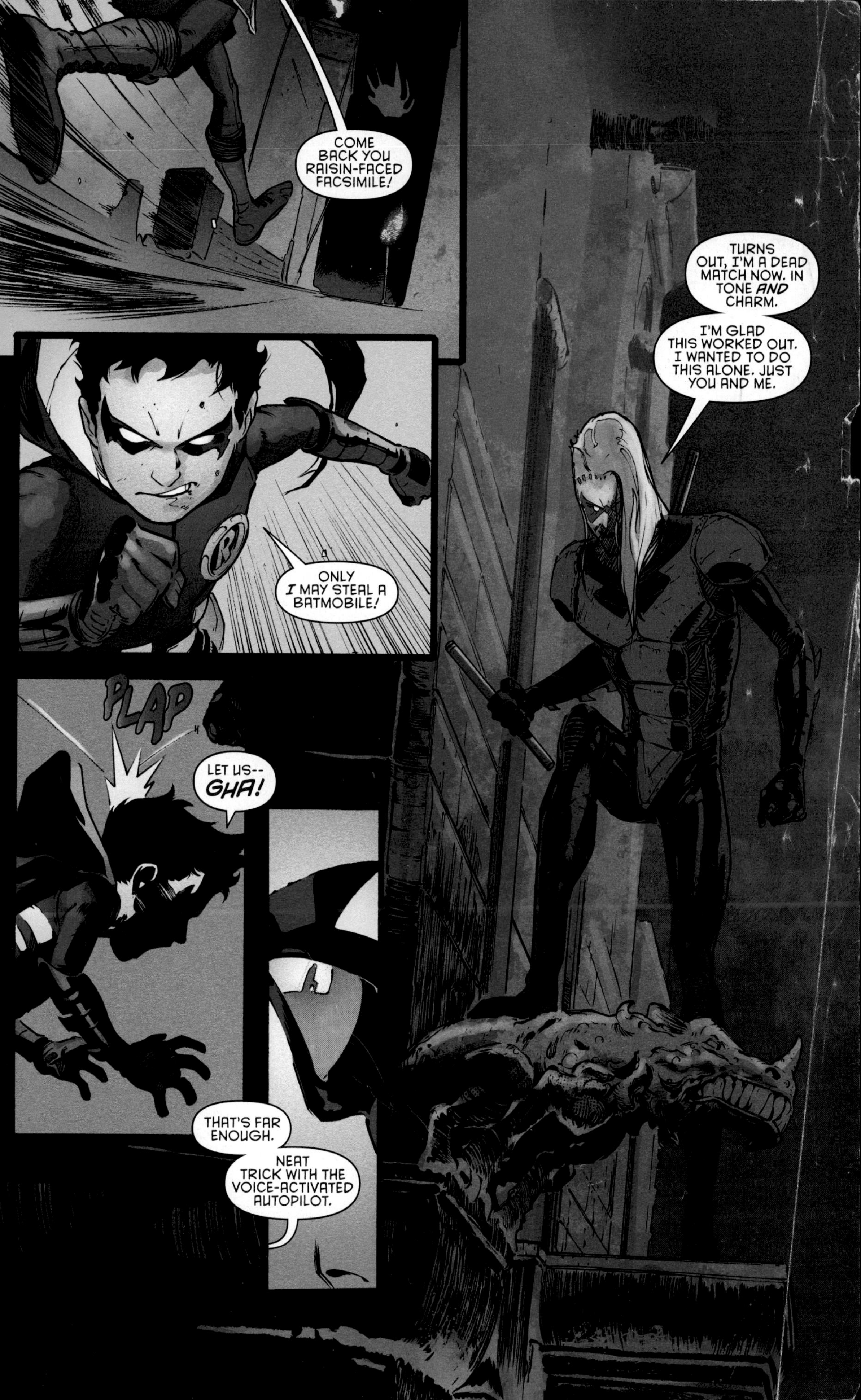
COME BACK YOU RAISIN-FACED FACSIMILE!
ONLY *I* MAY STEAL A BATMOBILE!
PLAP
LET US-- *GHA!*
THAT'S FAR ENOUGH.
NEAT TRICK WITH THE VOICE-ACTIVATED AUTOPILOT.
TURNS OUT, I'M A DEAD MATCH NOW. IN TONE *AND* CHARM.
I'M GLAD THIS WORKED OUT. I WANTED TO DO THIS ALONE. JUST YOU AND ME.

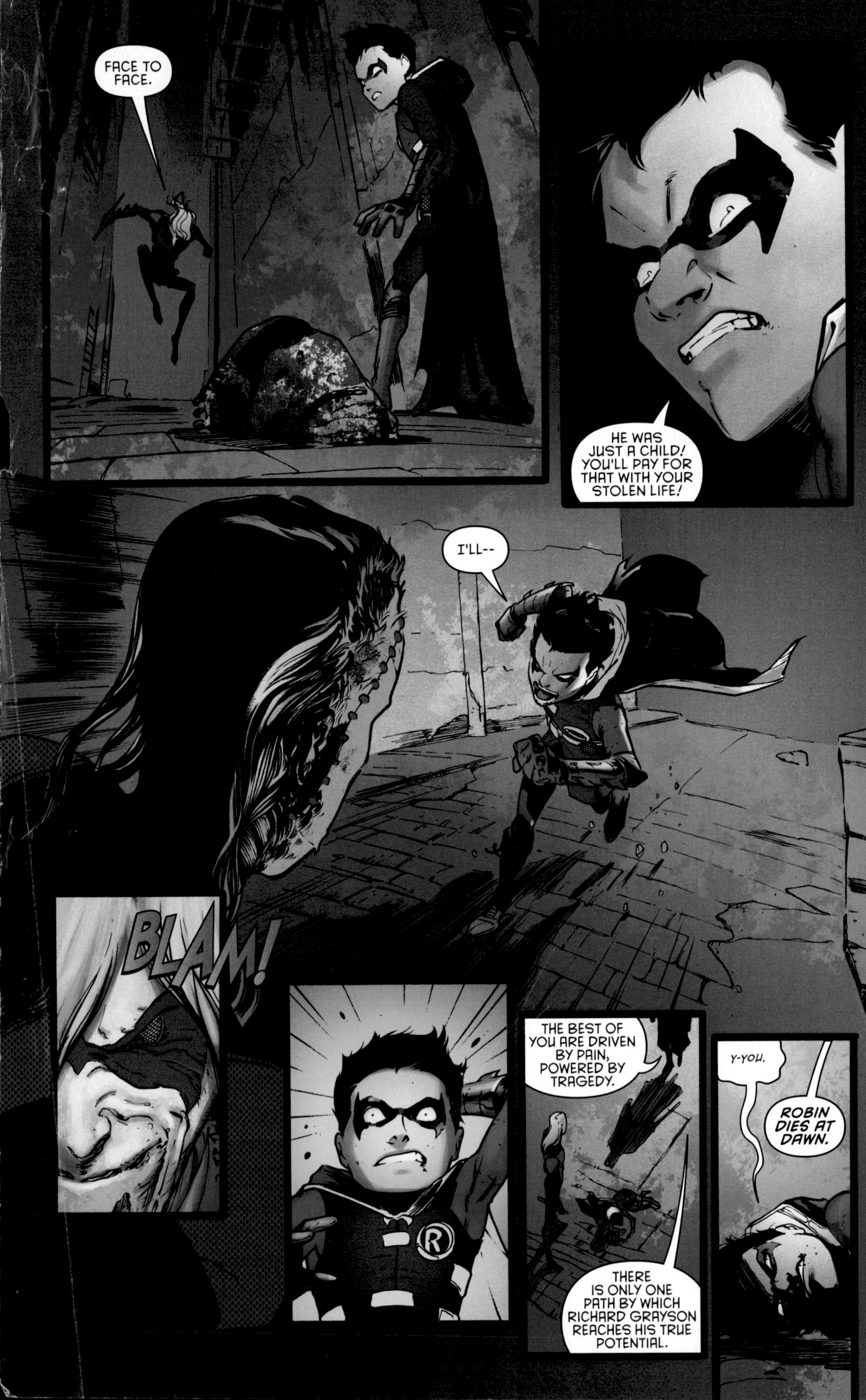
FACE TO FACE.
HE WAS JUST A CHILD! YOU'LL PAY FOR THAT WITH YOUR STOLEN LIFE!
I'LL--
BLAM!
THE BEST OF YOU ARE DRIVEN BY PAIN, POWERED BY TRAGEDY.
THERE IS ONLY ONE PATH BY WHICH RICHARD GRAYSON REACHES HIS TRUE POTENTIAL.
Y-YOU.
ROBIN DIES AT DAWN.

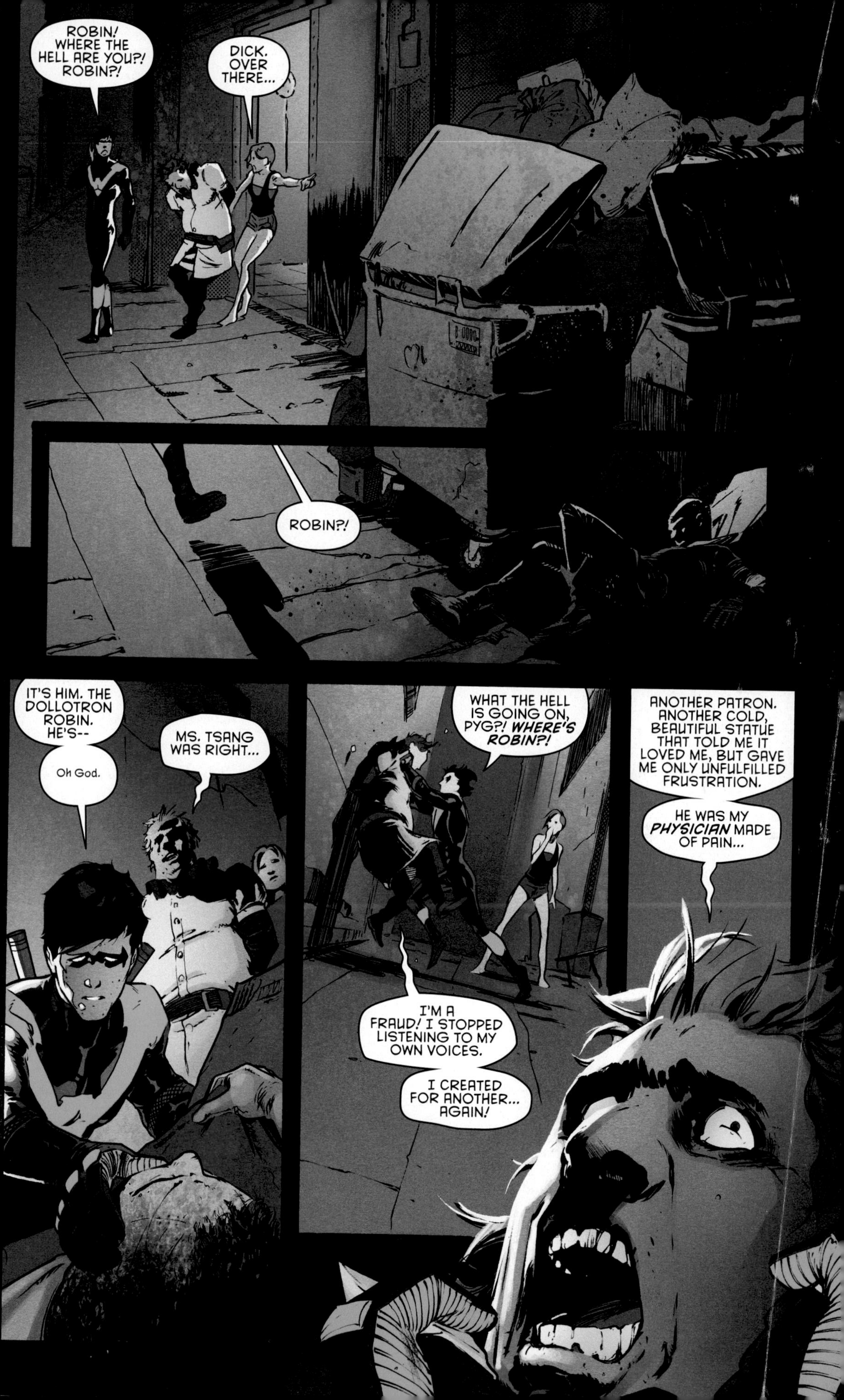
ROBIN! WHERE THE HELL ARE YOU?! ROBIN?!
DICK. OVER THERE...
ROBIN?!
IT'S HIM. THE DOLLOTRON ROBIN. HE'S--
Oh God.
MS. TSANG WAS RIGHT...
WHAT THE HELL IS GOING ON, PYG?! WHERE'S ROBIN?!
I'M A FRAUD! I STOPPED LISTENING TO MY OWN VOICES.
I CREATED FOR ANOTHER... AGAIN!
ANOTHER PATRON. ANOTHER COLD, BEAUTIFUL STATUE THAT TOLD ME IT LOVED ME, BUT GAVE ME ONLY UNFULFILLED FRUSTRATION.
HE WAS MY PHYSICIAN MADE OF PAIN...

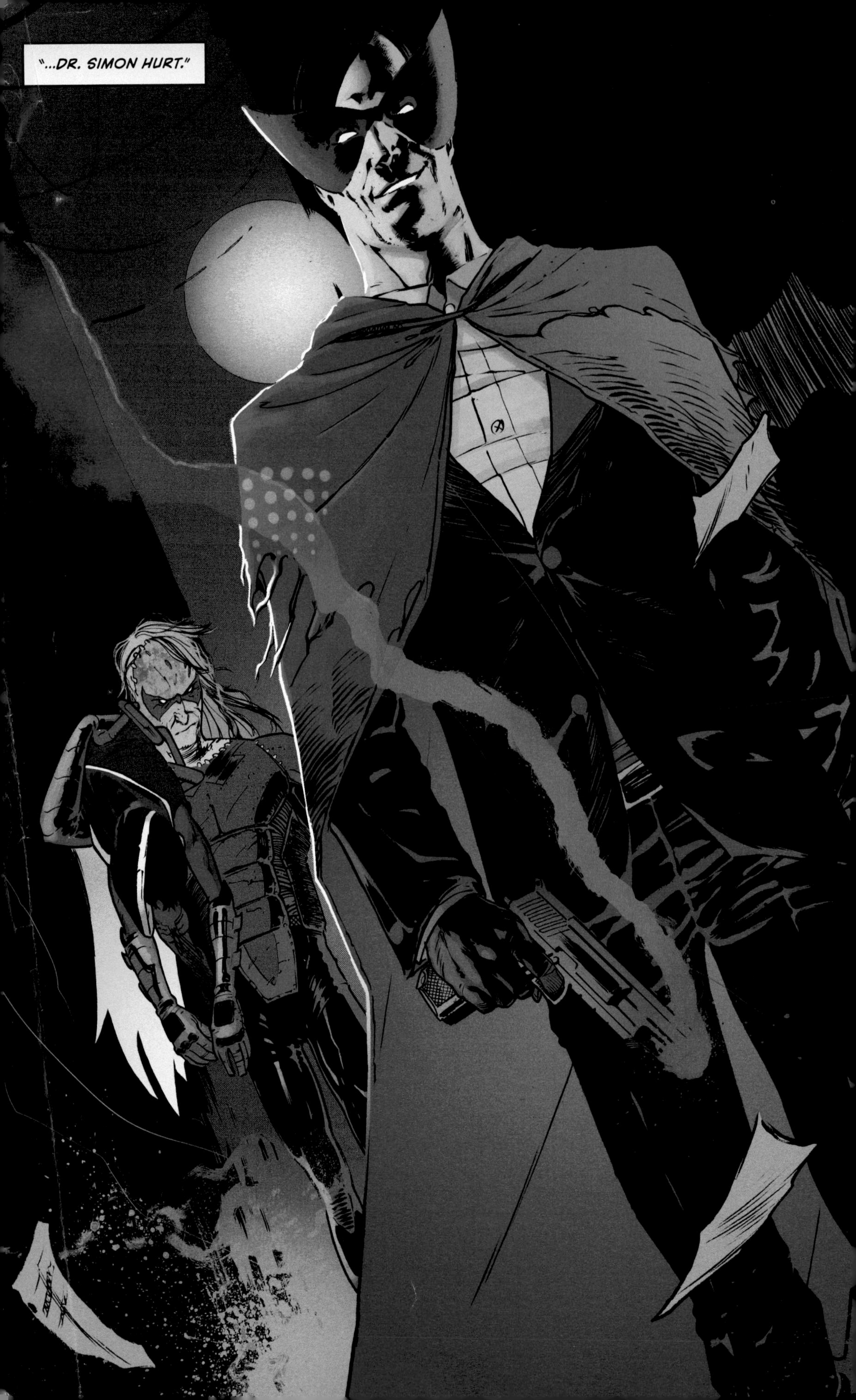
"...DR. SIMON HURT."

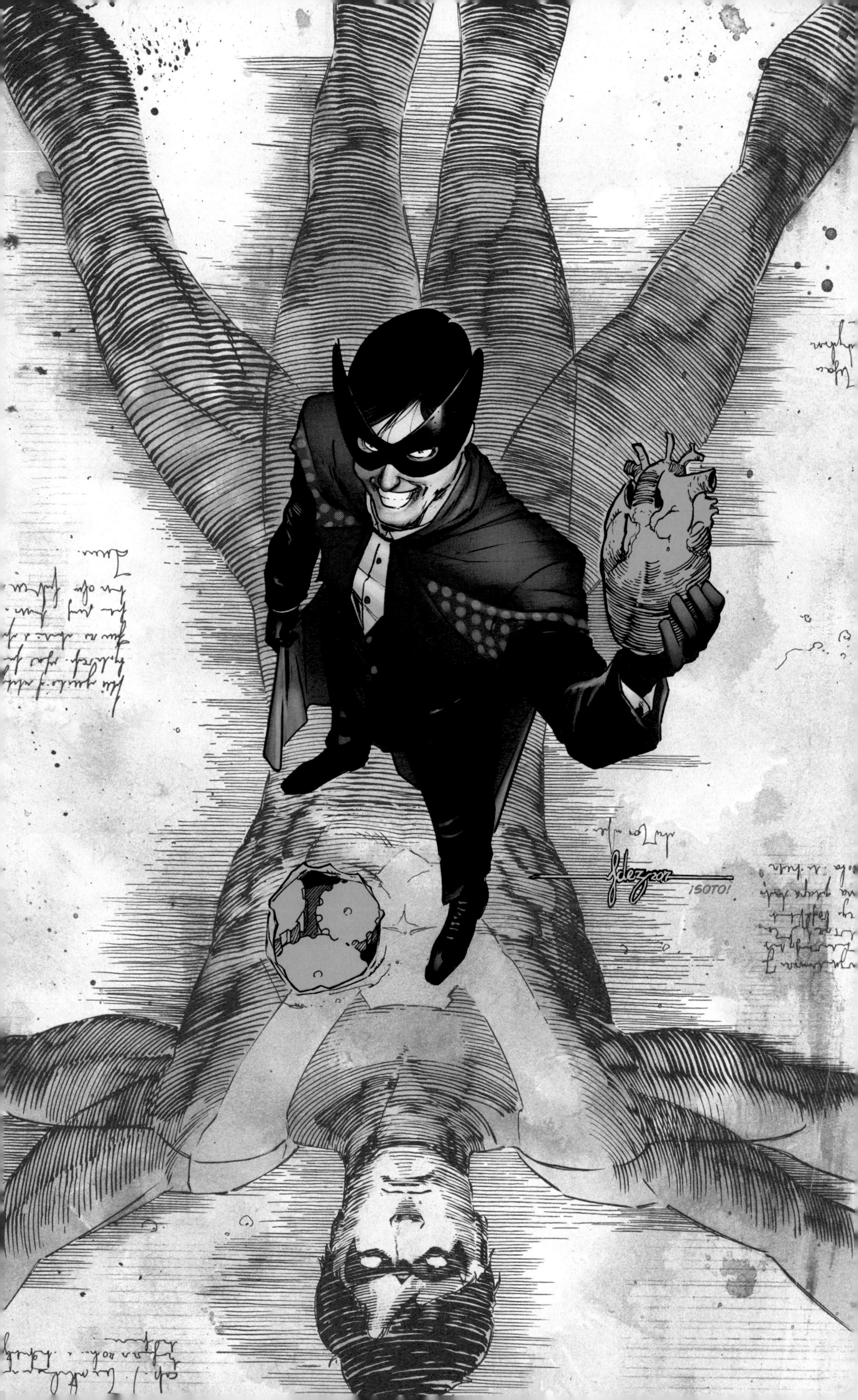
¡SOTO!

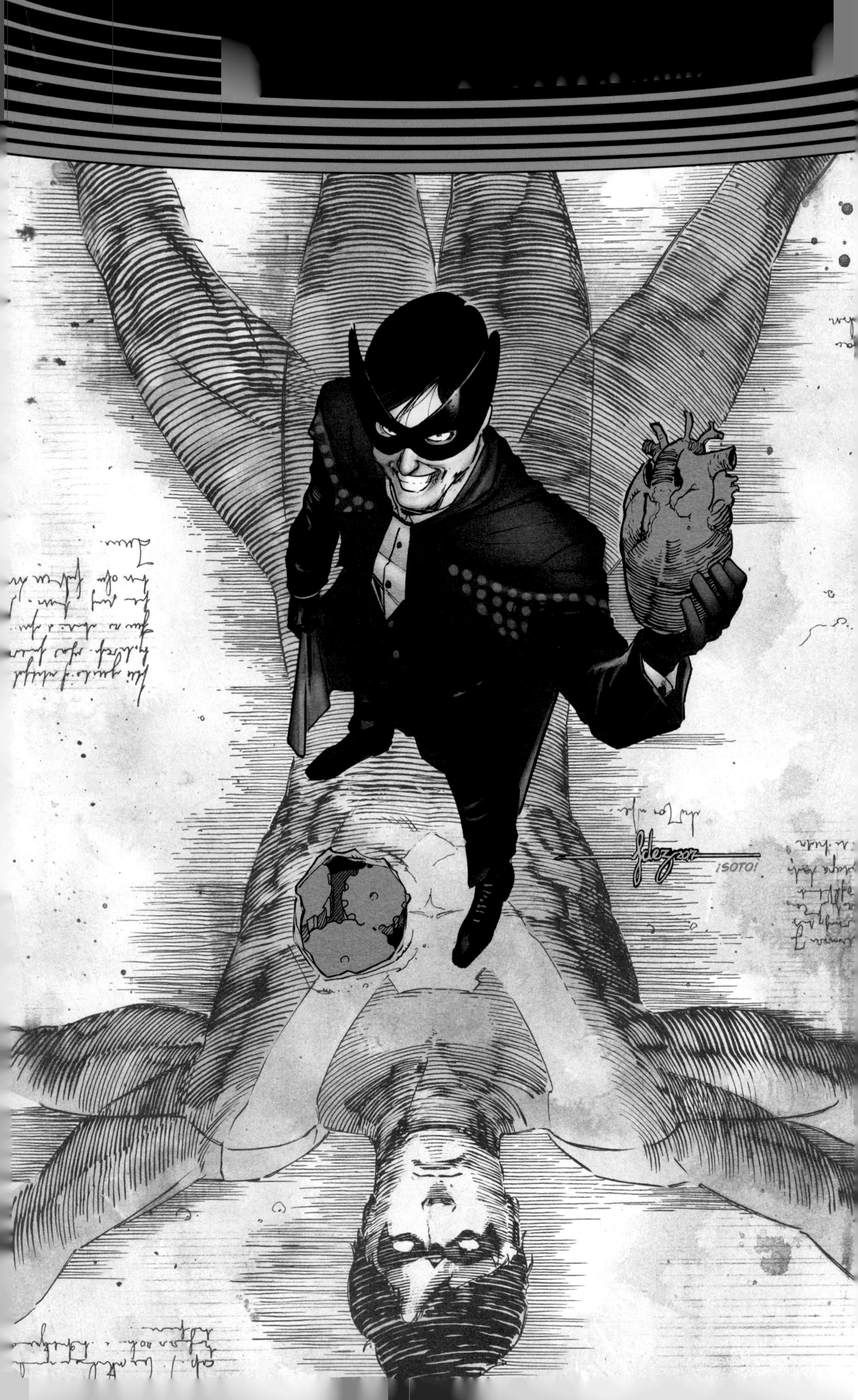
¡SOTO!

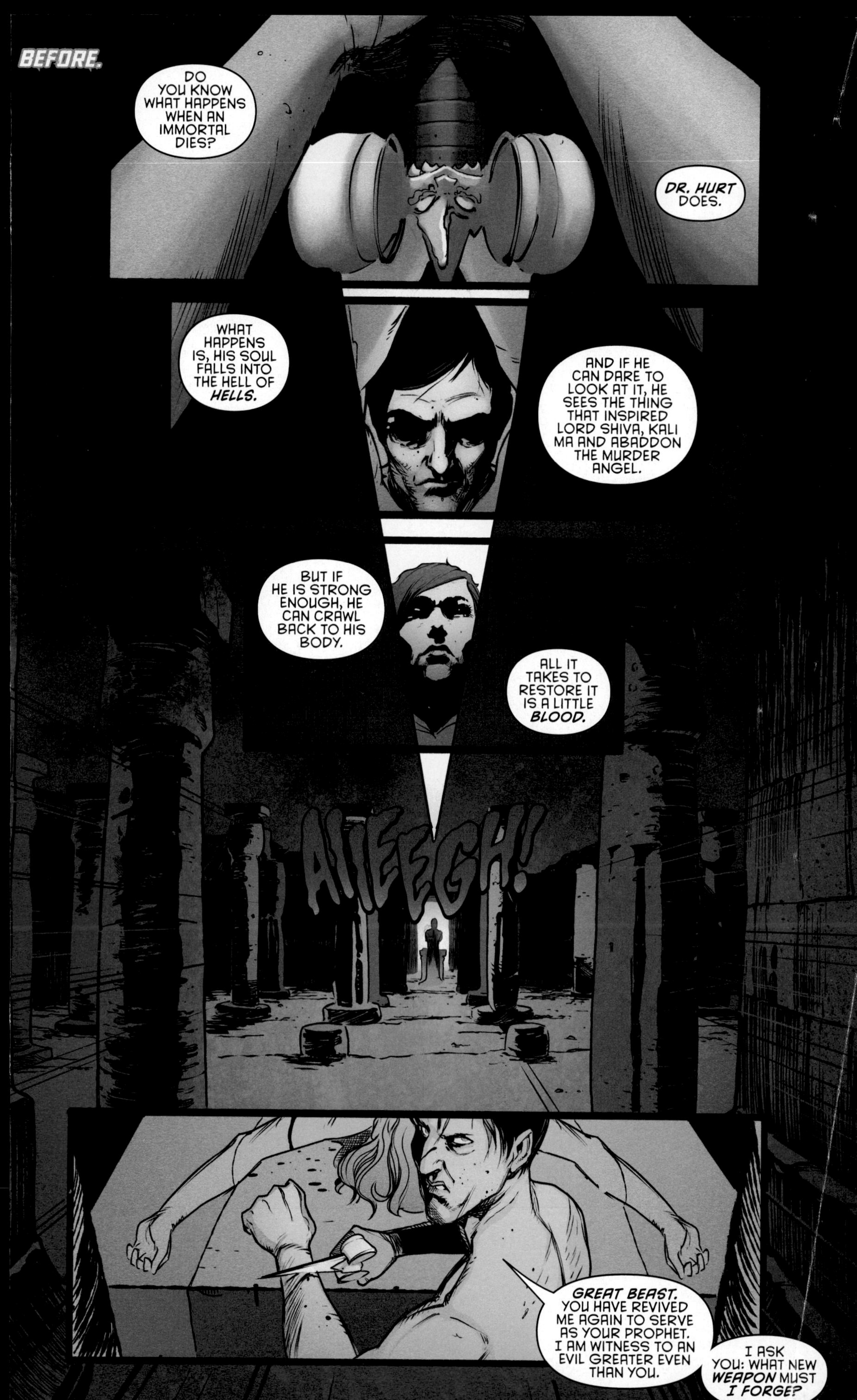
BEFORE.
DO YOU KNOW WHAT HAPPENS WHEN AN IMMORTAL DIES?
DR. HURT DOES.
WHAT HAPPENS IS, HIS SOUL FALLS INTO THE HELL OF HELLS.
AND IF HE CAN DARE TO LOOK AT IT, HE SEES THE THING THAT INSPIRED LORD SHIVA, KALI MA AND ABADDON THE MURDER ANGEL.
BUT IF HE IS STRONG ENOUGH, HE CAN CRAWL BACK TO HIS BODY.
ALL IT TAKES TO RESTORE IT IS A LITTLE BLOOD.
AIIEEGH!
GREAT BEAST. YOU HAVE REVIVED ME AGAIN TO SERVE AS YOUR PROPHET. I AM WITNESS TO AN EVIL GREATER EVEN THAN YOU.
I ASK YOU: WHAT NEW WEAPON MUST I FORGE?

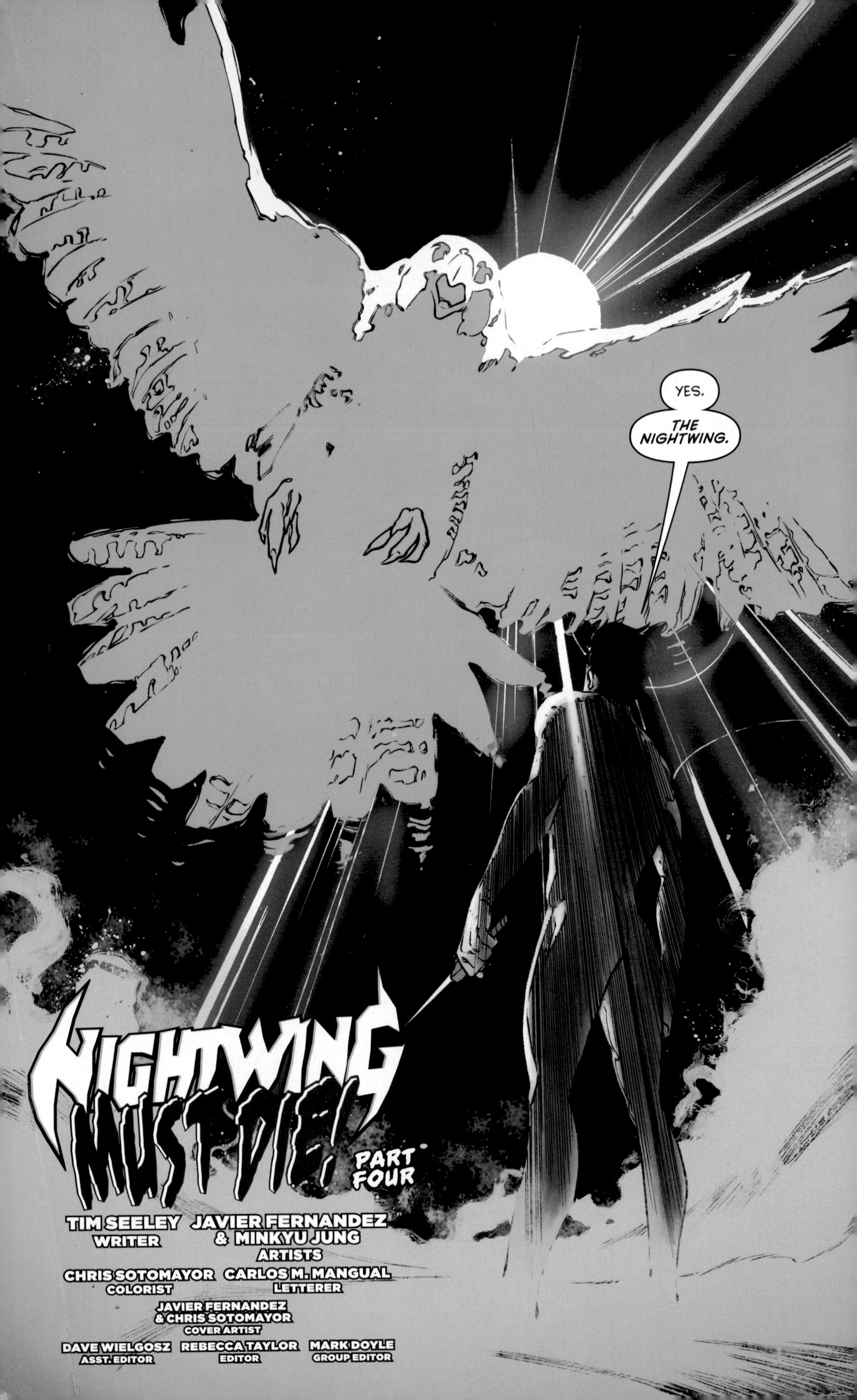
YES.
THE NIGHTWING.
NIGHTWING MUST DIE!
PART FOUR
TIM SEELEY WRITER
JAVIER FERNANDEZ & MINKYU JUNG ARTISTS
CHRIS SOTOMAYOR COLORIST
CARLOS M. MANGUAL LETTERER
JAVIER FERNANDEZ & CHRIS SOTOMAYOR COVER ARTIST
DAVE WIELGOSZ ASST. EDITOR
REBECCA TAYLOR EDITOR
MARK DOYLE GROUP EDITOR

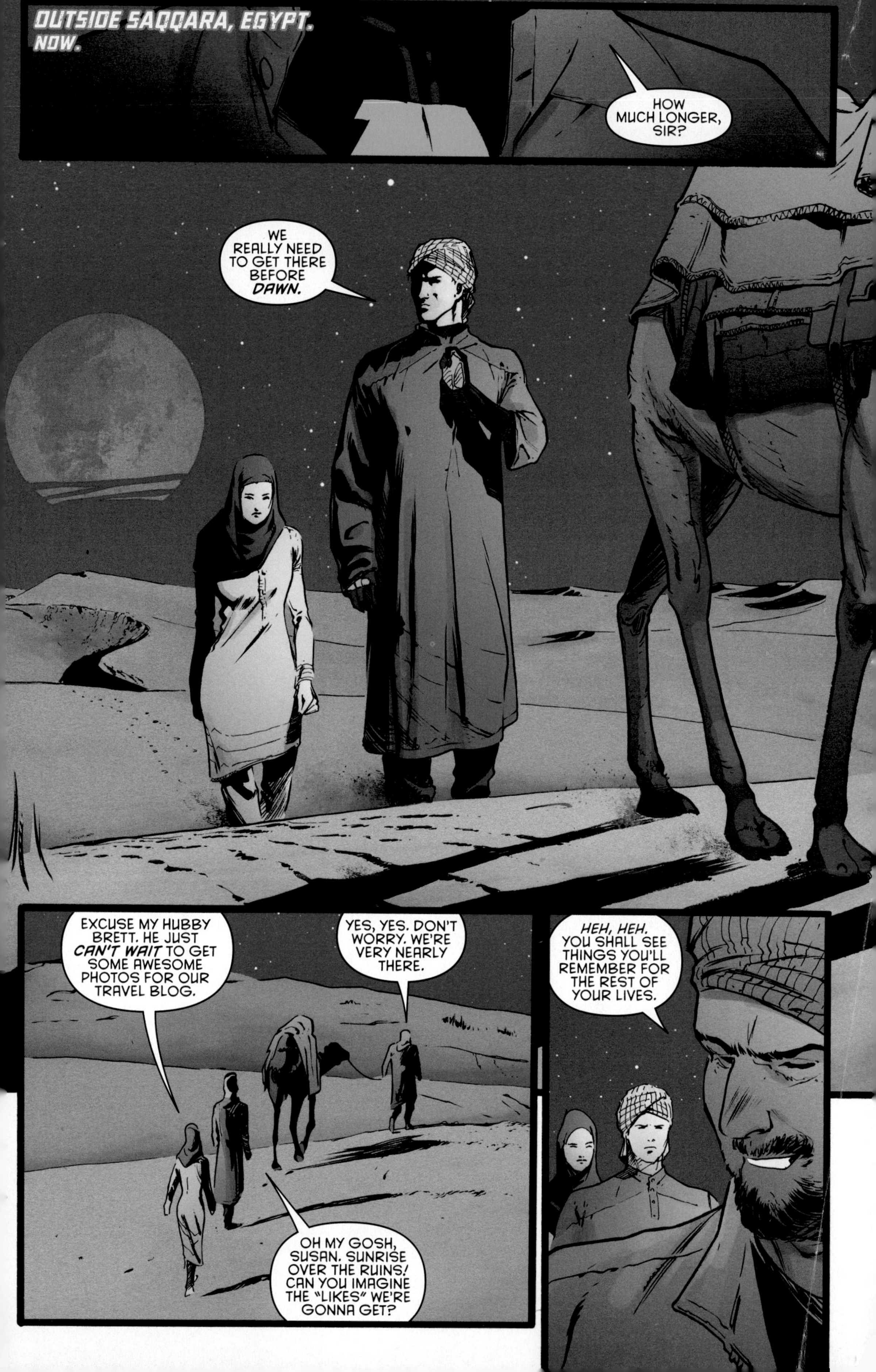
OUTSIDE SAQQARA, EGYPT. NOW.
HOW MUCH LONGER, SIR?
WE REALLY NEED TO GET THERE BEFORE *DAWN.*
EXCUSE MY HUBBY BRETT. HE JUST ***CAN'T WAIT*** TO GET SOME AWESOME PHOTOS FOR OUR TRAVEL BLOG.
YES, YES. DON'T WORRY. WE'RE VERY NEARLY THERE.
OH MY GOSH, SUSAN. SUNRISE OVER THE RUINS! CAN YOU IMAGINE THE "LIKES" WE'RE GONNA GET?
HEH, HEH. YOU SHALL SEE THINGS YOU'LL REMEMBER FOR THE REST OF YOUR LIVES.

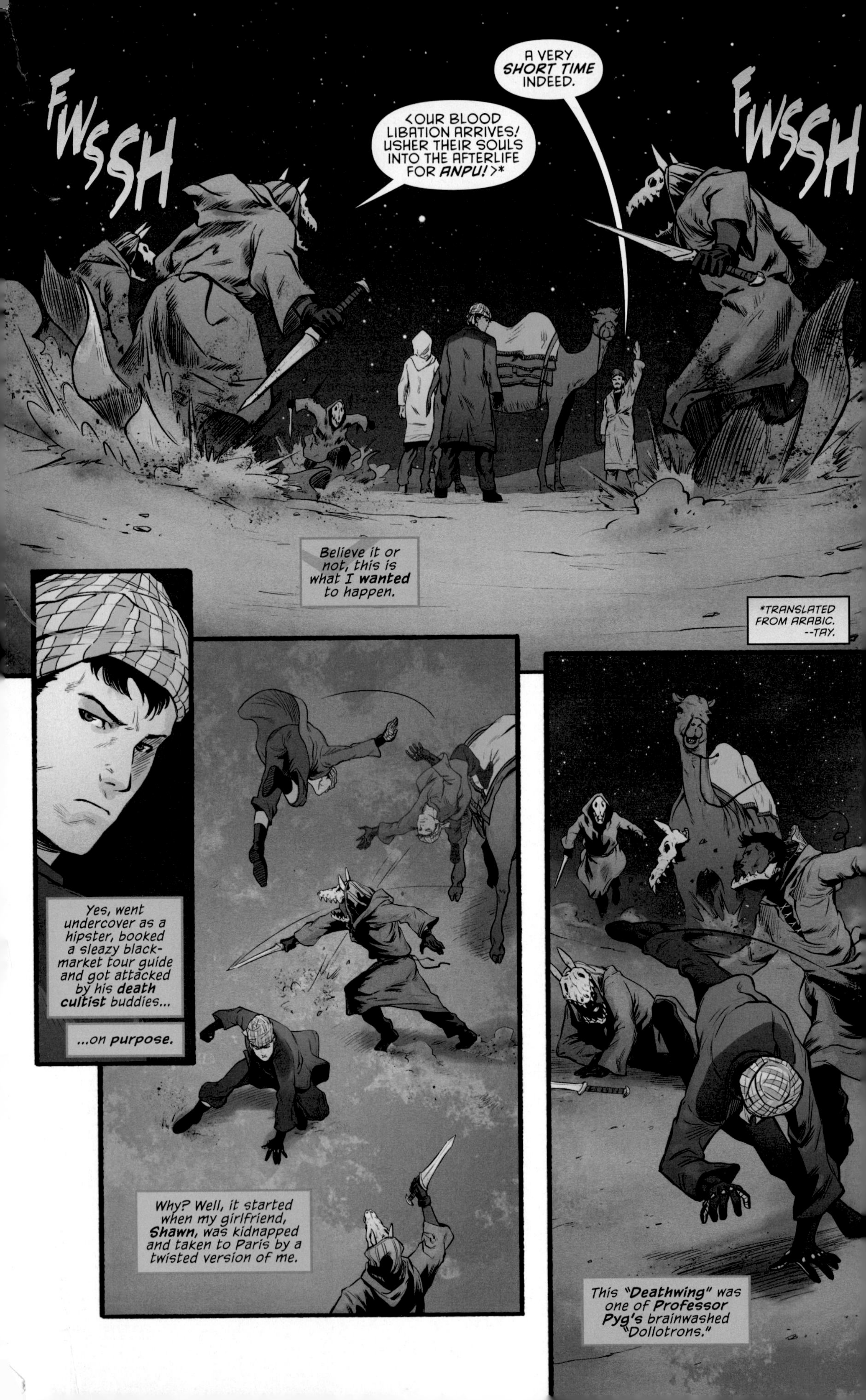
FWSSH
<OUR BLOOD LIBATION ARRIVES! USHER THEIR SOULS INTO THE AFTERLIFE FOR ANPU!>*
A VERY SHORT TIME INDEED.
FWSSH
Believe it or not, this is what I wanted to happen.
*TRANSLATED FROM ARABIC. --TAY.
Yes, went undercover as a hipster, booked a sleazy black-market tour guide and got attacked by his death cultist buddies...
...on purpose.
Why? Well, it started when my girlfriend, Shawn, was kidnapped and taken to Paris by a twisted version of me.
This "Deathwing" was one of Professor Pyg's brainwashed "Dollotrons."

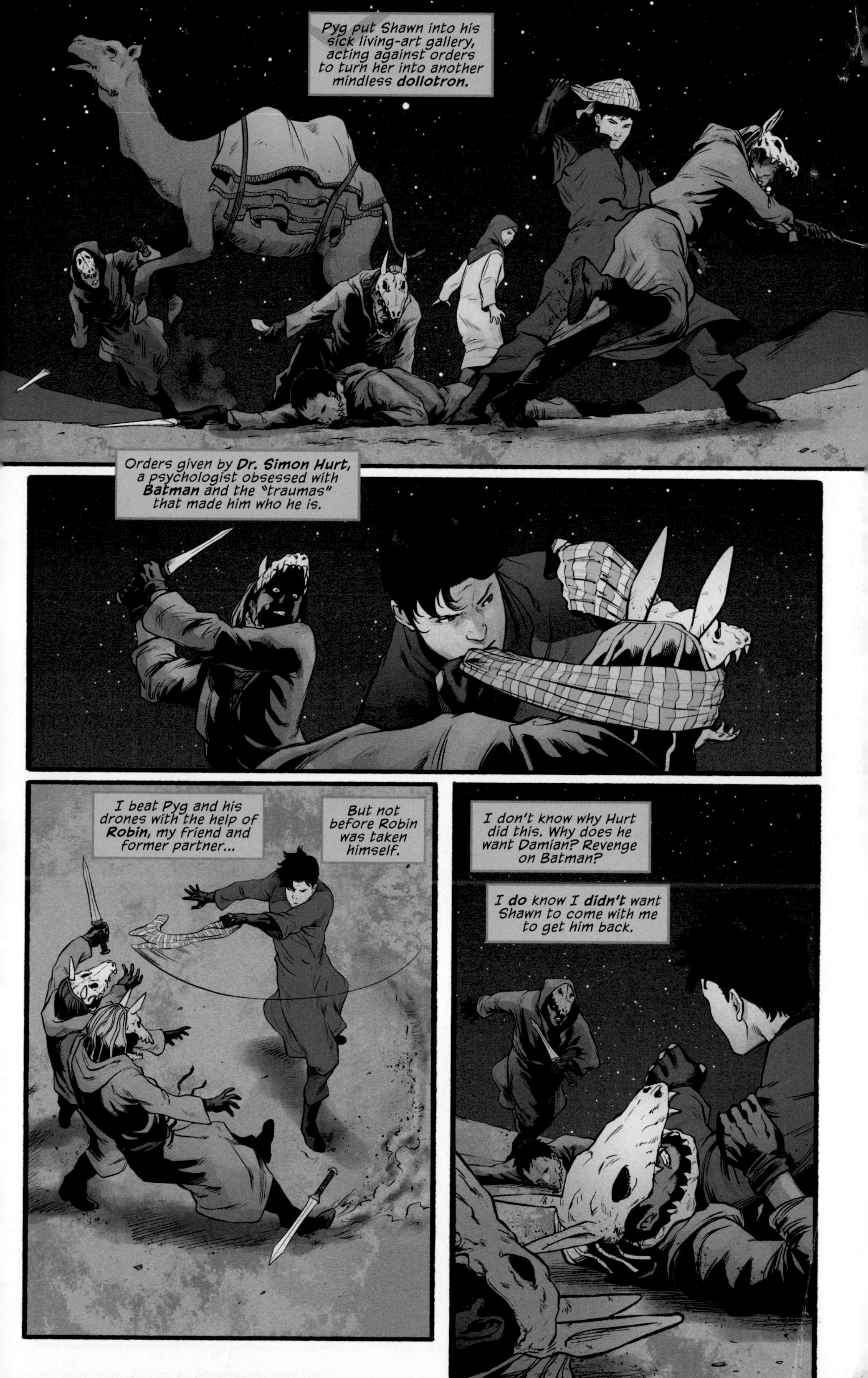
Pyg put Shawn into his sick living-art gallery, acting against orders to turn her into another mindless **dollotron.**
Orders given by **Dr. Simon Hurt,** a psychologist obsessed with **Batman** and the "traumas" that made him who he is.
I beat Pyg and his drones with the help of **Robin,** my friend and former partner...
But not before Robin was taken himself.
I don't know why Hurt did this. Why does he want Damian? Revenge on Batman?
I **do** know I **didn't** want Shawn to come with me to get him back.

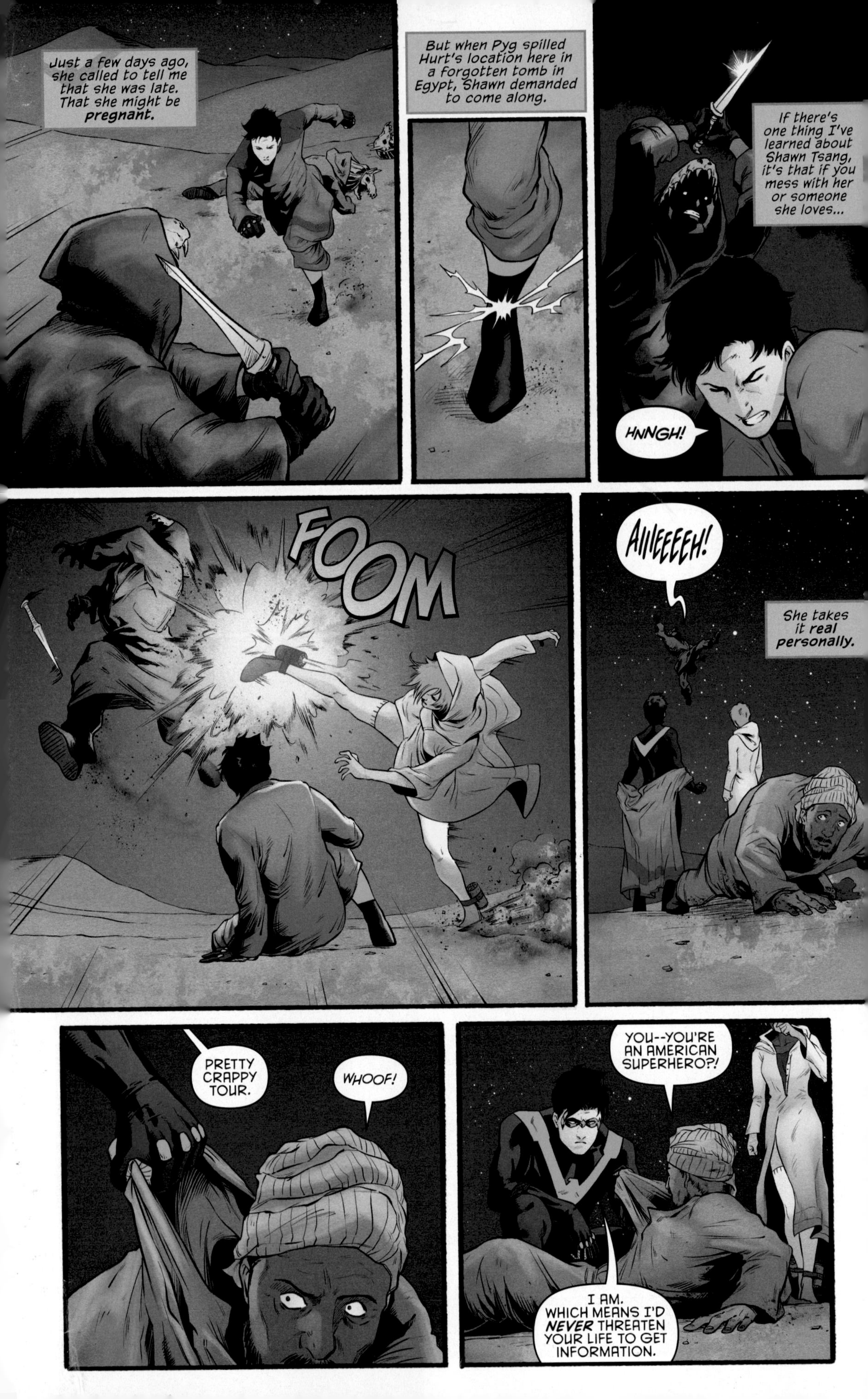
Just a few days ago, she called to tell me that she was late. That she might be **pregnant.**
But when Pyg spilled Hurt's location here in a forgotten tomb in Egypt, Shawn demanded to come along.
If there's one thing I've learned about Shawn Tsang, it's that if you mess with her or someone she loves...
HNNGH!
FOOM
AIIIEEEEH!
She takes it *real* personally.
PRETTY CRAPPY TOUR.
WHOOF!
YOU--YOU'RE AN AMERICAN SUPERHERO?!
I AM. WHICH MEANS I'D ***NEVER*** THREATEN YOUR LIFE TO GET INFORMATION.

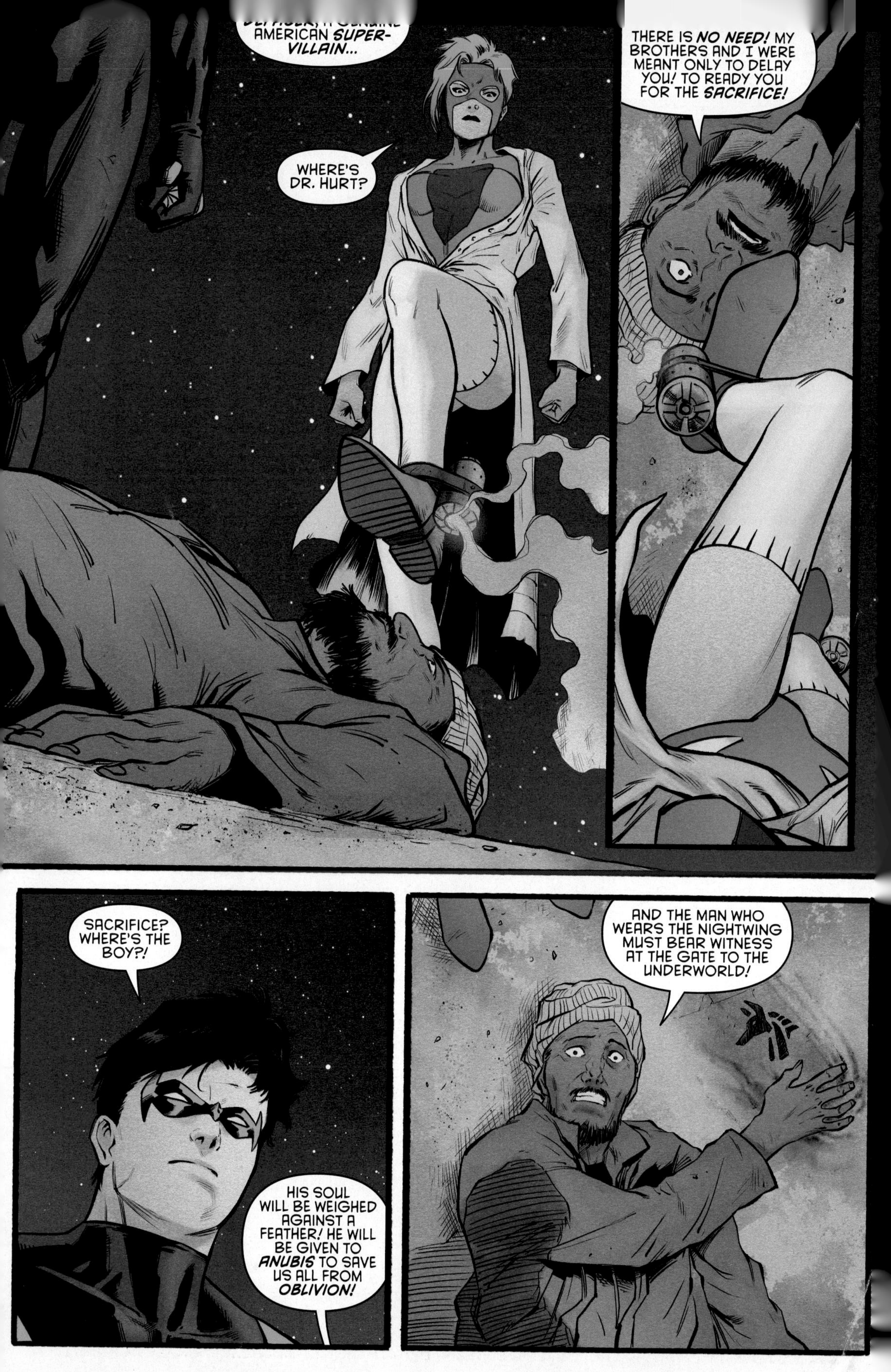
AMERICAN SUPER-VILLAIN...
WHERE'S DR. HURT?
THERE IS NO NEED! MY BROTHERS AND I WERE MEANT ONLY TO DELAY YOU! TO READY YOU FOR THE SACRIFICE!
SACRIFICE? WHERE'S THE BOY?!
HIS SOUL WILL BE WEIGHED AGAINST A FEATHER! HE WILL BE GIVEN TO ANUBIS TO SAVE US ALL FROM OBLIVION!
AND THE MAN WHO WEARS THE NIGHTWING MUST BEAR WITNESS AT THE GATE TO THE UNDERWORLD!

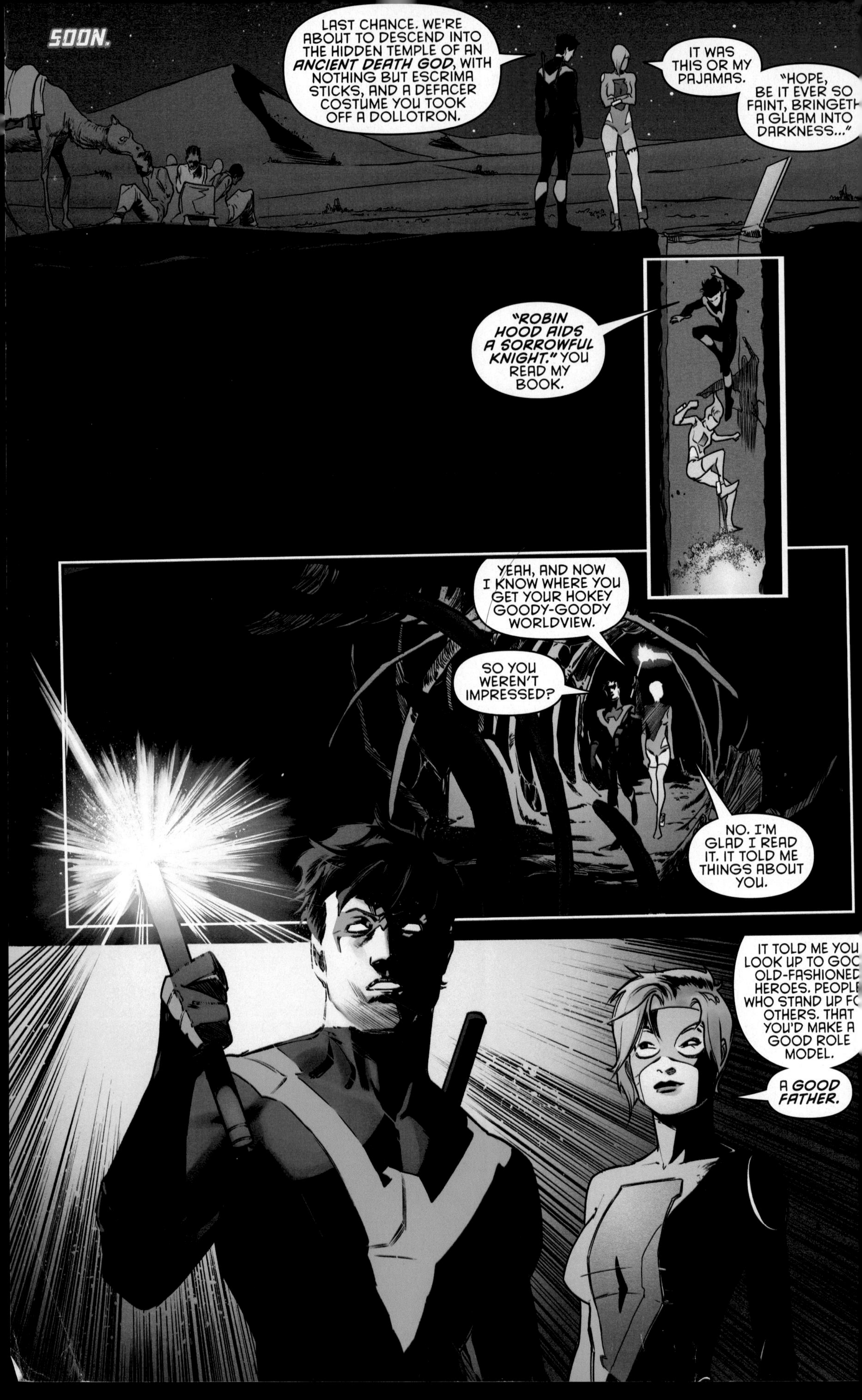

SOON.
LAST CHANCE. WE'RE ABOUT TO DESCEND INTO THE HIDDEN TEMPLE OF AN *ANCIENT DEATH GOD*, WITH NOTHING BUT ESCRIMA STICKS, AND A DEFACER COSTUME YOU TOOK OFF A DOLLOTRON.
IT WAS THIS OR MY PAJAMAS.
"HOPE, BE IT EVER SO FAINT, BRINGETH A GLEAM INTO DARKNESS..."
"ROBIN HOOD AIDS A SORROWFUL KNIGHT." YOU READ MY BOOK.
YEAH, AND NOW I KNOW WHERE YOU GET YOUR HOKEY GOODY-GOODY WORLDVIEW.
SO YOU WEREN'T IMPRESSED?
NO. I'M GLAD I READ IT. IT TOLD ME THINGS ABOUT YOU.
IT TOLD ME YOU LOOK UP TO GOOD OLD-FASHIONED HEROES. PEOPLE WHO STAND UP FOR OTHERS. THAT YOU'D MAKE A GOOD ROLE MODEL.
A *GOOD FATHER.*

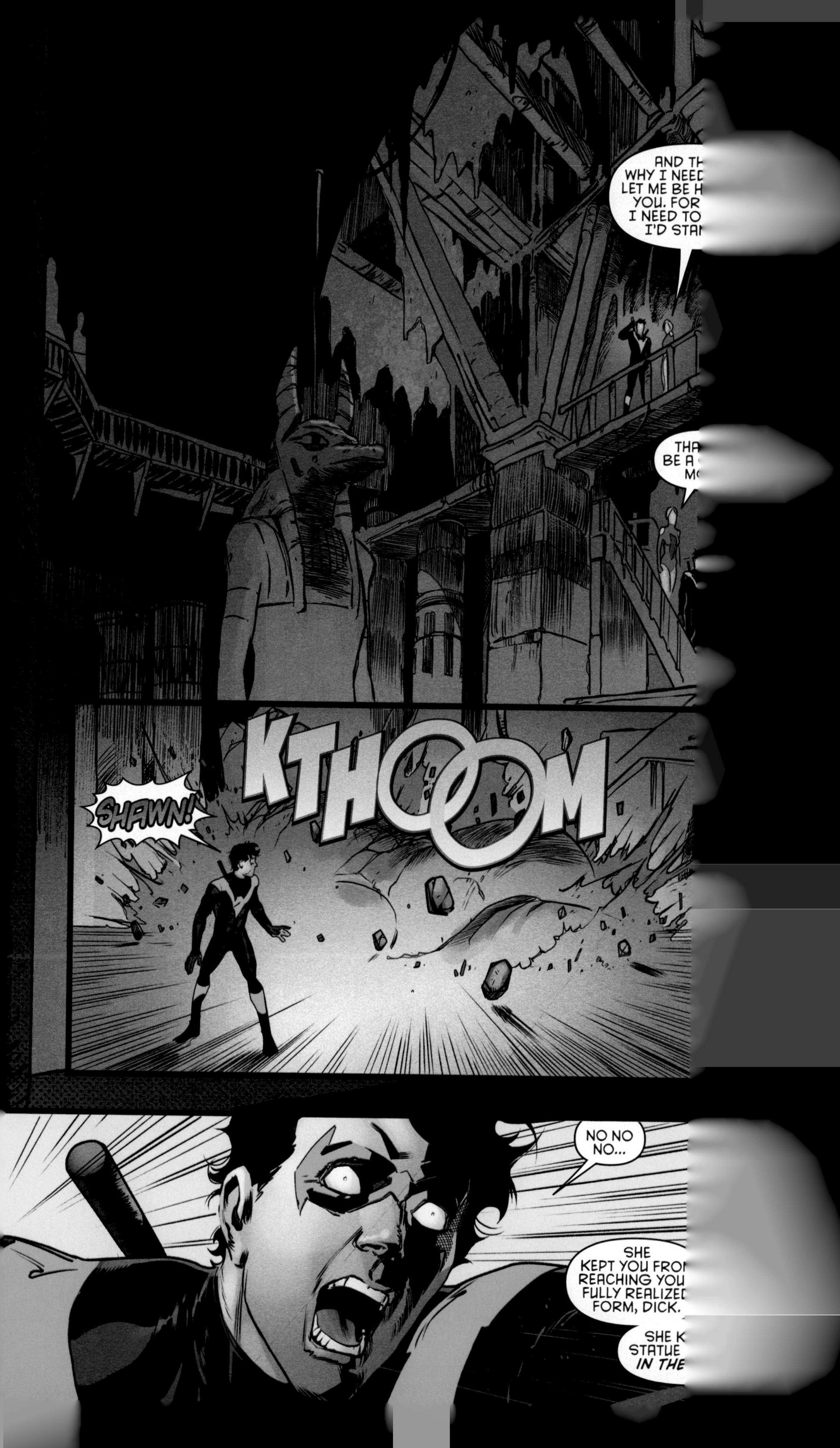
AND TH
WHY I NEED
LET ME BE H
YOU. FOR
I NEED TO
I'D STAN
THA
BE A
M
KTHOOM
SHAWN!
NO NO NO...
SHE KEPT YOU FROM REACHING YOU FULLY REALIZED FORM, DICK.
SHE K
STATUE
IN THE

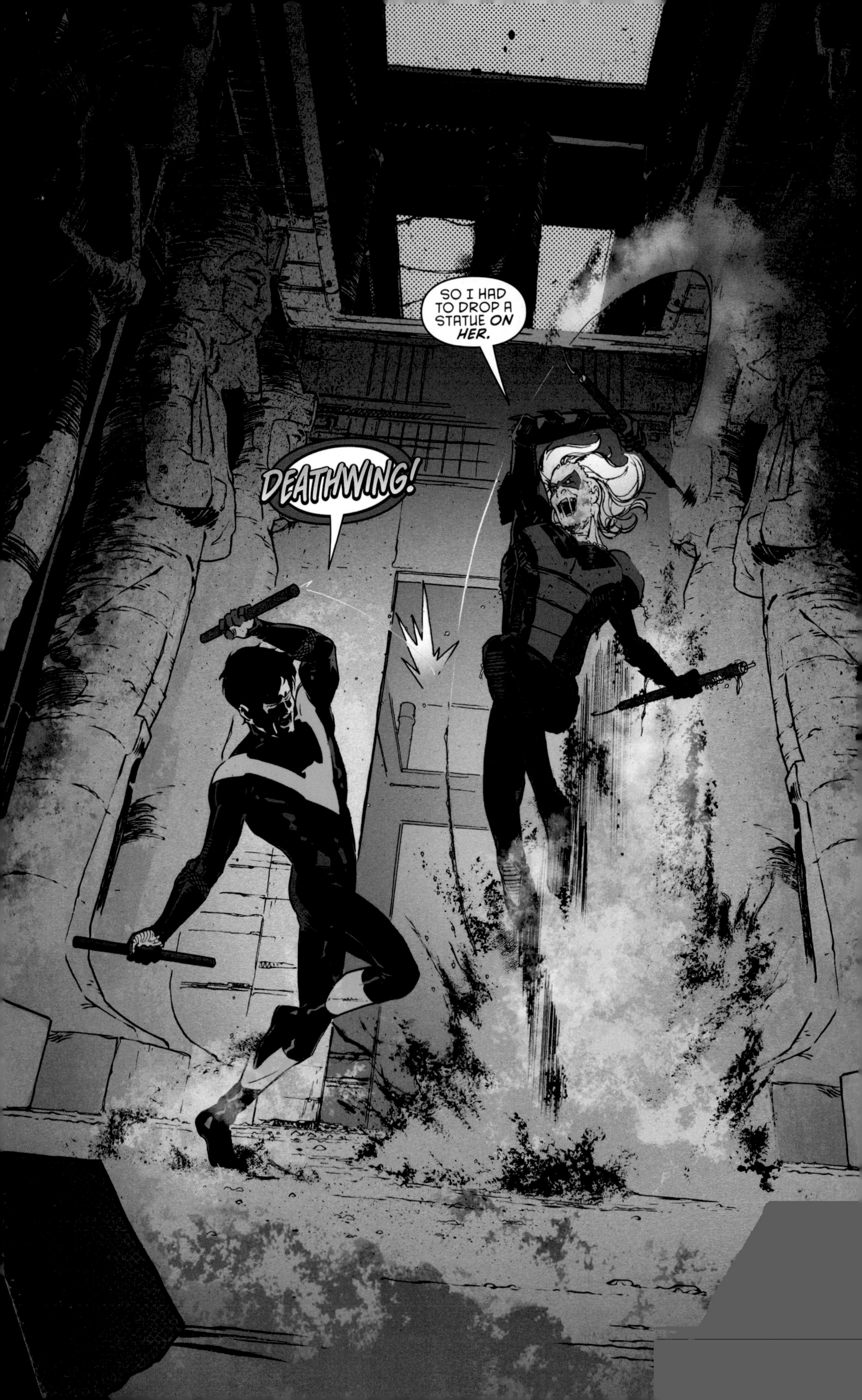
SO I HAD TO DROP A STATUE ON HER.
DEATHWING!

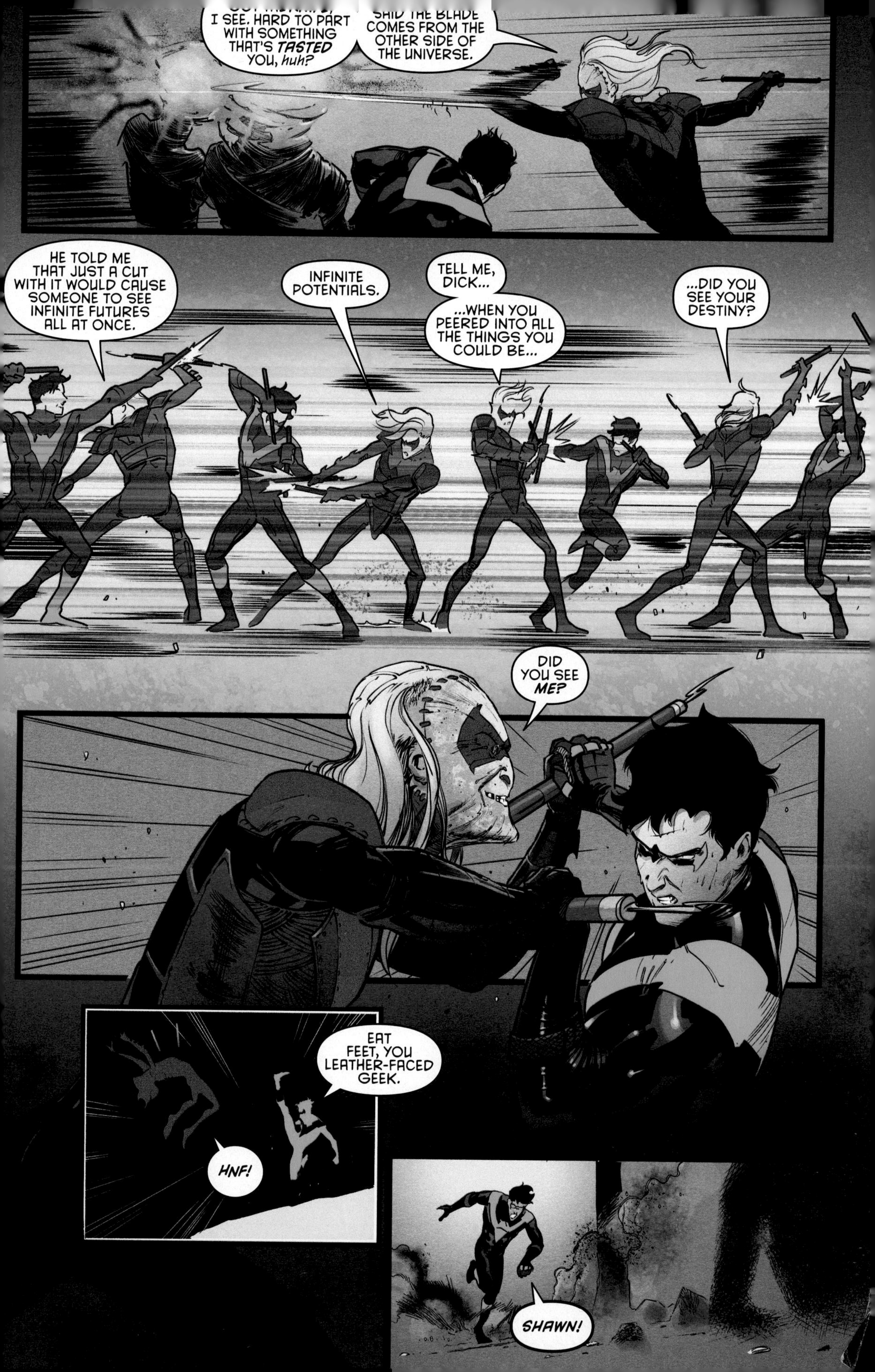
I SEE. HARD TO PART WITH SOMETHING THAT'S TASTED YOU, huh?
SAID THE BLADE COMES FROM THE OTHER SIDE OF THE UNIVERSE.
HE TOLD ME THAT JUST A CUT WITH IT WOULD CAUSE SOMEONE TO SEE INFINITE FUTURES ALL AT ONCE.
INFINITE POTENTIALS.
TELL ME, DICK...
...WHEN YOU PEERED INTO ALL THE THINGS YOU COULD BE...
...DID YOU SEE YOUR DESTINY?
DID YOU SEE ME?
EAT FEET, YOU LEATHER-FACED GEEK.
HNF!
SHAWN!

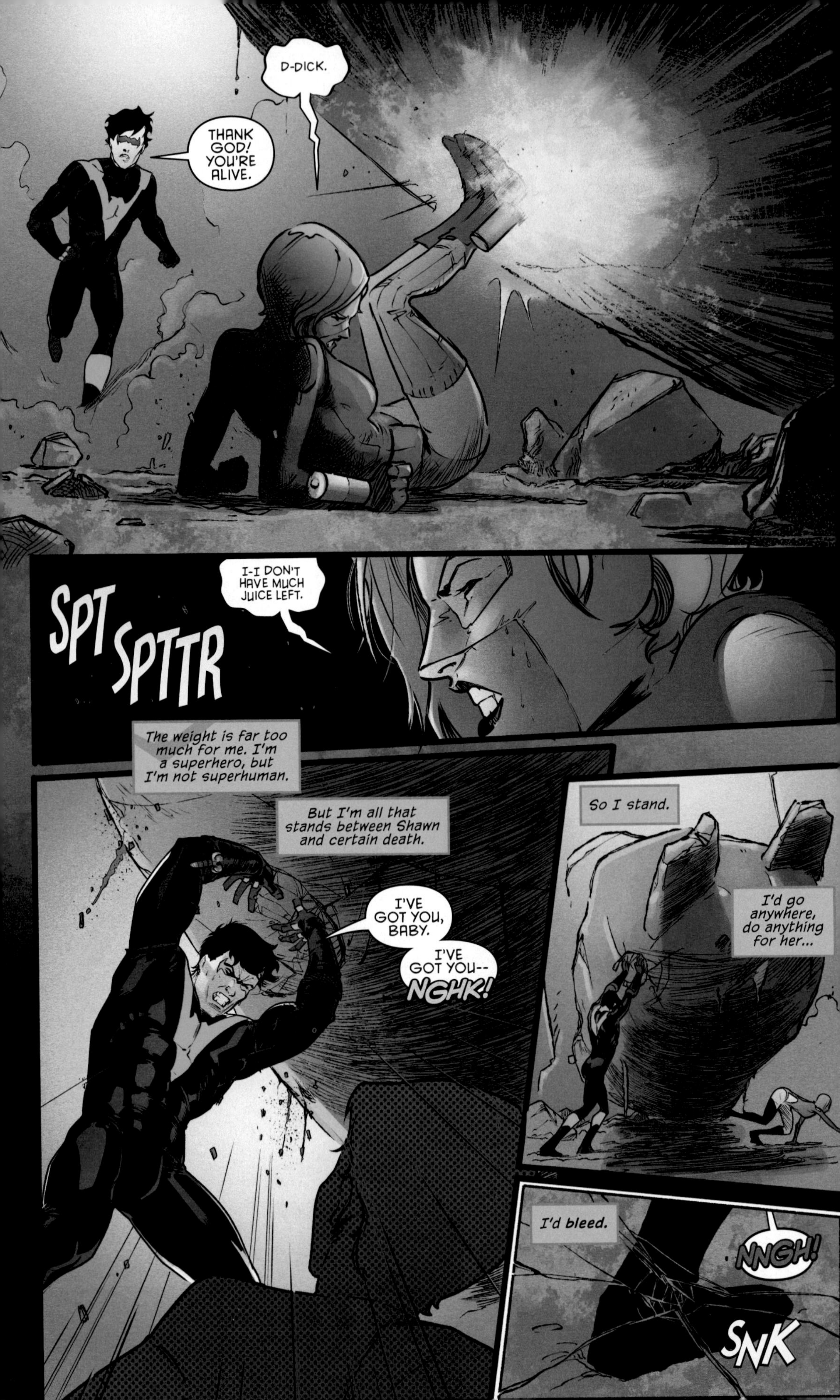
D-DICK.
THANK GOD! YOU'RE ALIVE.
SPT SPTTR
I-I DON'T HAVE MUCH JUICE LEFT.
The weight is far too much for me. I'm a superhero, but I'm not superhuman.
But I'm all that stands between Shawn and certain death.
I'VE GOT YOU, BABY.
I'VE GOT YOU-- NGHK!
So I stand.
I'd go anywhere, do anything for her...
I'd bleed.
NNGH!
SNK

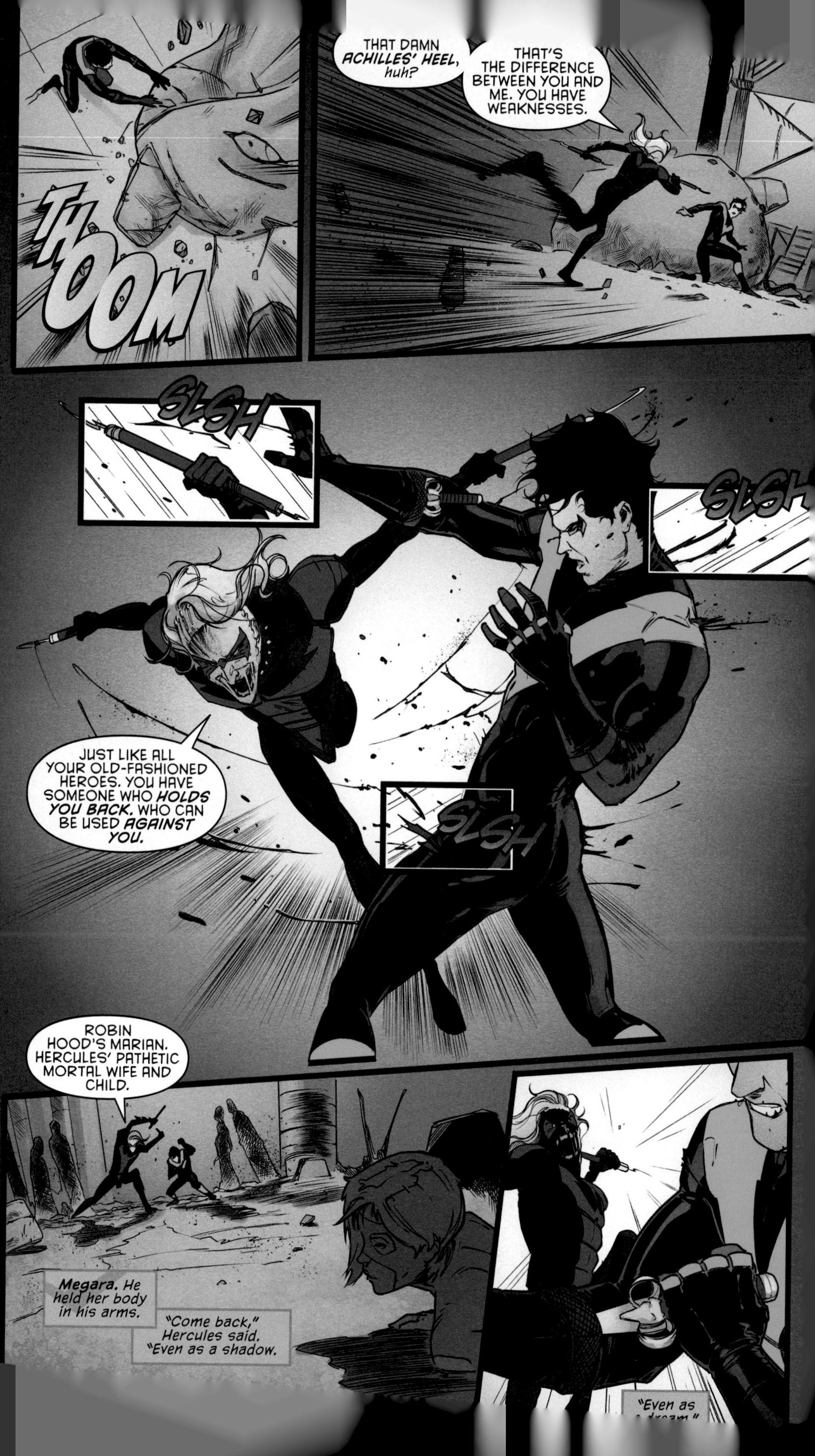
THOOM
THAT DAMN ACHILLES' HEEL, huh?
THAT'S THE DIFFERENCE BETWEEN YOU AND ME. YOU HAVE WEAKNESSES.
SLSH
SLSH
JUST LIKE ALL YOUR OLD-FASHIONED HEROES. YOU HAVE SOMEONE WHO HOLDS YOU BACK. WHO CAN BE USED AGAINST YOU.
SLSH
ROBIN HOOD'S MARIAN. HERCULES' PATHETIC MORTAL WIFE AND CHILD.
Megara. He held her body in his arms.
"Come back," Hercules said. "Even as a shadow.
"Even as

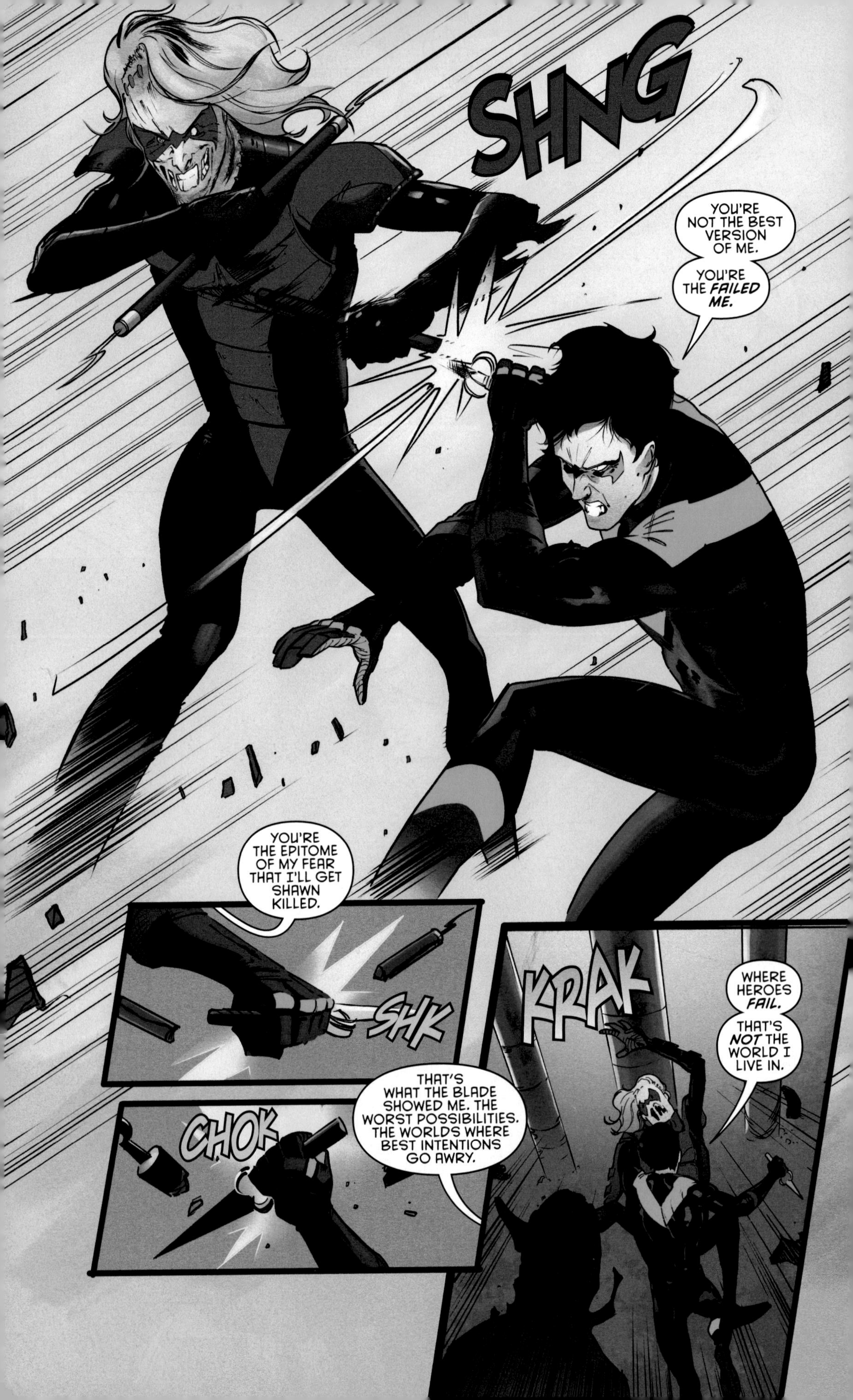
SHNG
YOU'RE NOT THE BEST VERSION OF ME.
YOU'RE THE *FAILED ME.*
YOU'RE THE EPITOME OF MY FEAR THAT I'LL GET SHAWN KILLED.
SHK
CHOK
THAT'S WHAT THE BLADE SHOWED ME. THE WORST POSSIBILITIES. THE WORLDS WHERE BEST INTENTIONS GO AWRY.
KRAK
WHERE HEROES *FAIL.*
THAT'S *NOT* THE WORLD I LIVE IN.

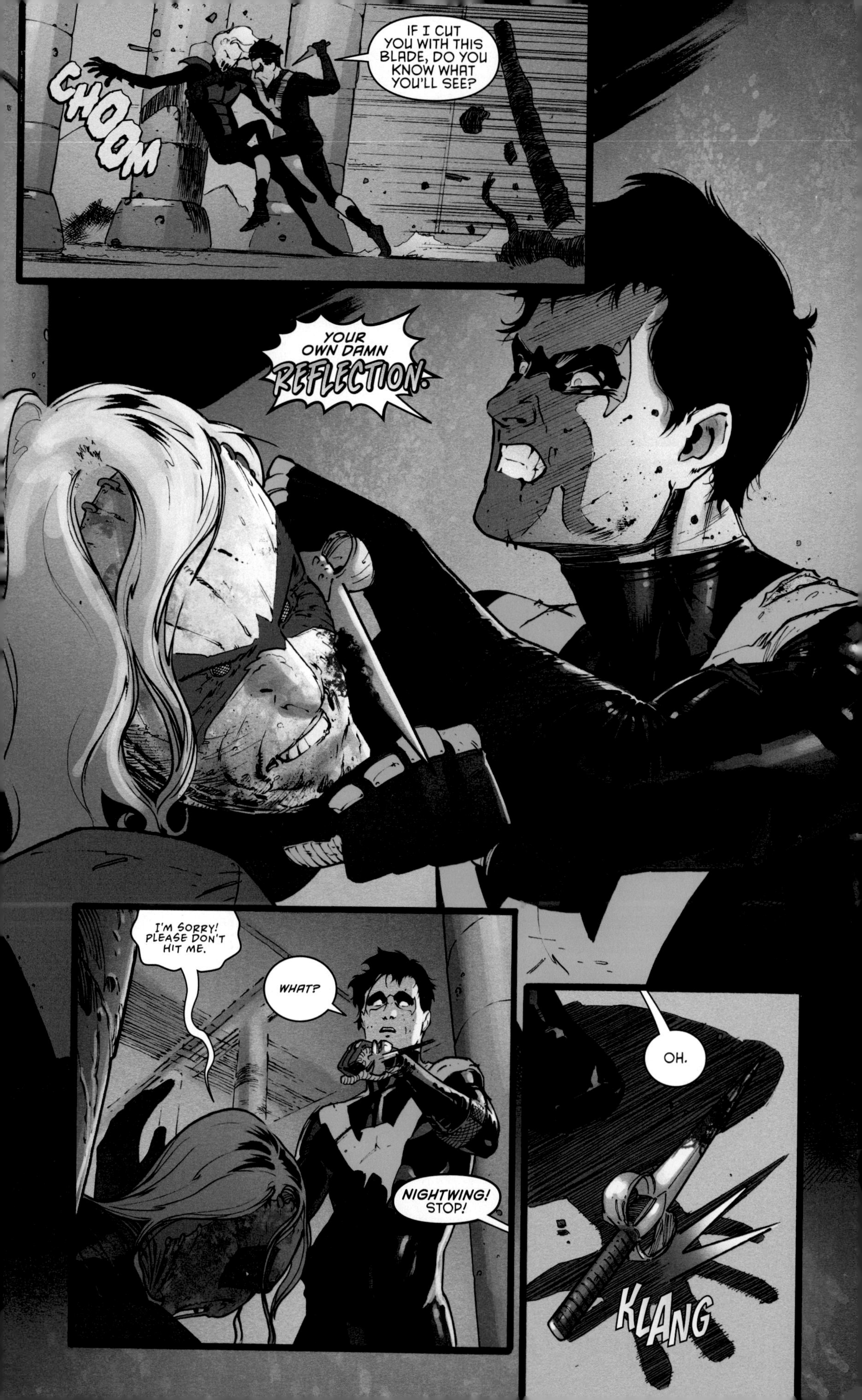

CHOOM
IF I CUT YOU WITH THIS BLADE, DO YOU KNOW WHAT YOU'LL SEE?
YOUR OWN DAMN REFLECTION.
I'M SORRY! PLEASE DON'T HIT ME.
WHAT?
NIGHTWING! STOP!
OH.
KLANG

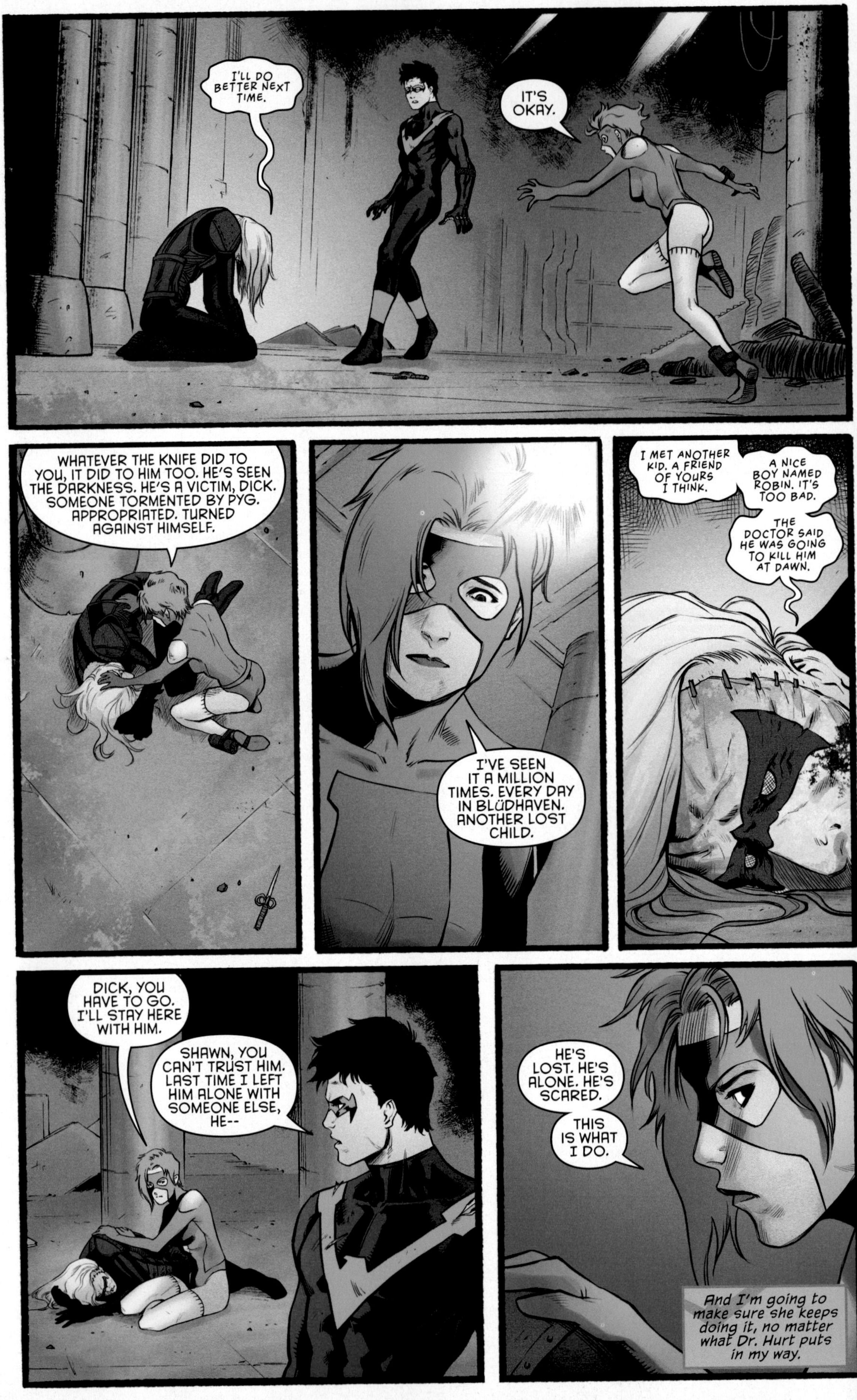
I'LL DO BETTER NEXT TIME.
IT'S OKAY.
WHATEVER THE KNIFE DID TO YOU, IT DID TO HIM TOO. HE'S SEEN THE DARKNESS. HE'S A VICTIM, DICK. SOMEONE TORMENTED BY PYG. APPROPRIATED. TURNED AGAINST HIMSELF.
I'VE SEEN IT A MILLION TIMES. EVERY DAY IN BLÜDHAVEN. ANOTHER LOST CHILD.
I MET ANOTHER KID. A FRIEND OF YOURS I THINK.
A NICE BOY NAMED ROBIN. IT'S TOO BAD.
THE DOCTOR SAID HE WAS GOING TO KILL HIM AT DAWN.
DICK, YOU HAVE TO GO. I'LL STAY HERE WITH HIM.
SHAWN, YOU CAN'T TRUST HIM. LAST TIME I LEFT HIM ALONE WITH SOMEONE ELSE, HE--
HE'S LOST. HE'S ALONE. HE'S SCARED.
THIS IS WHAT I DO.
And I'm going to make sure she keeps doing it, no matter what Dr. Hurt puts in my way.

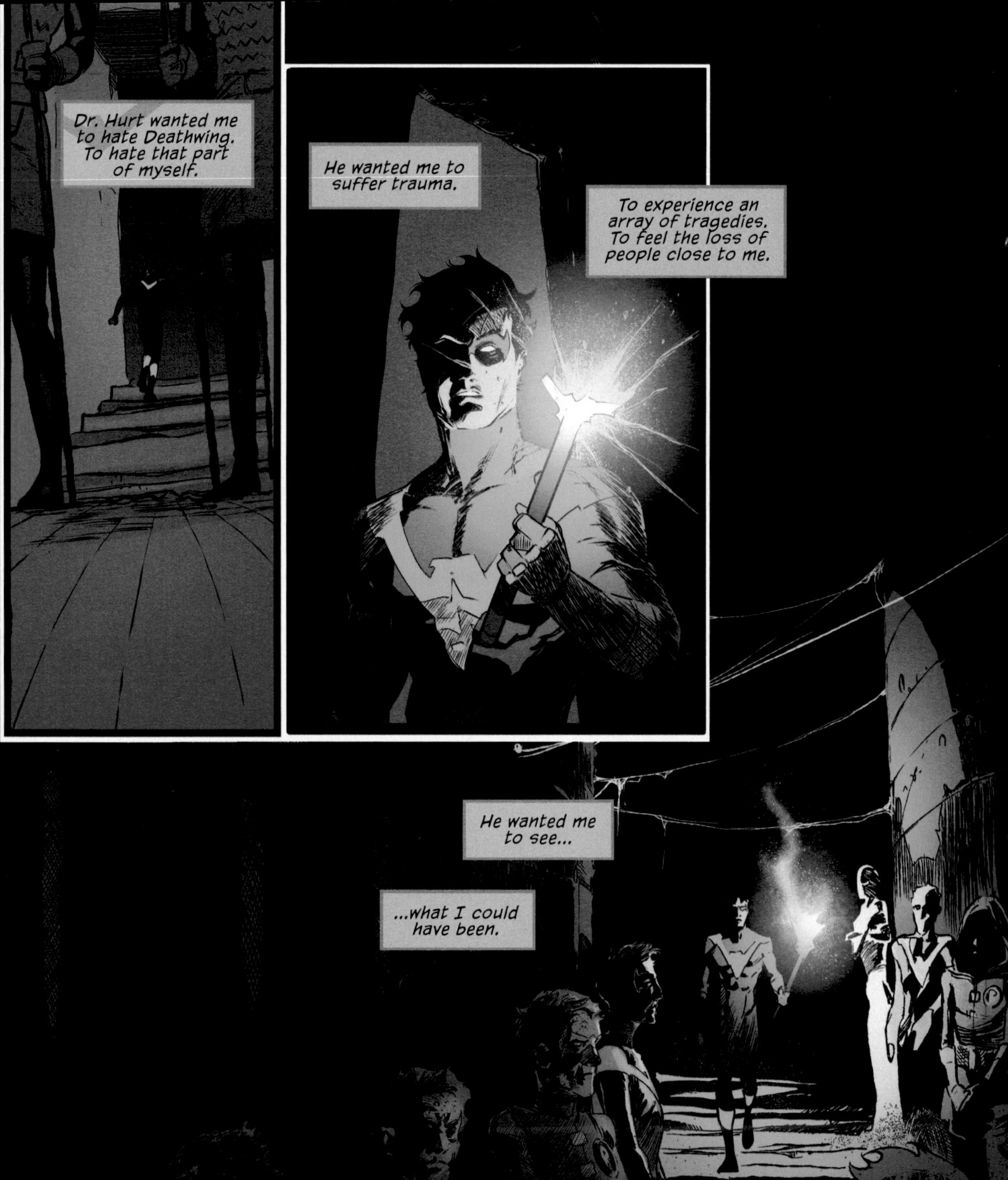
Dr. Hurt wanted me to hate Deathwing. To hate that part of myself.
He wanted me to suffer trauma.
To experience an array of tragedies. To feel the loss of people close to me.
He wanted me to see...
...what I could have been.

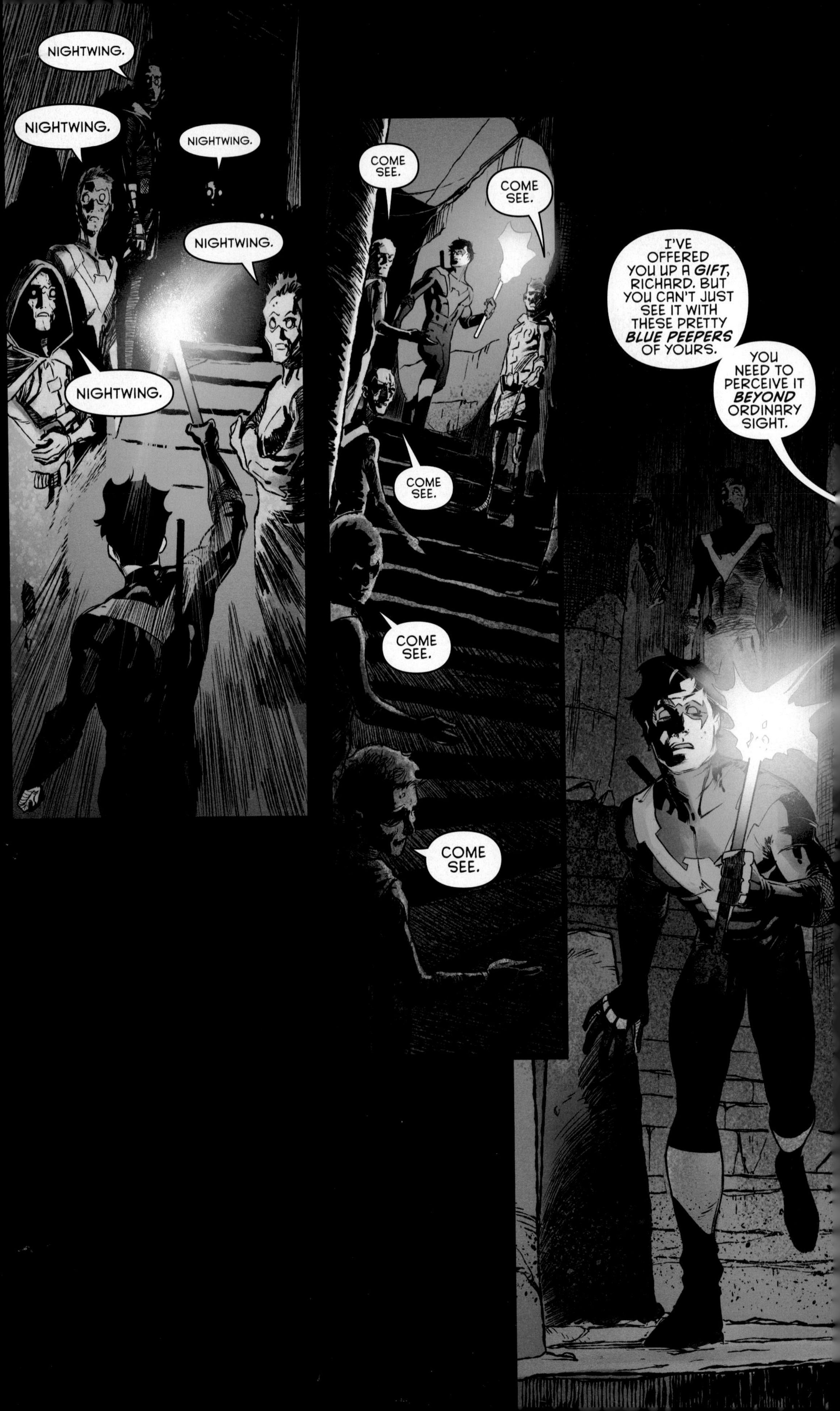
NIGHTWING.
NIGHTWING.
NIGHTWING.
NIGHTWING.
NIGHTWING.
COME SEE.
COME SEE.
COME SEE.
COME SEE.
COME SEE.
I'VE OFFERED YOU UP A GIFT, RICHARD. BUT YOU CAN'T JUST SEE IT WITH THESE PRETTY BLUE PEEPERS OF YOURS.
YOU NEED TO PERCEIVE IT BEYOND ORDINARY SIGHT.

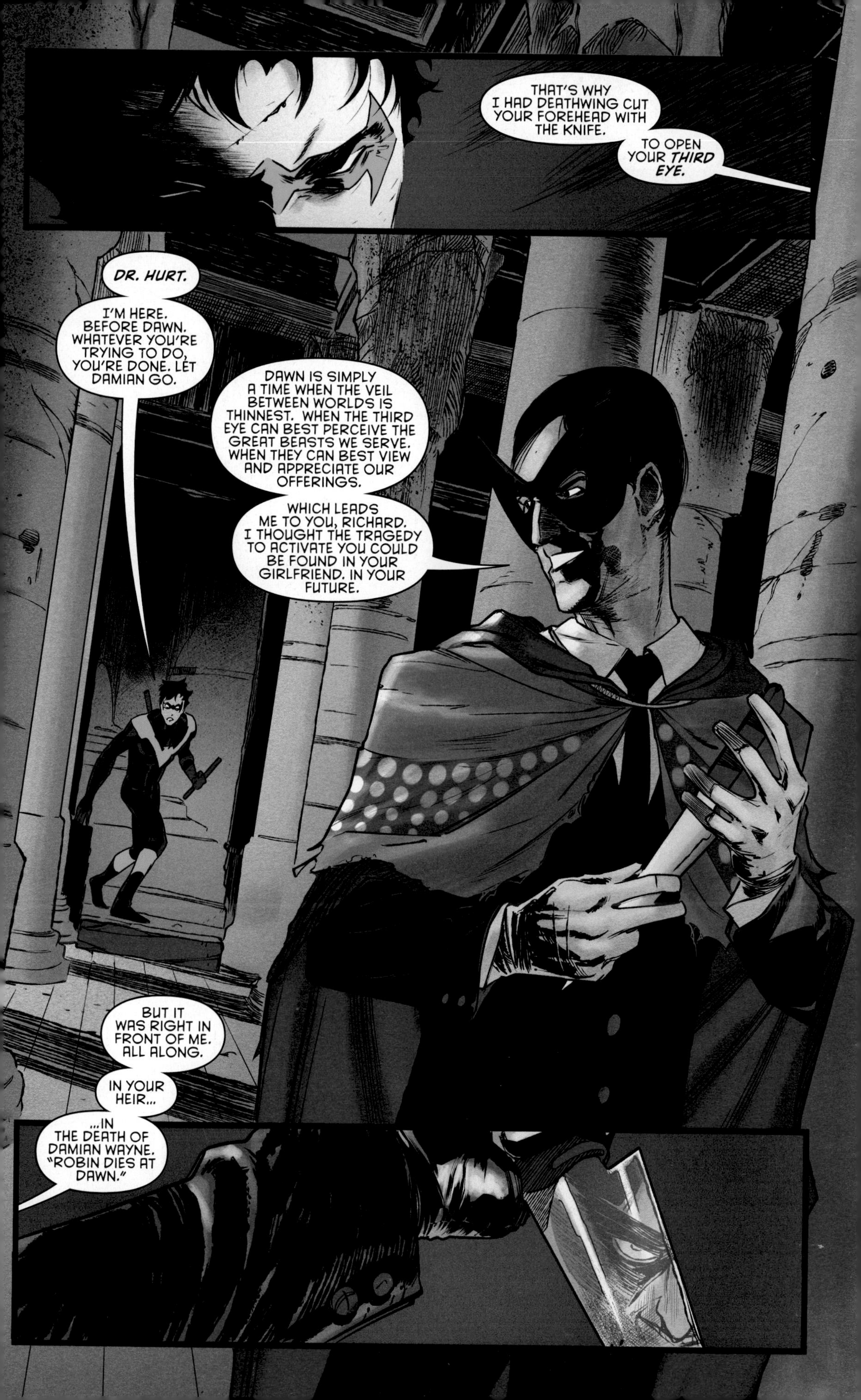

THAT'S WHY I HAD DEATHWING CUT YOUR FOREHEAD WITH THE KNIFE.
TO OPEN YOUR *THIRD EYE.*
DR. HURT.
I'M HERE. BEFORE DAWN. WHATEVER YOU'RE TRYING TO DO, YOU'RE DONE. LET DAMIAN GO.
DAWN IS SIMPLY A TIME WHEN THE VEIL BETWEEN WORLDS IS THINNEST. WHEN THE THIRD EYE CAN BEST PERCEIVE THE GREAT BEASTS WE SERVE. WHEN THEY CAN BEST VIEW AND APPRECIATE OUR OFFERINGS.
WHICH LEADS ME TO YOU, RICHARD. I THOUGHT THE TRAGEDY TO ACTIVATE YOU COULD BE FOUND IN YOUR GIRLFRIEND. IN YOUR FUTURE.
BUT IT WAS RIGHT IN FRONT OF ME. ALL ALONG.
IN YOUR HEIR...
...IN THE DEATH OF DAMIAN WAYNE. "ROBIN DIES AT DAWN."

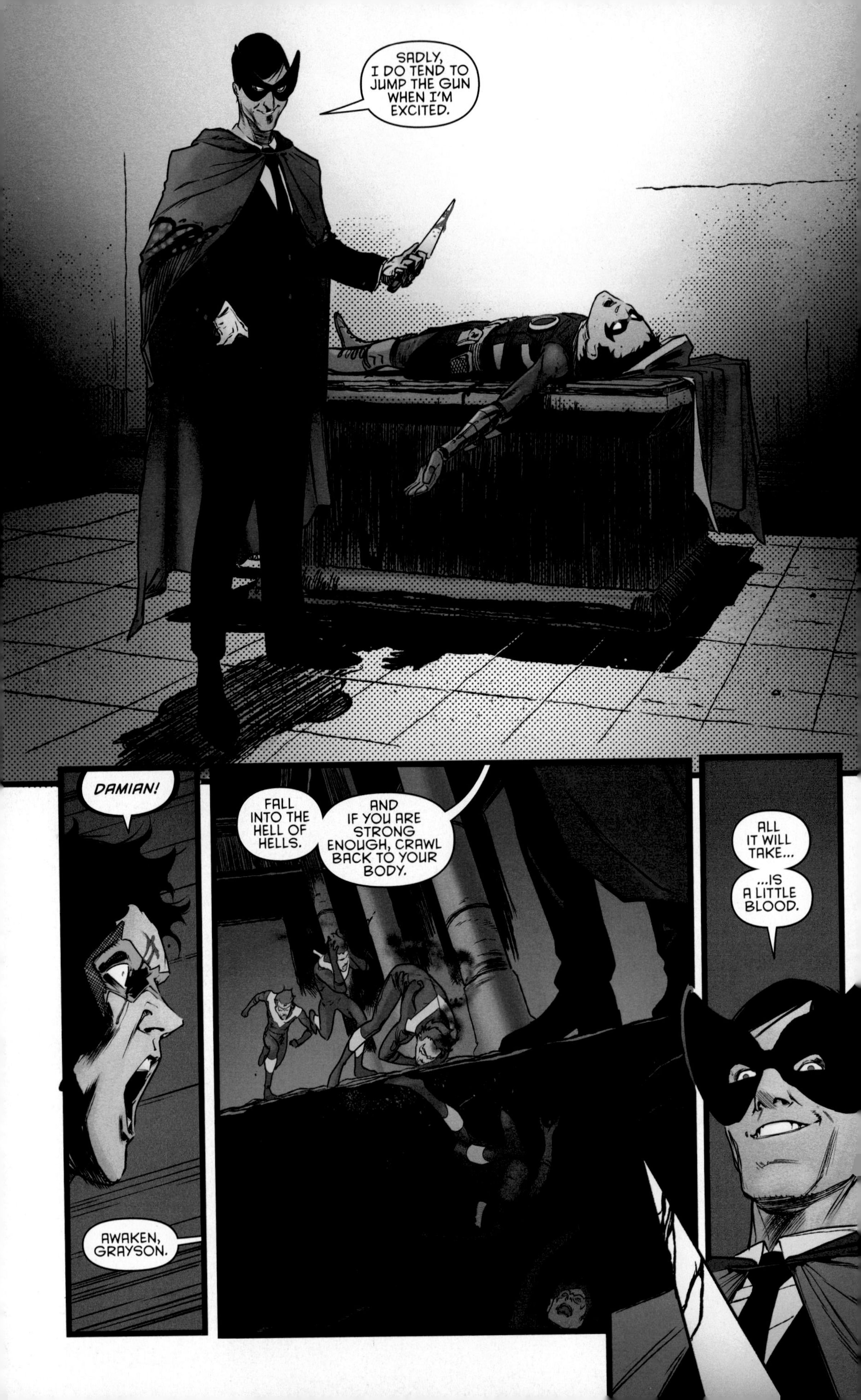
SADLY, I DO TEND TO JUMP THE GUN WHEN I'M EXCITED.
DAMIAN!
AWAKEN, GRAYSON.
FALL INTO THE HELL OF HELLS.
AND IF YOU ARE STRONG ENOUGH, CRAWL BACK TO YOUR BODY.
ALL IT WILL TAKE...
...IS A LITTLE BLOOD.

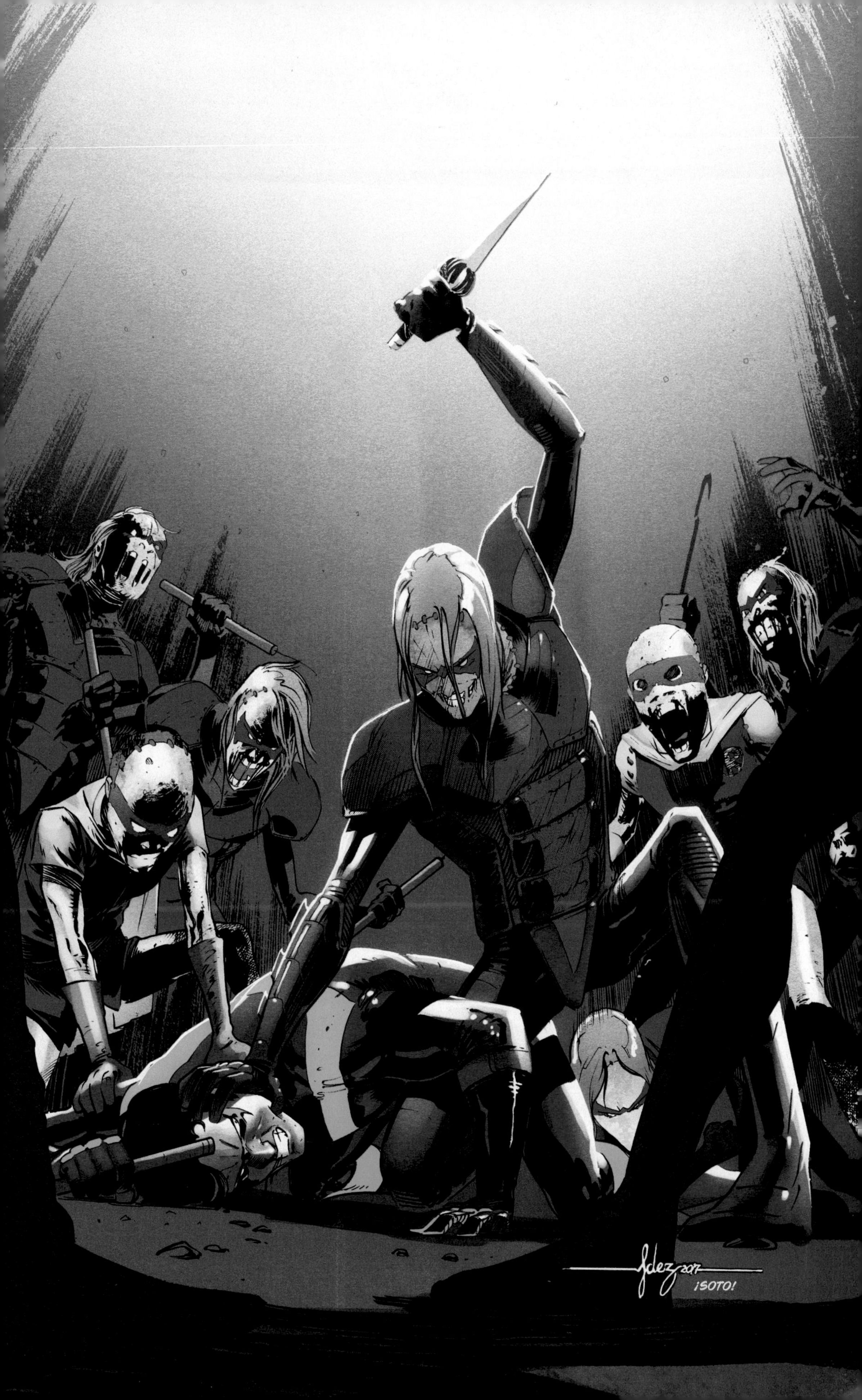
¡SOTO!

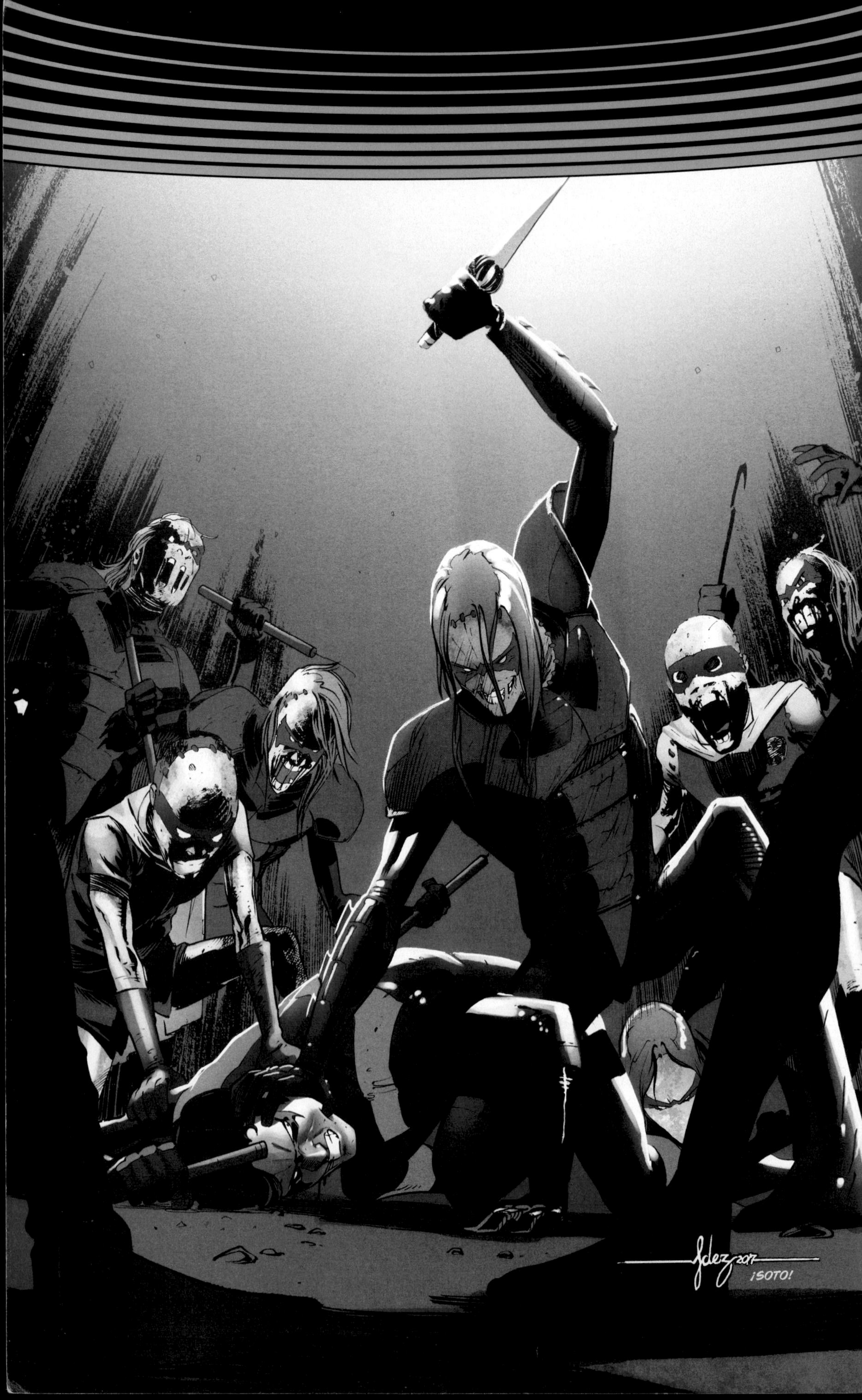
fdez 2017
¡SOTO!

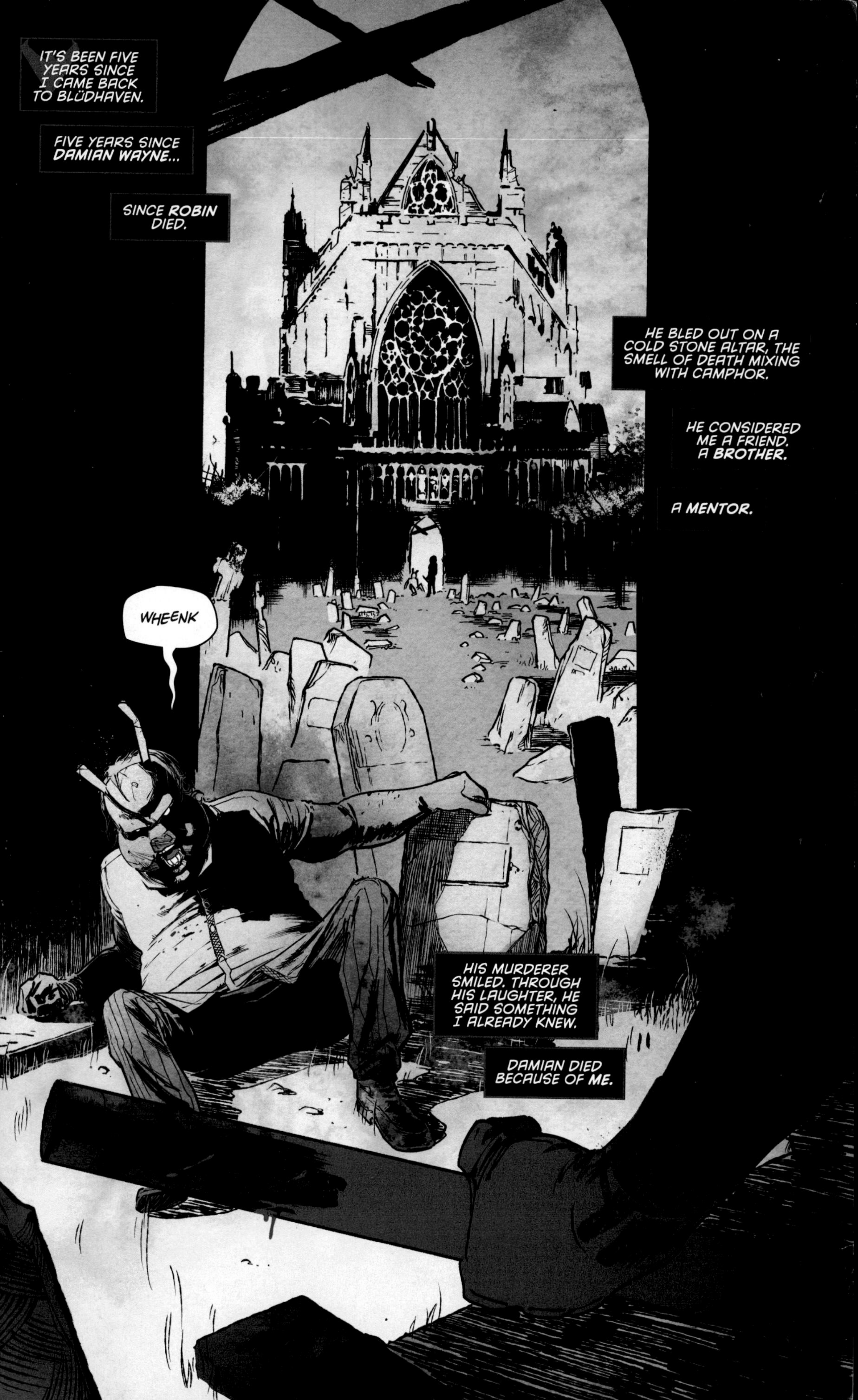
IT'S BEEN FIVE YEARS SINCE I CAME BACK TO BLÜDHAVEN.
FIVE YEARS SINCE DAMIAN WAYNE...
SINCE ROBIN DIED.
HE BLED OUT ON A COLD STONE ALTAR, THE SMELL OF DEATH MIXING WITH CAMPHOR.
HE CONSIDERED ME A FRIEND. A BROTHER.
A MENTOR.
WHEENK
HIS MURDERER SMILED. THROUGH HIS LAUGHTER, HE SAID SOMETHING I ALREADY KNEW.
DAMIAN DIED BECAUSE OF ME.

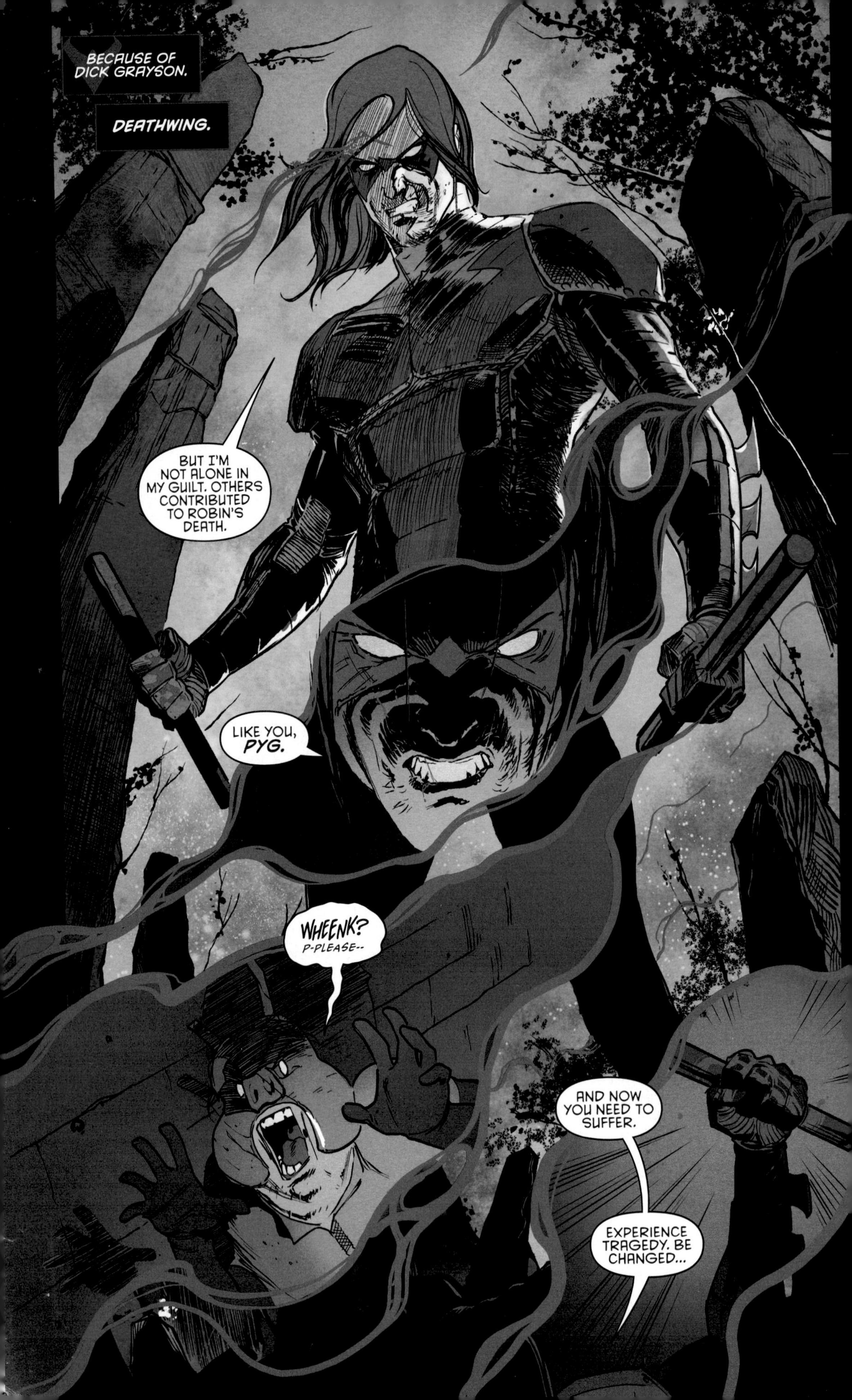

BECAUSE OF DICK GRAYSON.
DEATHWING.
BUT I'M NOT ALONE IN MY GUILT. OTHERS CONTRIBUTED TO ROBIN'S DEATH.
LIKE YOU, *PYG.*
WHEENK? P-PLEASE--
AND NOW YOU NEED TO SUFFER.
EXPERIENCE TRAGEDY. BE CHANGED...

...UNTIL YOU NO LONGER RECOGNIZE YOUR OWN FACE.

YOU WILL LIVE THIS TRAGEDY OVER AND OVER, NIGHTWING. IT WILL *POWER* YOU. *PREPARE* YOU.

YOU MUST BE A FINELY TEMPERED WEAPON.

IF YOU ARE TO SURVIVE THE DAWN TO COME.

NIGHTWING MUST DIE!

FINALE

TIM SEELEY WRITER **JAVIER FERNANDEZ** ARTIST
CHRIS SOTOMAYOR COLORIST **CARLOS M. MANGUAL** LETTERER
JAVIER FERNANDEZ & CHRIS SOTOMAYOR COVER
DAVE WIELGOSZ ASST. EDITOR **REBECCA TAYLOR** EDITOR **MARK DOYLE** GROUP EDITOR
NIGHTWING CREATED BY MARV WOLFMAN & GEORGE PÉREZ

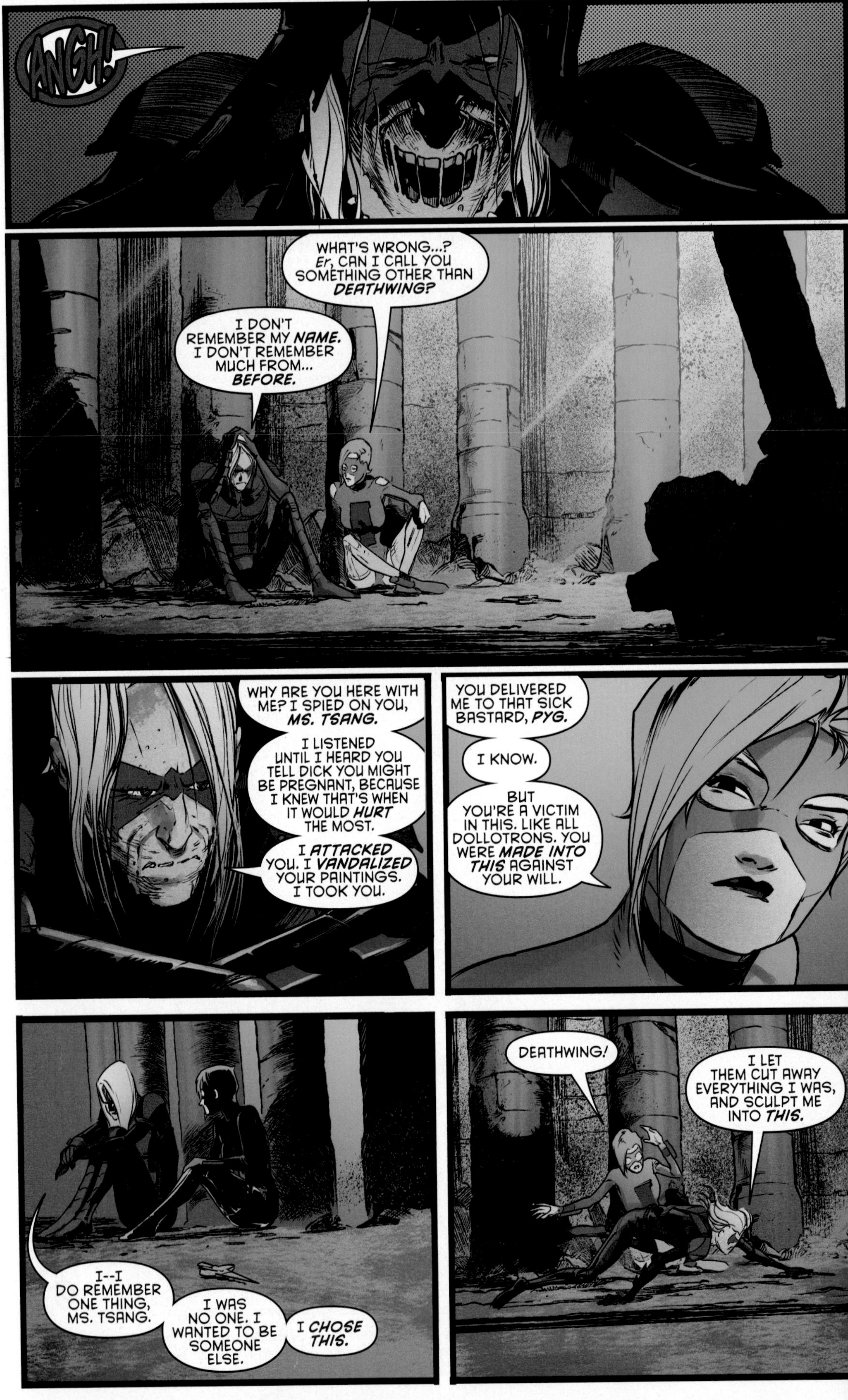
ANGH!
WHAT'S WRONG...? Er, CAN I CALL YOU SOMETHING OTHER THAN DEATHWING?
I DON'T REMEMBER MY NAME. I DON'T REMEMBER MUCH FROM... BEFORE.
WHY ARE YOU HERE WITH ME? I SPIED ON YOU, MS. TSANG.
I LISTENED UNTIL I HEARD YOU TELL DICK YOU MIGHT BE PREGNANT, BECAUSE I KNEW THAT'S WHEN IT WOULD HURT THE MOST.
I ATTACKED YOU. I VANDALIZED YOUR PAINTINGS. I TOOK YOU.
YOU DELIVERED ME TO THAT SICK BASTARD, PYG.
I KNOW.
BUT YOU'RE A VICTIM IN THIS. LIKE ALL DOLLOTRONS. YOU WERE MADE INTO THIS AGAINST YOUR WILL.
I--I DO REMEMBER ONE THING, MS. TSANG.
I WAS NO ONE. I WANTED TO BE SOMEONE ELSE.
I CHOSE THIS.
DEATHWING!
I LET THEM CUT AWAY EVERYTHING I WAS, AND SCULPT ME INTO THIS.

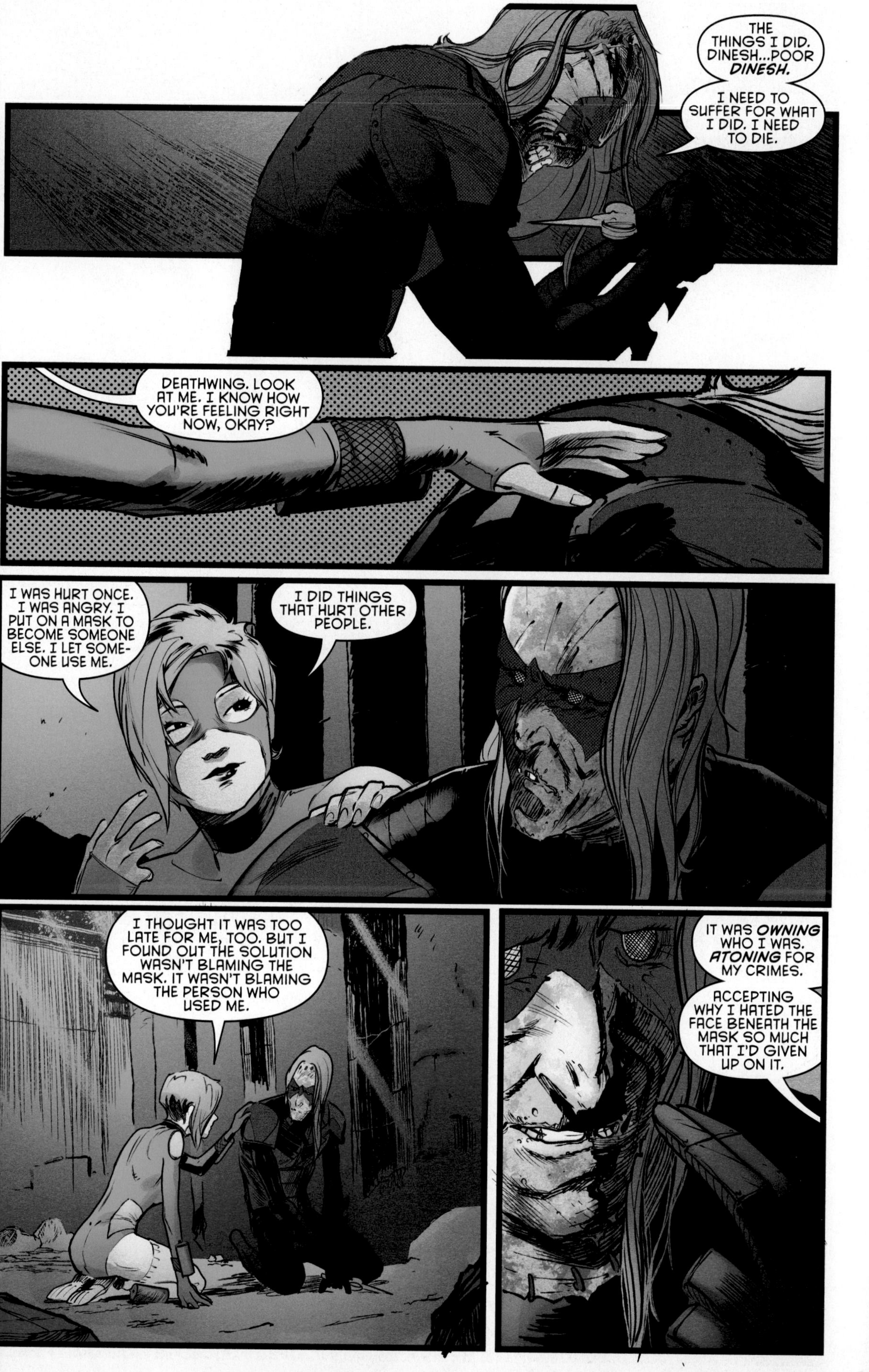
THE THINGS I DID. DINESH...POOR DINESH.
I NEED TO SUFFER FOR WHAT I DID. I NEED TO DIE.
DEATHWING. LOOK AT ME. I KNOW HOW YOU'RE FEELING RIGHT NOW, OKAY?
I WAS HURT ONCE. I WAS ANGRY. I PUT ON A MASK TO BECOME SOMEONE ELSE. I LET SOME-ONE USE ME.
I DID THINGS THAT HURT OTHER PEOPLE.
I THOUGHT IT WAS TOO LATE FOR ME, TOO. BUT I FOUND OUT THE SOLUTION WASN'T BLAMING THE MASK. IT WASN'T BLAMING THE PERSON WHO USED ME.
IT WAS OWNING WHO I WAS. ATONING FOR MY CRIMES.
ACCEPTING WHY I HATED THE FACE BENEATH THE MASK SO MUCH THAT I'D GIVEN UP ON IT.

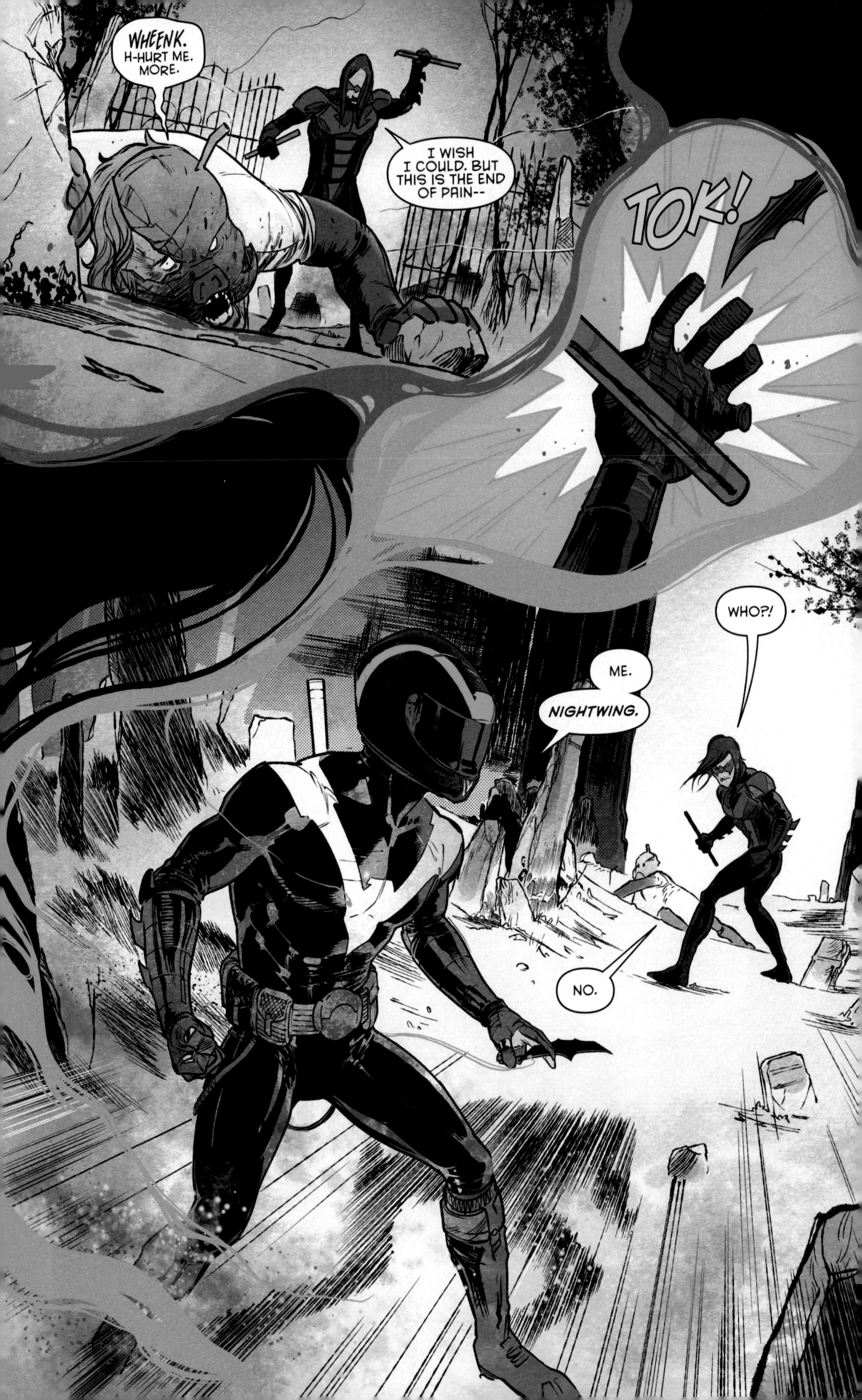
WHEENK. H-HURT ME. MORE.
I WISH I COULD. BUT THIS IS THE END OF PAIN--
TOK!
WHO?!
ME.
NIGHTWING.
NO.

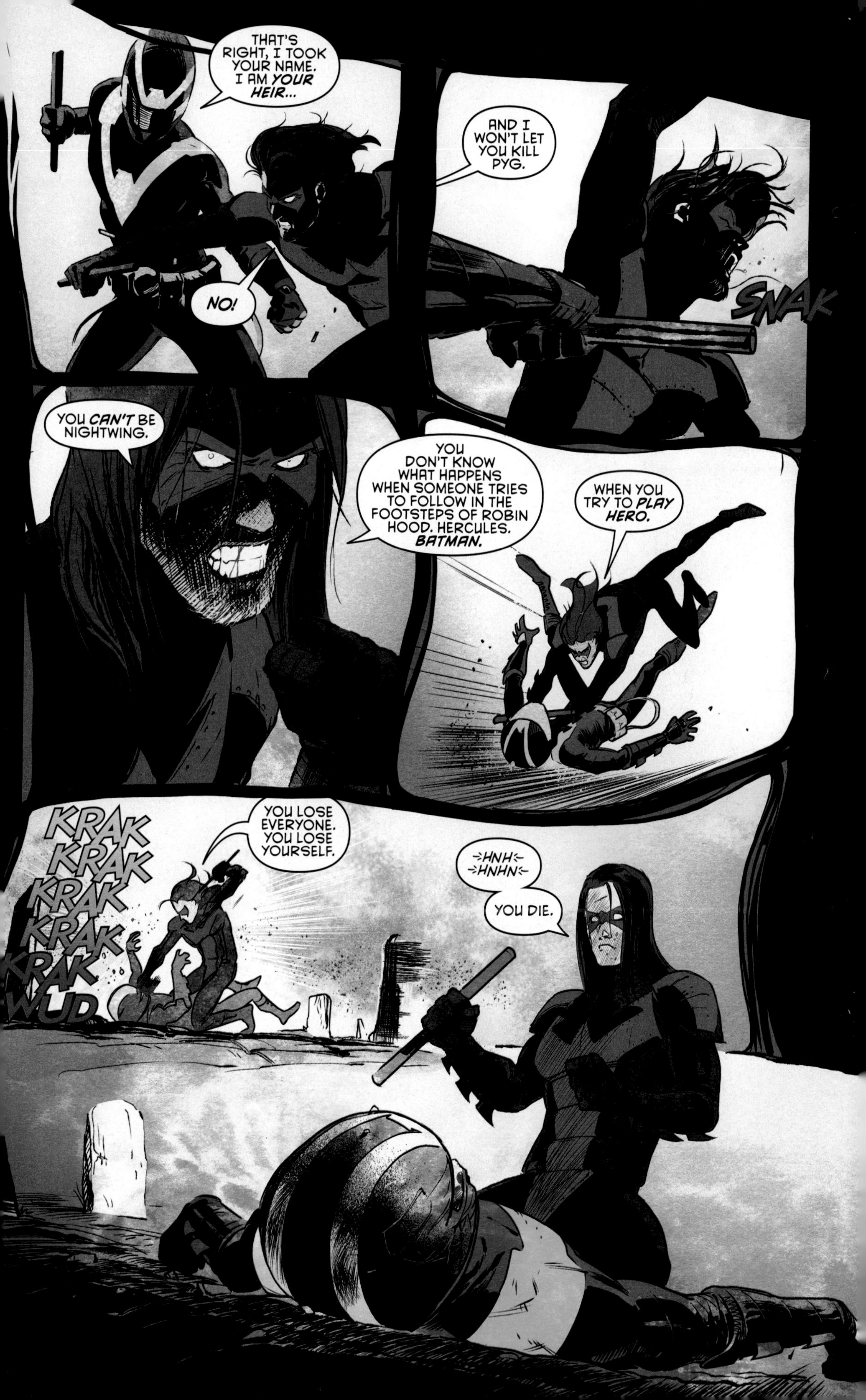
THAT'S RIGHT, I TOOK YOUR NAME. I AM YOUR HEIR...
NO!
AND I WON'T LET YOU KILL PYG.
SNAK
YOU CAN'T BE NIGHTWING.
YOU DON'T KNOW WHAT HAPPENS WHEN SOMEONE TRIES TO FOLLOW IN THE FOOTSTEPS OF ROBIN HOOD. HERCULES. BATMAN.
WHEN YOU TRY TO PLAY HERO.
KRAK KRAK KRAK KRAK KRAK WUD
YOU LOSE EVERYONE. YOU LOSE YOURSELF.
HNH HNHN
YOU DIE.

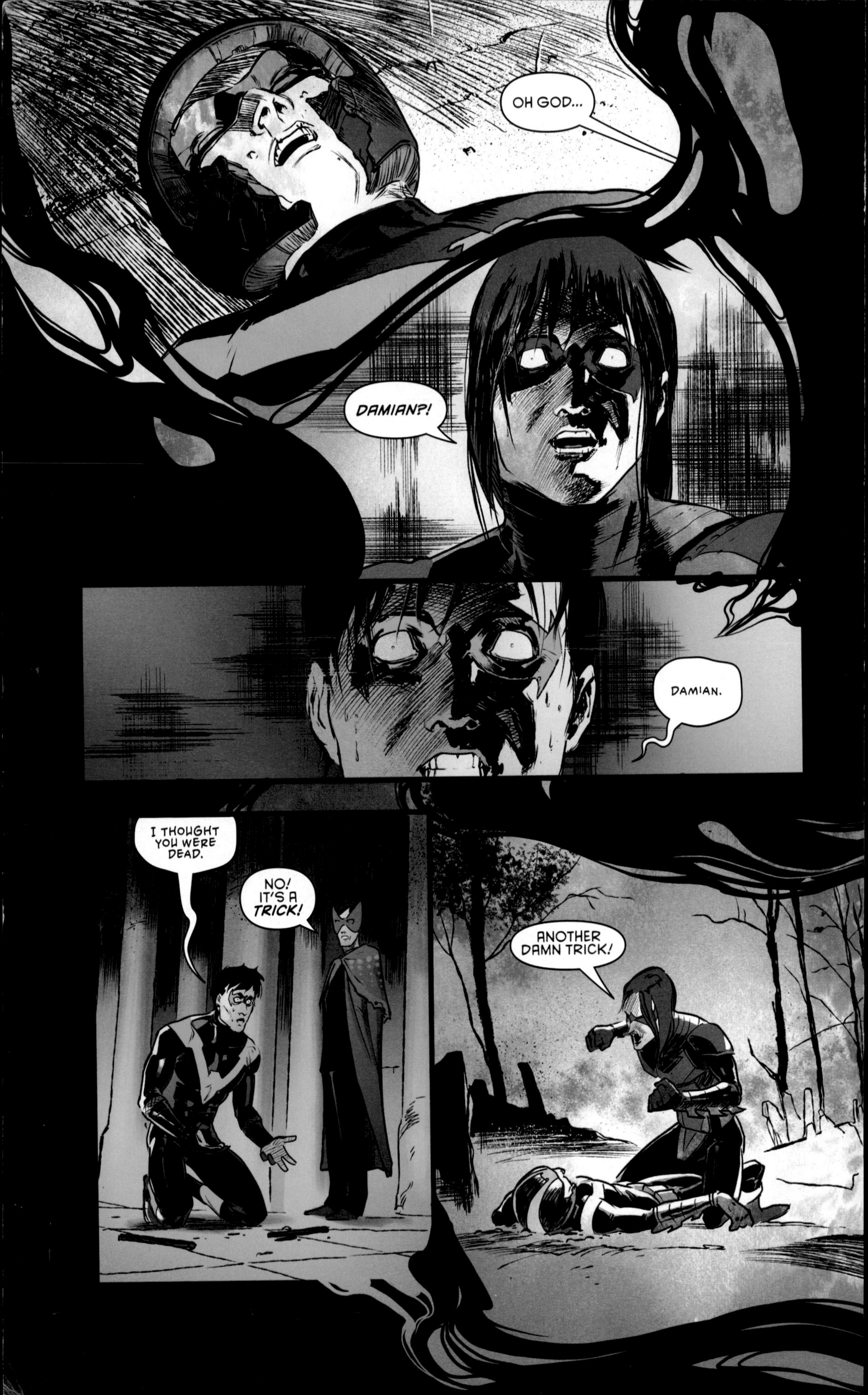
OH GOD...
DAMIAN?!
DAMIAN.
I THOUGHT YOU WERE DEAD.
NO! IT'S A TRICK!
ANOTHER DAMN TRICK!

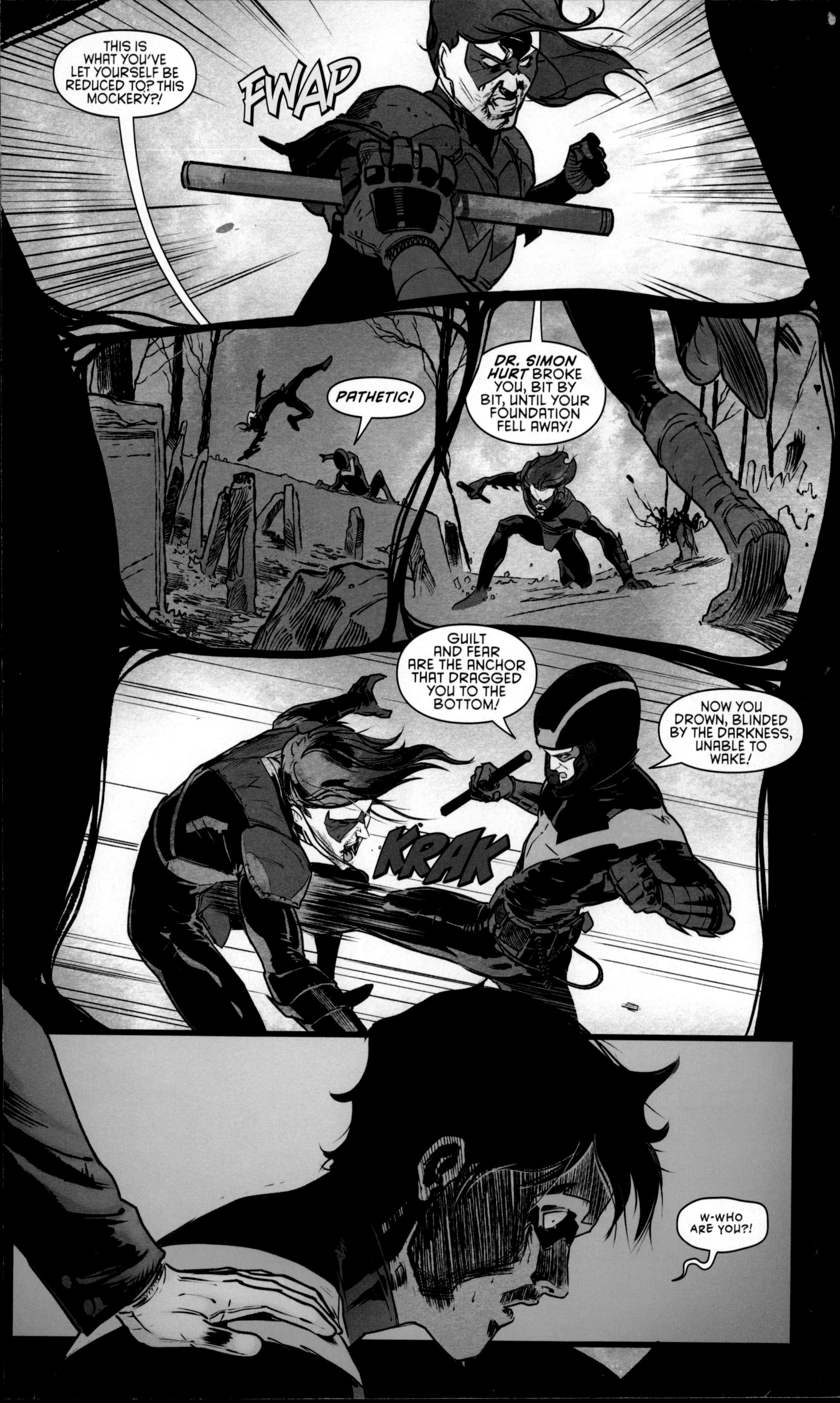

THIS IS WHAT YOU'VE LET YOURSELF BE REDUCED TO? THIS MOCKERY?!
FWAP
PATHETIC!
DR. SIMON HURT BROKE YOU, BIT BY BIT, UNTIL YOUR FOUNDATION FELL AWAY!
GUILT AND FEAR ARE THE ANCHOR THAT DRAGGED YOU TO THE BOTTOM!
NOW YOU DROWN, BLINDED BY THE DARKNESS, UNABLE TO WAKE!
KRAK
W-WHO ARE YOU?!

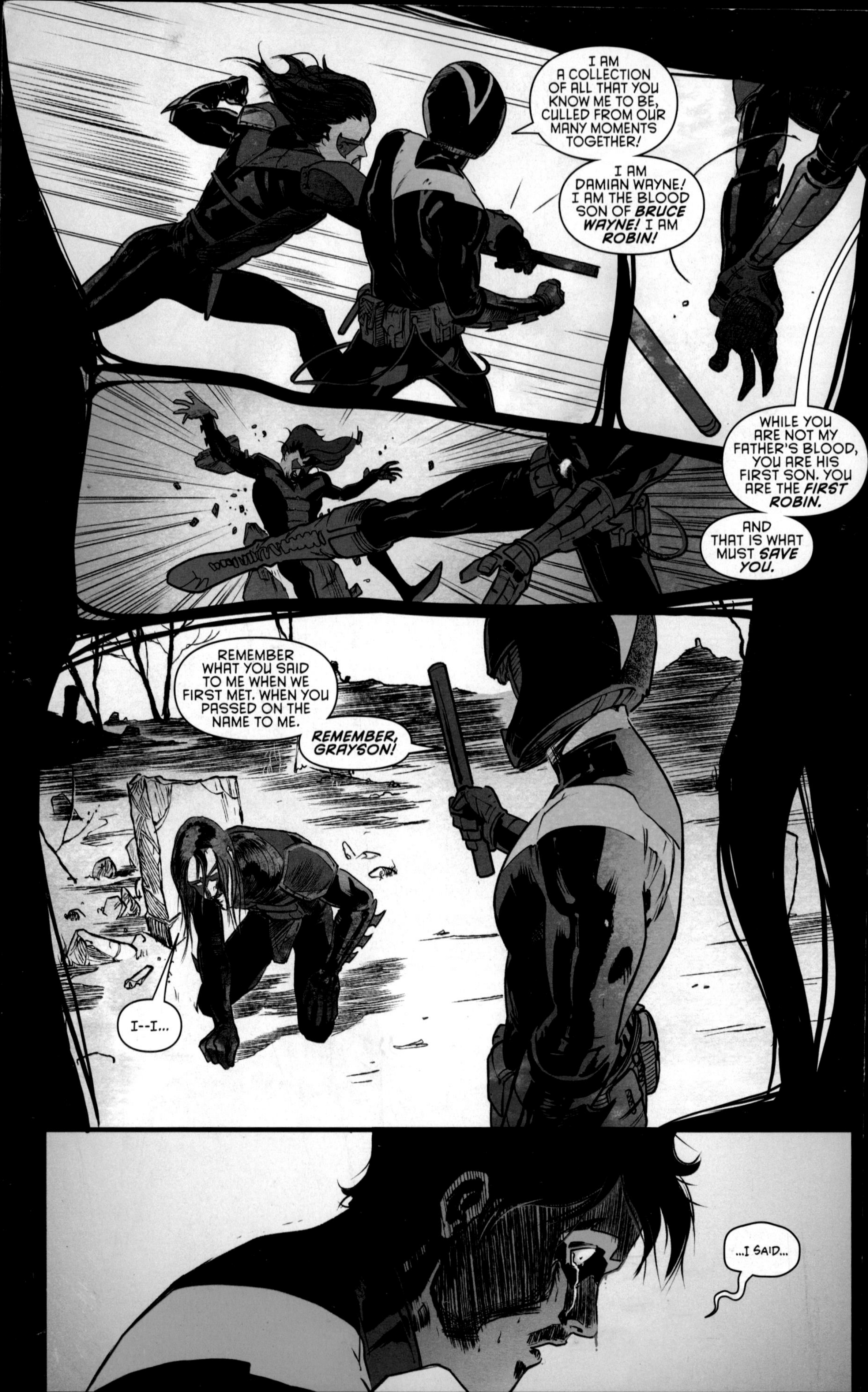
I AM A COLLECTION OF ALL THAT YOU KNOW ME TO BE, CULLED FROM OUR MANY MOMENTS TOGETHER!
I AM DAMIAN WAYNE! I AM THE BLOOD SON OF BRUCE WAYNE! I AM ROBIN!
WHILE YOU ARE NOT MY FATHER'S BLOOD, YOU ARE HIS FIRST SON. YOU ARE THE FIRST ROBIN.
AND THAT IS WHAT MUST SAVE YOU.
REMEMBER WHAT YOU SAID TO ME WHEN WE FIRST MET. WHEN YOU PASSED ON THE NAME TO ME.
REMEMBER, GRAYSON!
I--I...
...I SAID...

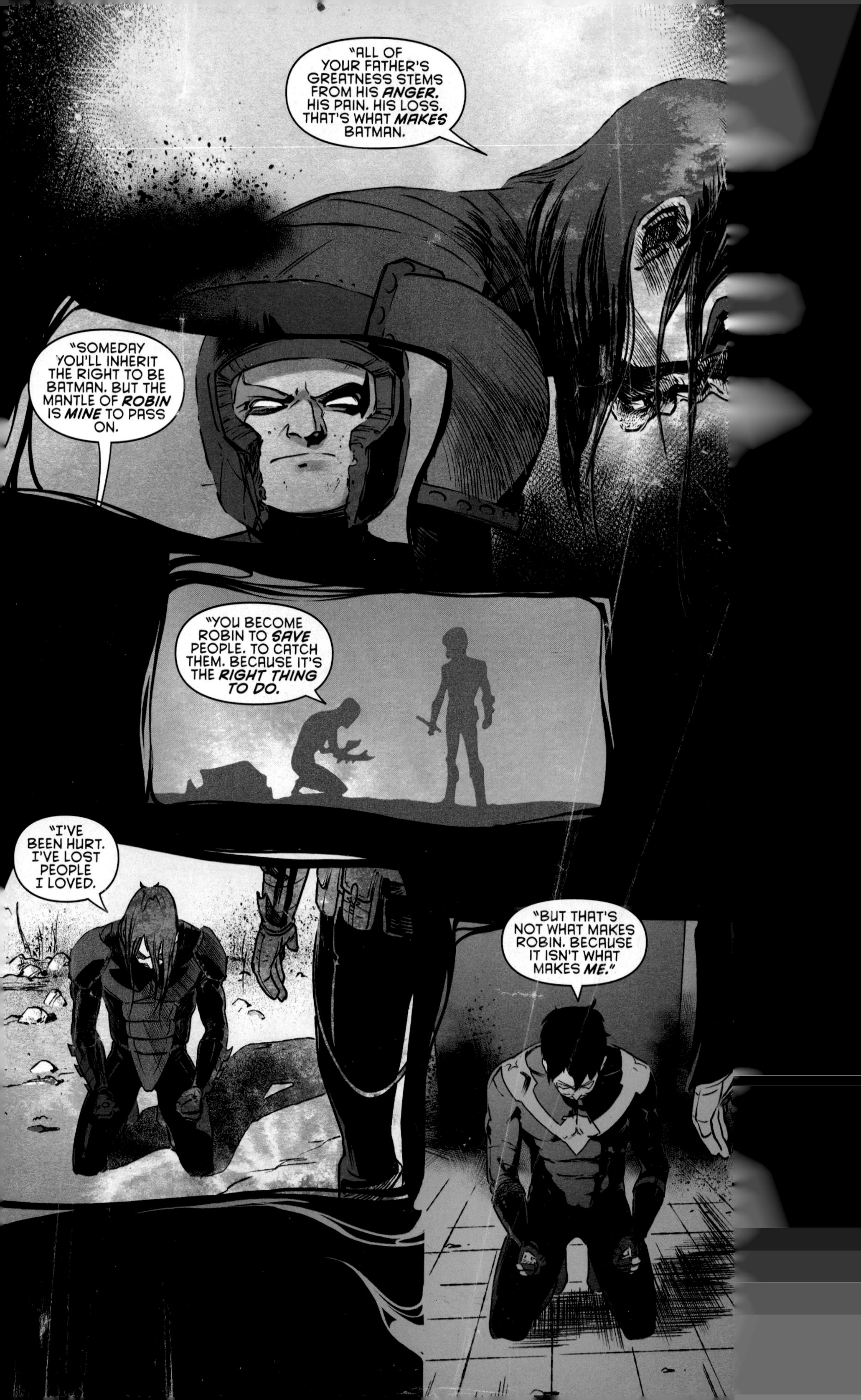
"ALL OF YOUR FATHER'S GREATNESS STEMS FROM HIS ANGER. HIS PAIN. HIS LOSS. THAT'S WHAT MAKES BATMAN.
"SOMEDAY YOU'LL INHERIT THE RIGHT TO BE BATMAN. BUT THE MANTLE OF ROBIN IS MINE TO PASS ON.
"YOU BECOME ROBIN TO SAVE PEOPLE. TO CATCH THEM. BECAUSE IT'S THE RIGHT THING TO DO.
"I'VE BEEN HURT. I'VE LOST PEOPLE I LOVED.
"BUT THAT'S NOT WHAT MAKES ROBIN. BECAUSE IT ISN'T WHAT MAKES ME."

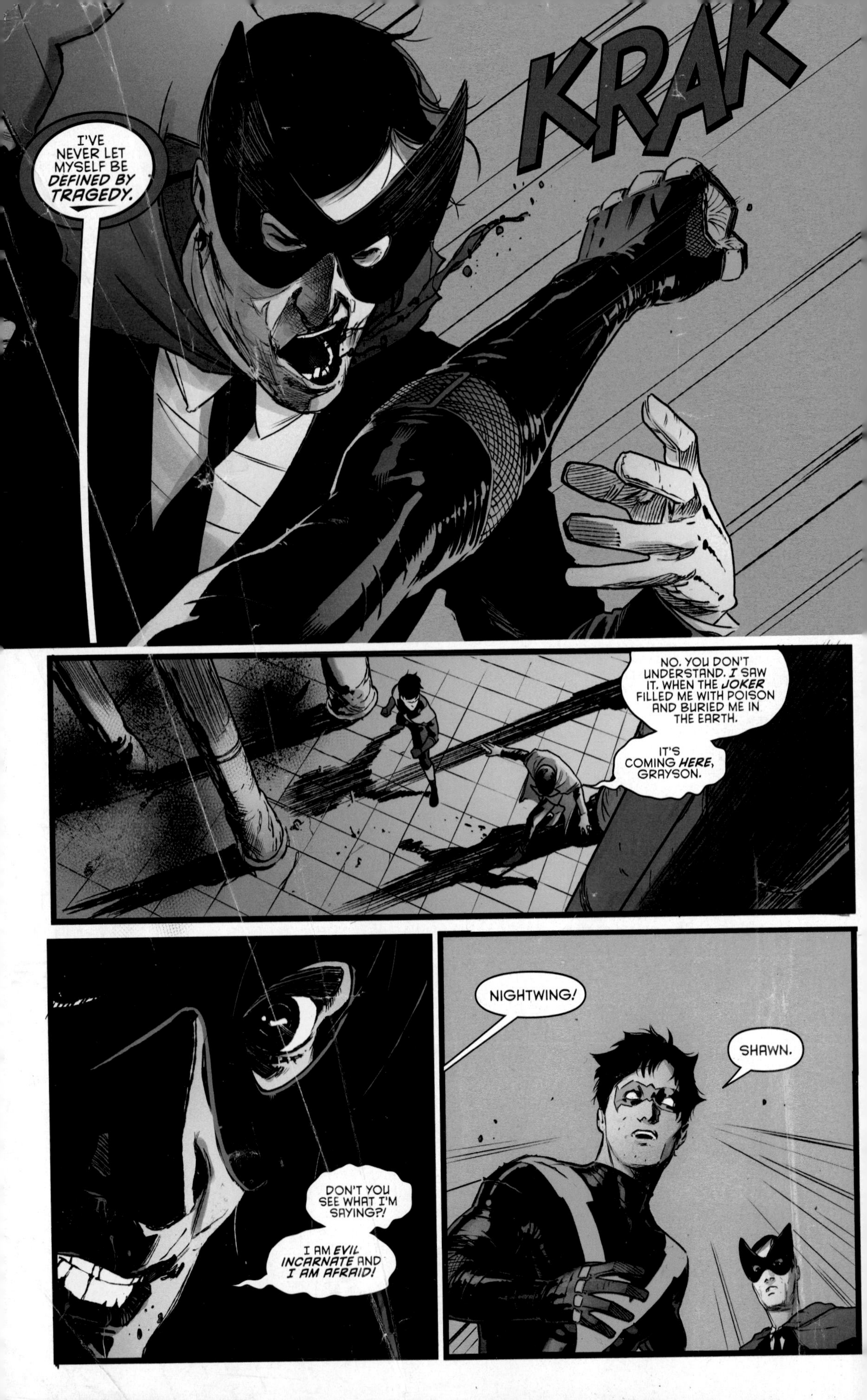
KRAK
I'VE NEVER LET MYSELF BE DEFINED BY TRAGEDY.
NO. YOU DON'T UNDERSTAND. I SAW IT. WHEN THE JOKER FILLED ME WITH POISON AND BURIED ME IN THE EARTH.
IT'S COMING HERE, GRAYSON.
DON'T YOU SEE WHAT I'M SAYING?!
I AM EVIL INCARNATE AND I AM AFRAID!
NIGHTWING!
SHAWN.

ROBIN. HE'S...HE'S STILL ALIVE.

ROBIN!

COME ON, WAKE UP, MAN!

GRAYSON. YOU--YOU... ...ARE AN IDIOT.

I WAS SIMPLY IN A DEEP TRANCE, REPAIRING THE DAMAGE CAUSED BY THE HEMATOMA.

BUT--BUT HE STABBED YOU. LIKE, IN THE DEATH PARTS.

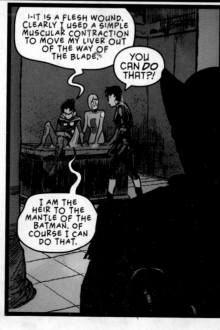

I-IT IS A FLESH WOUND. CLEARLY I USED A SIMPLE MUSCULAR CONTRACTION TO MOVE MY LIVER OUT OF THE WAY OF THE BLADE.

YOU CAN DO THAT?!

I AM THE HEIR TO THE MANTLE OF THE BATMAN. OF COURSE I CAN DO THAT.

NO. ROBIN WILL BE OF NO USE IN THE DAYS TO COME. I TESTED IT MANY TIMES. HE'S TOO STUBBORN. TOO PROUD OF HIS FATHER.

REMINDS ME OF A KID I MET NAMED DINESH.

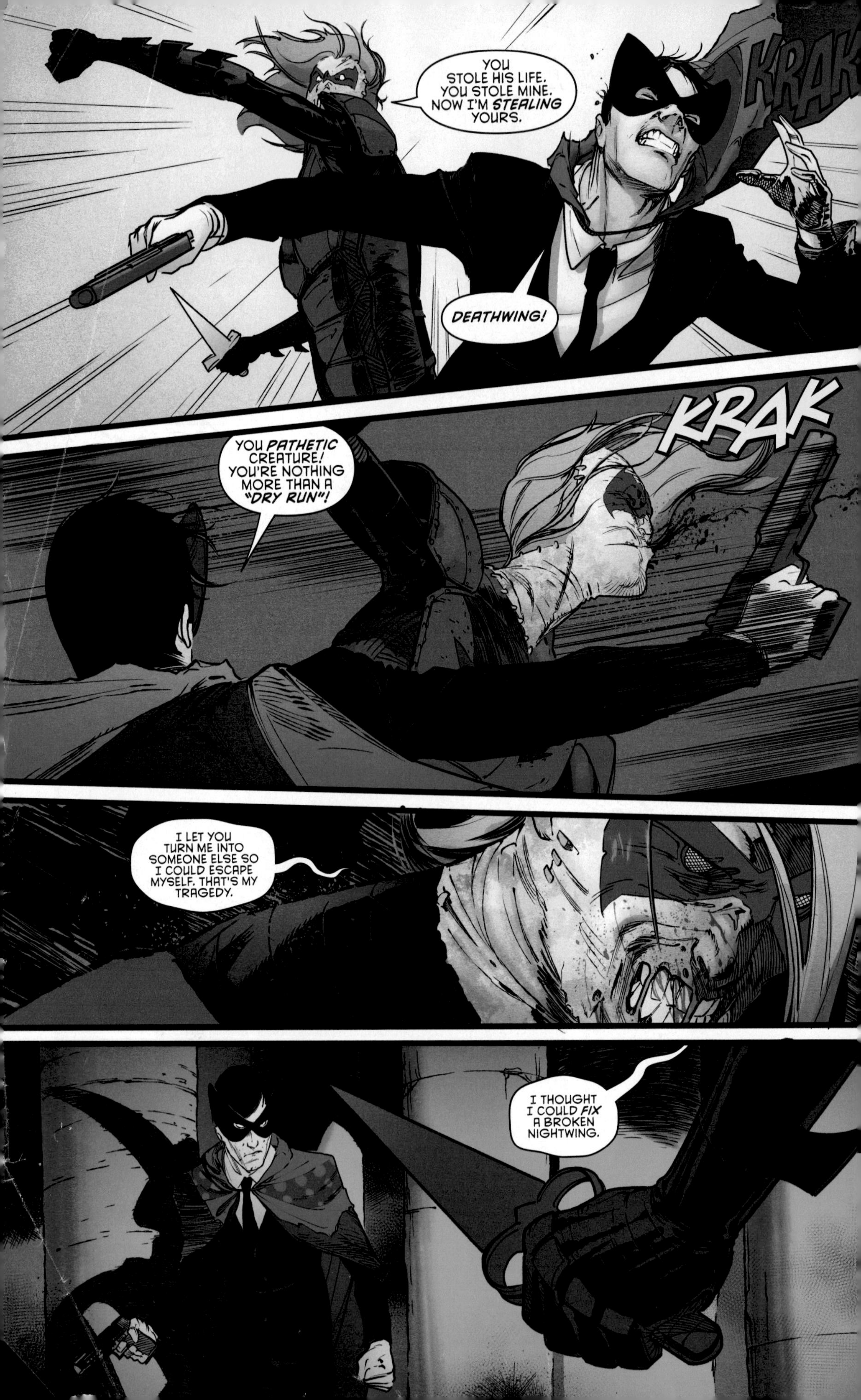
KRAK
YOU STOLE HIS LIFE. YOU STOLE MINE. NOW I'M STEALING YOURS.
DEATHWING!
KRAK
YOU PATHETIC CREATURE! YOU'RE NOTHING MORE THAN A "DRY RUN"!
I LET YOU TURN ME INTO SOMEONE ELSE SO I COULD ESCAPE MYSELF. THAT'S MY TRAGEDY.
I THOUGHT I COULD FIX A BROKEN NIGHTWING.

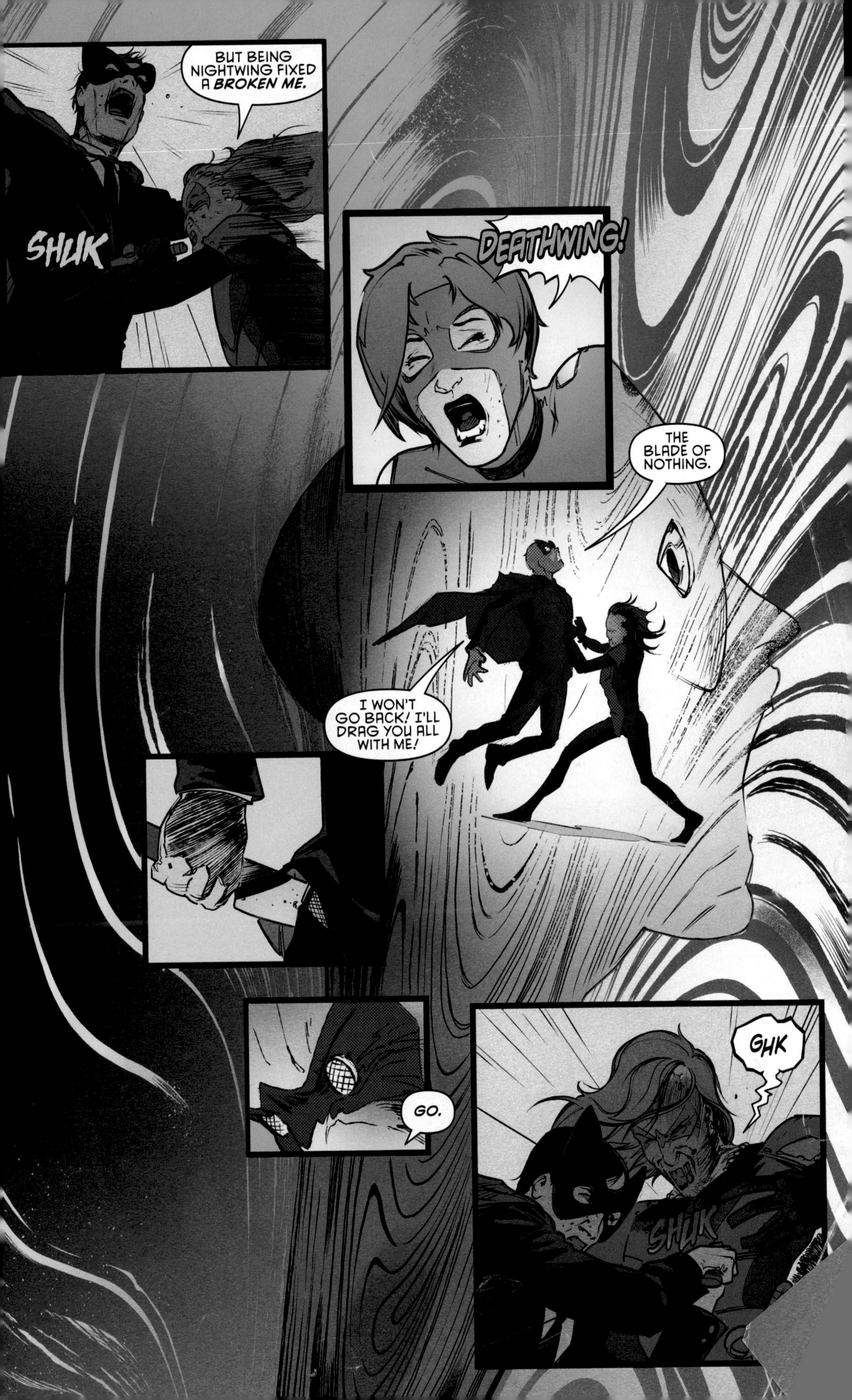
BUT BEING NIGHTWING FIXED A BROKEN ME.
SHUK
DEATHWING!
THE BLADE OF NOTHING.
I WON'T GO BACK! I'LL DRAG YOU ALL WITH ME!
GO.
GHK
SHUK

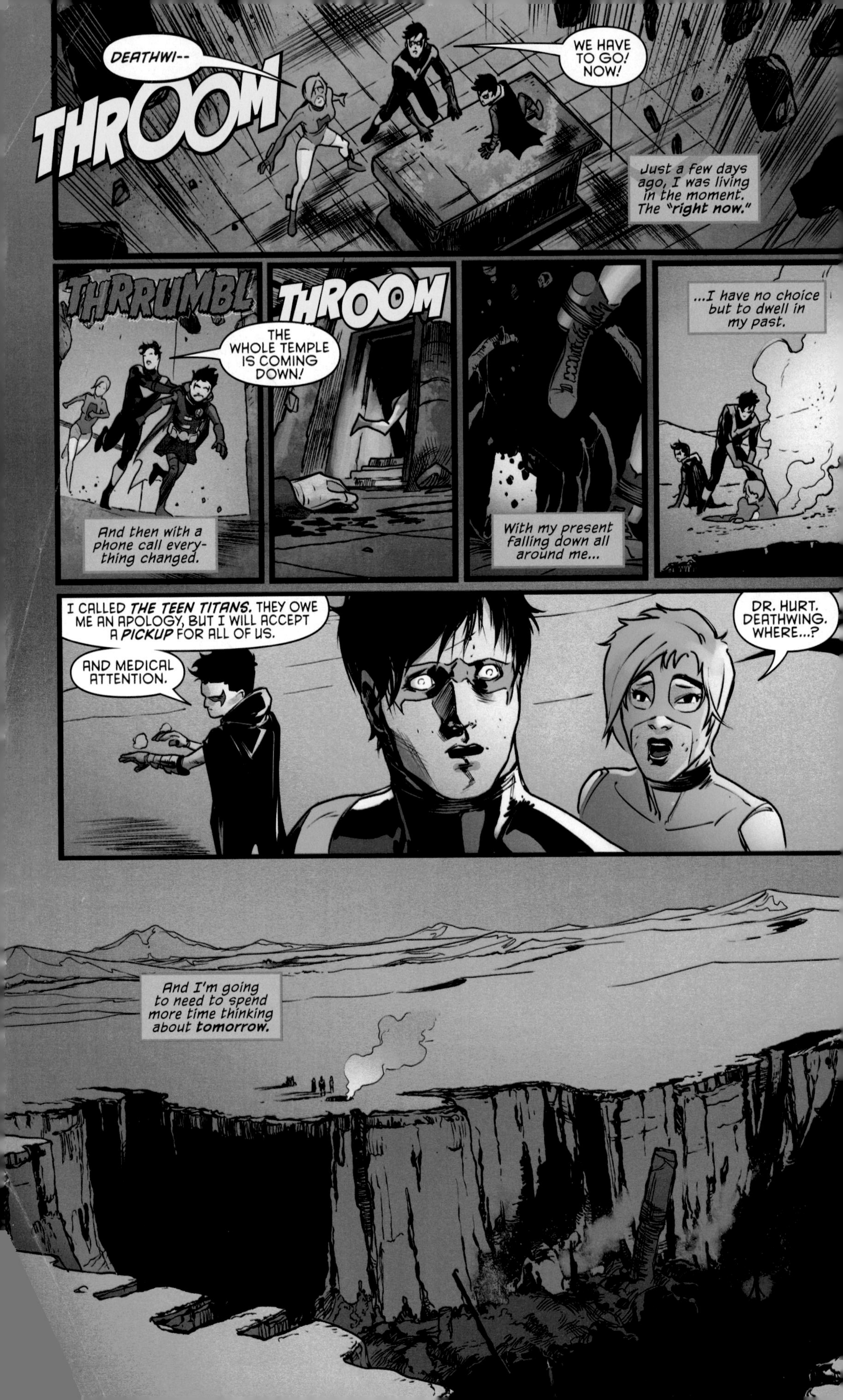
DEATHWI--
THROOM
WE HAVE TO GO! NOW!
Just a few days ago, I was living in the moment. The "right now."
THRRUMBL
And then with a phone call everything changed.
THROOM
THE WHOLE TEMPLE IS COMING DOWN!
With my present falling down all around me...
...I have no choice but to dwell in my past.
I CALLED THE TEEN TITANS. THEY OWE ME AN APOLOGY, BUT I WILL ACCEPT A PICKUP FOR ALL OF US.
AND MEDICAL ATTENTION.
DR. HURT. DEATHWING. WHERE...?
And I'm going to need to spend more time thinking about tomorrow.

BLÜDHAVEN.
A FEW DAYS LATER.

The bad thing about waiting for a pregnancy test is...

YOU CAN COME IN NOW.

...you're not sure whether to be excited or upset about either possibility.

And you know you're going to be surprised...

IT'S NEGATIVE. I'M NOT PREGNANT.

...no matter what your reaction is.

DICK? CAN I HAVE A LITTLE SPACE? JUST FOR A BIT.

OF COURSE. WHATEVER YOU NEED.

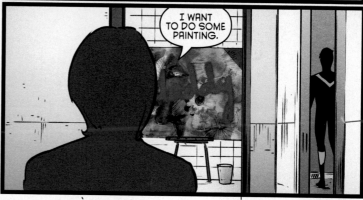

I WANT TO DO SOME PAINTING.

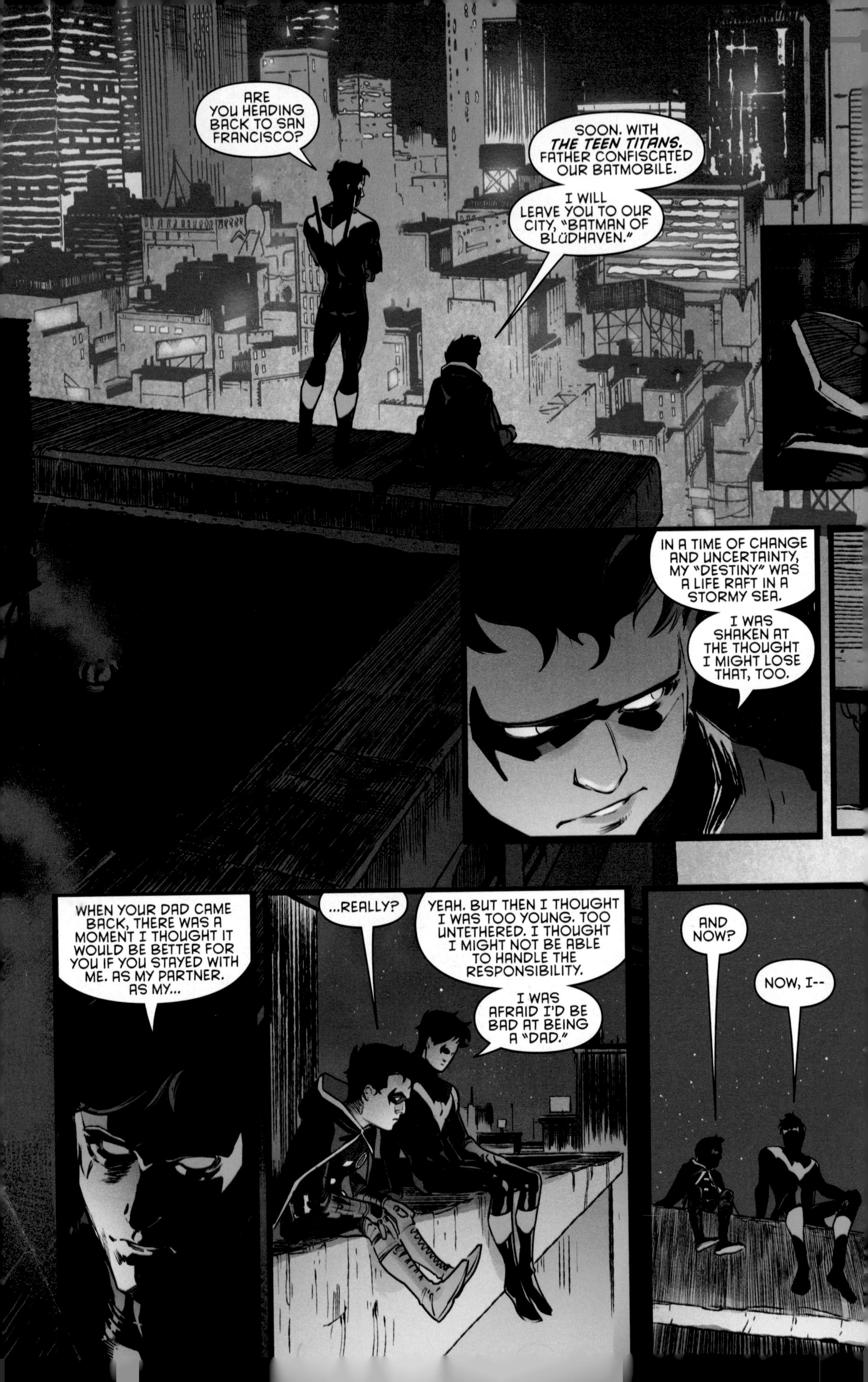
ARE YOU HEADING BACK TO SAN FRANCISCO?
SOON. WITH *THE TEEN TITANS.* FATHER CONFISCATED OUR BATMOBILE.
I WILL LEAVE YOU TO OUR CITY, "BATMAN OF BLÜDHAVEN."
IN A TIME OF CHANGE AND UNCERTAINTY, MY "DESTINY" WAS A LIFE RAFT IN A STORMY SEA.
I WAS SHAKEN AT THE THOUGHT I MIGHT LOSE THAT, TOO.
WHEN YOUR DAD CAME BACK, THERE WAS A MOMENT I THOUGHT IT WOULD BE BETTER FOR YOU IF YOU STAYED WITH ME. AS MY PARTNER. AS MY...
...REALLY?
YEAH. BUT THEN I THOUGHT I WAS TOO YOUNG. TOO UNTETHERED. I THOUGHT I MIGHT NOT BE ABLE TO HANDLE THE RESPONSIBILITY.
I WAS AFRAID I'D BE BAD AT BEING A "DAD."
AND NOW?
NOW, I--

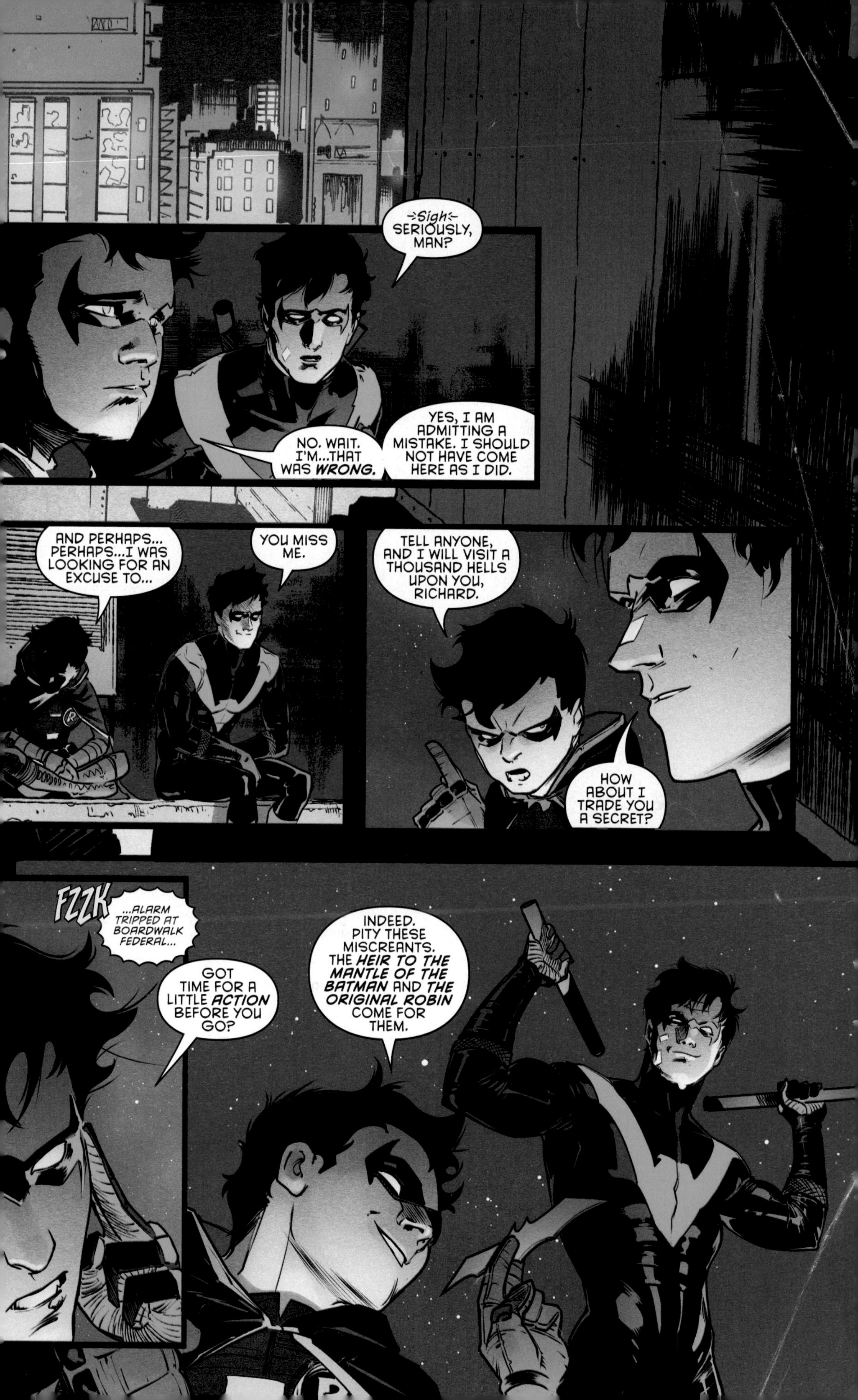

-Sigh- SERIOUSLY, MAN?
NO. WAIT. I'M...THAT WAS WRONG.
YES, I AM ADMITTING A MISTAKE. I SHOULD NOT HAVE COME HERE AS I DID.
AND PERHAPS... PERHAPS...I WAS LOOKING FOR AN EXCUSE TO...
YOU MISS ME.
TELL ANYONE, AND I WILL VISIT A THOUSAND HELLS UPON YOU, RICHARD.
HOW ABOUT I TRADE YOU A SECRET?
FZZK
...ALARM TRIPPED AT BOARDWALK FEDERAL...
GOT TIME FOR A LITTLE ACTION BEFORE YOU GO?
INDEED. PITY THESE MISCREANTS. THE HEIR TO THE MANTLE OF THE BATMAN AND THE ORIGINAL ROBIN COME FOR THEM.

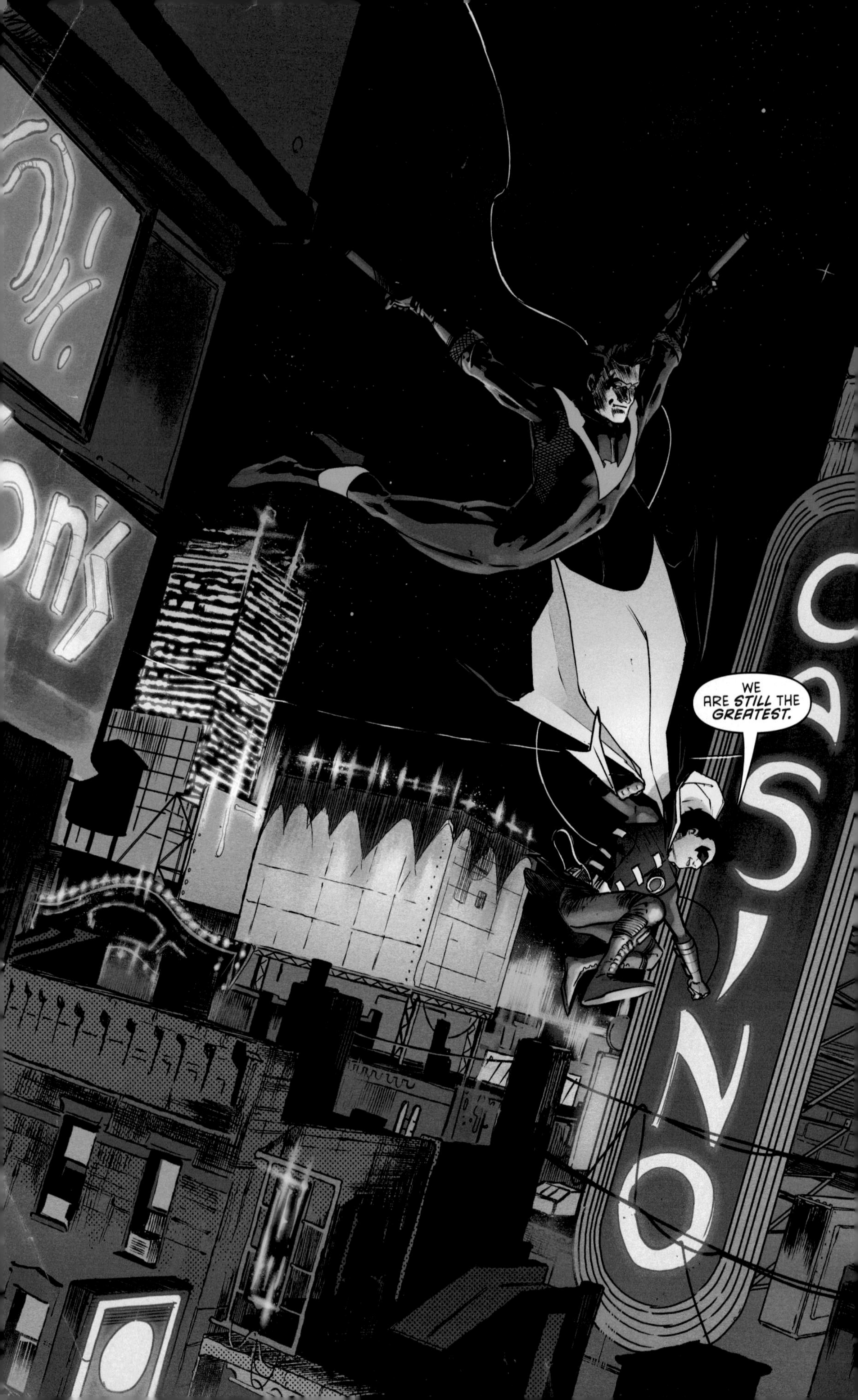
WE ARE STILL THE GREATEST.

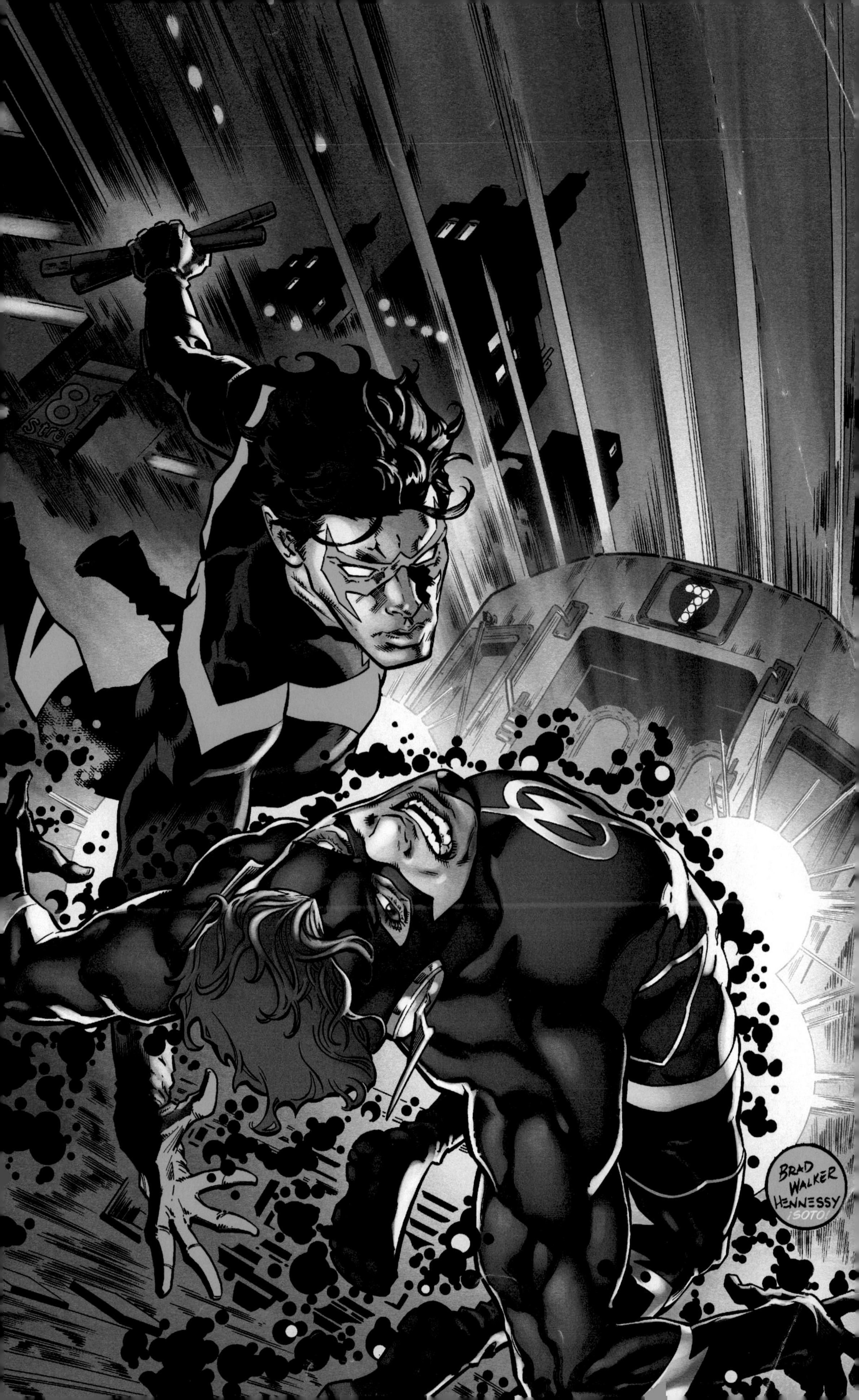
7
BRAD
WALKER
HENNESSY
¡SOTO!

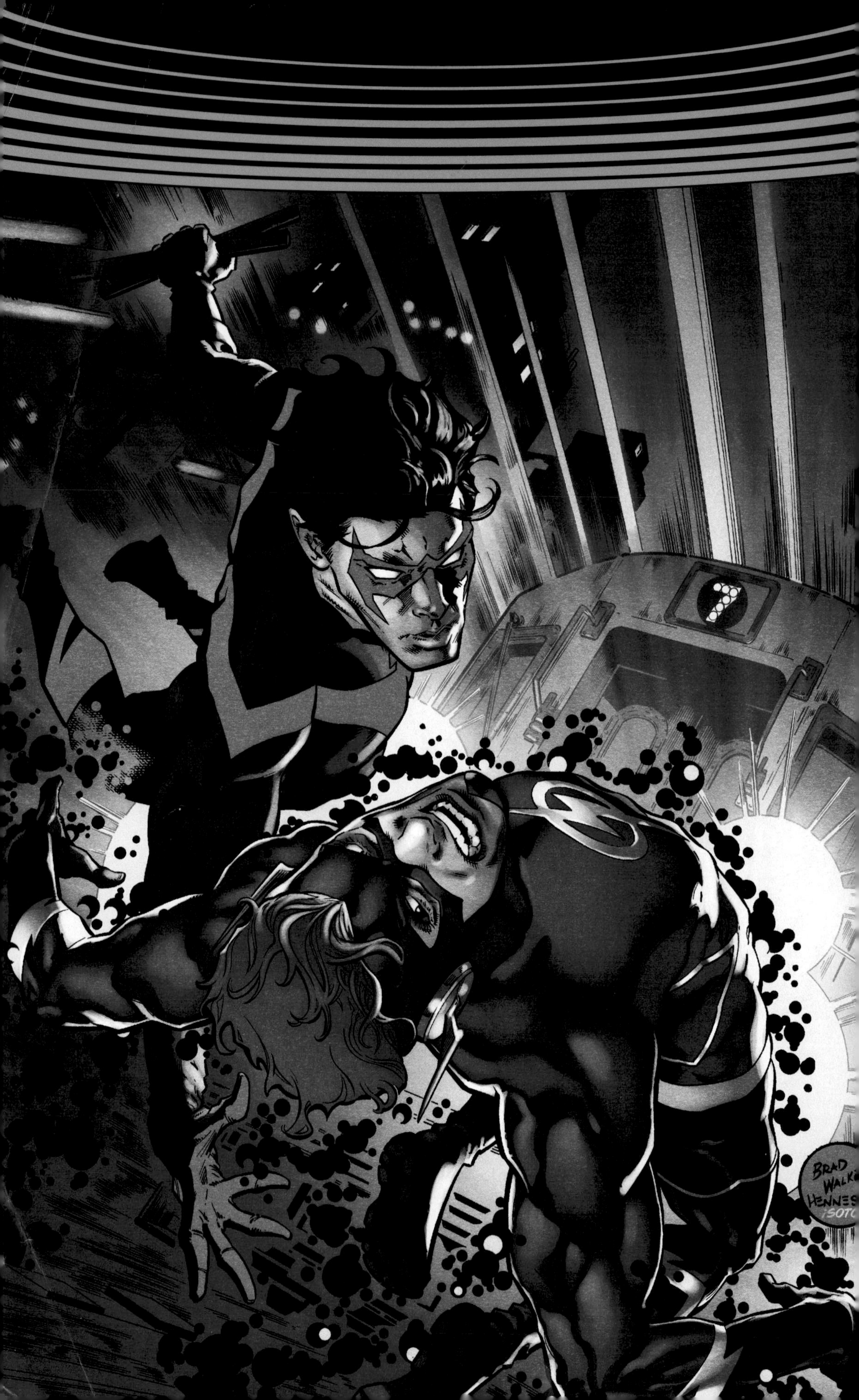
7
BRAD

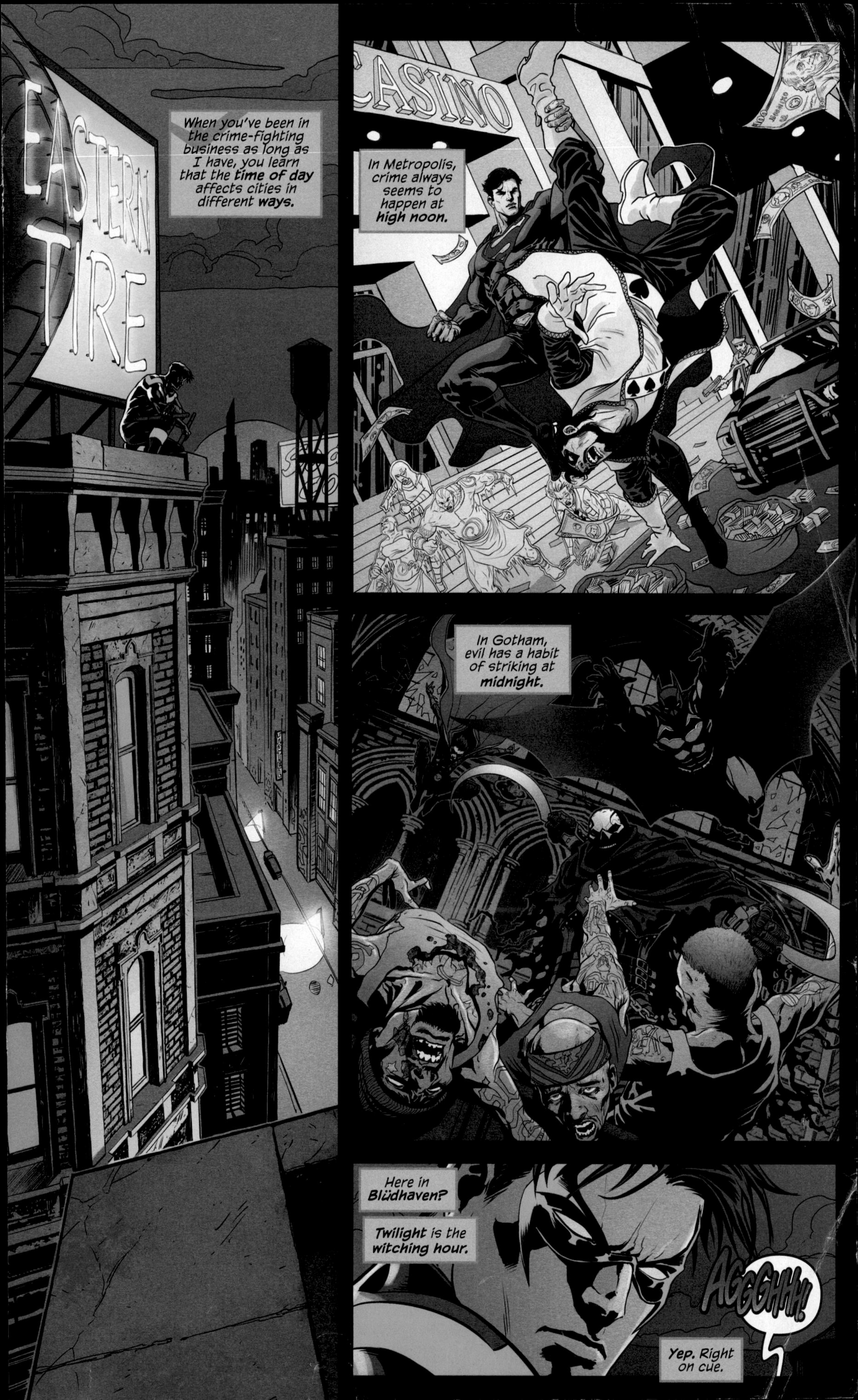

EASTERN TIRE
When you've been in the crime-fighting business as long as I have, you learn that the **time of day** affects cities in different **ways.**
CASINO
In Metropolis, crime always seems to happen at **high noon.**
In Gotham, evil has a habit of striking at **midnight.**
Here in **Blüdhaven?**
Twilight is the **witching hour.**
AGGGHHH!
Yep. Right on cue.

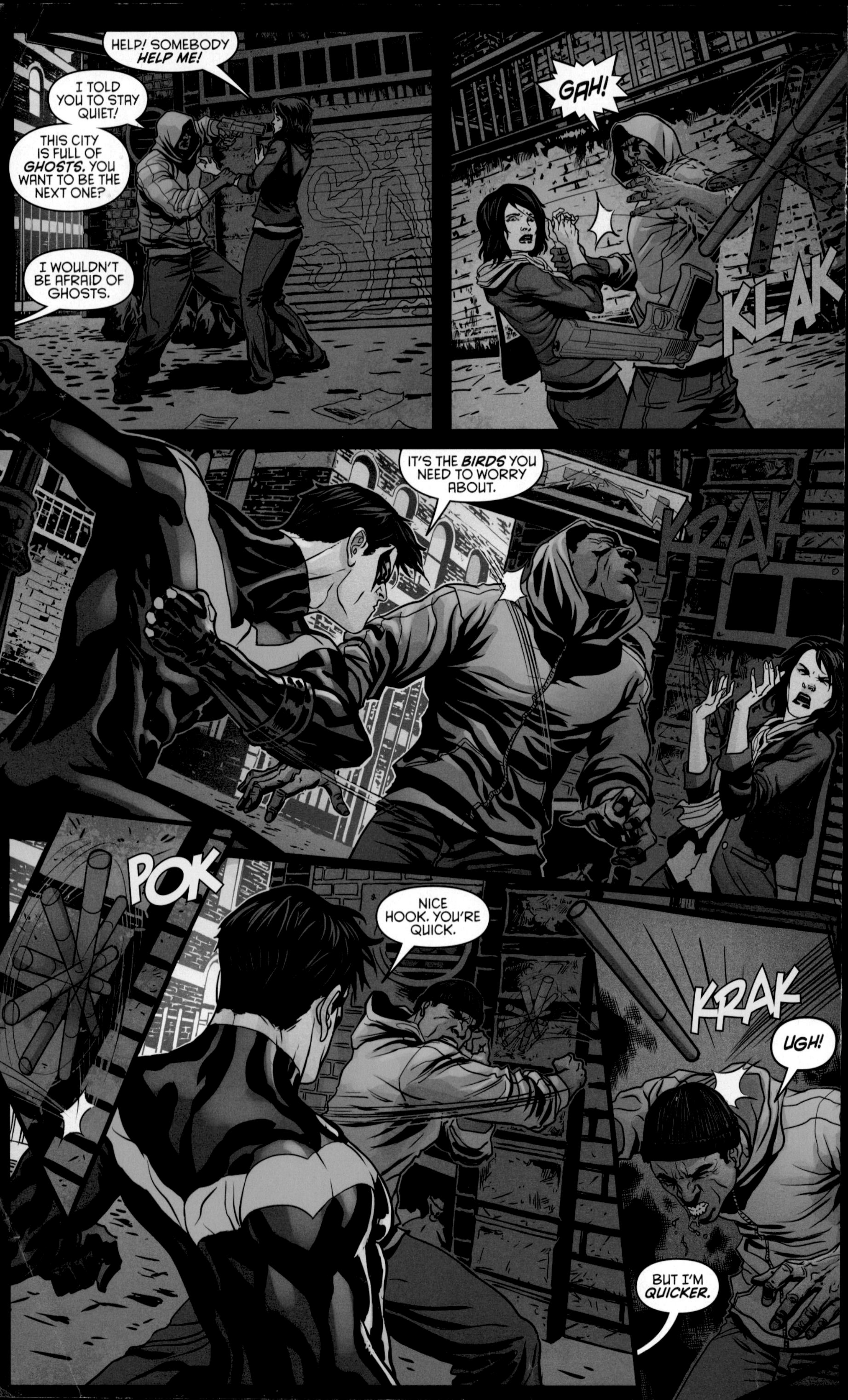
HELP! SOMEBODY HELP ME!
I TOLD YOU TO STAY QUIET!
THIS CITY IS FULL OF GHOSTS. YOU WANT TO BE THE NEXT ONE?
I WOULDN'T BE AFRAID OF GHOSTS.
GAH!
KLAK
IT'S THE BIRDS YOU NEED TO WORRY ABOUT.
KRAK
POK
NICE HOOK. YOU'RE QUICK.
KRAK
UGH!
BUT I'M QUICKER.

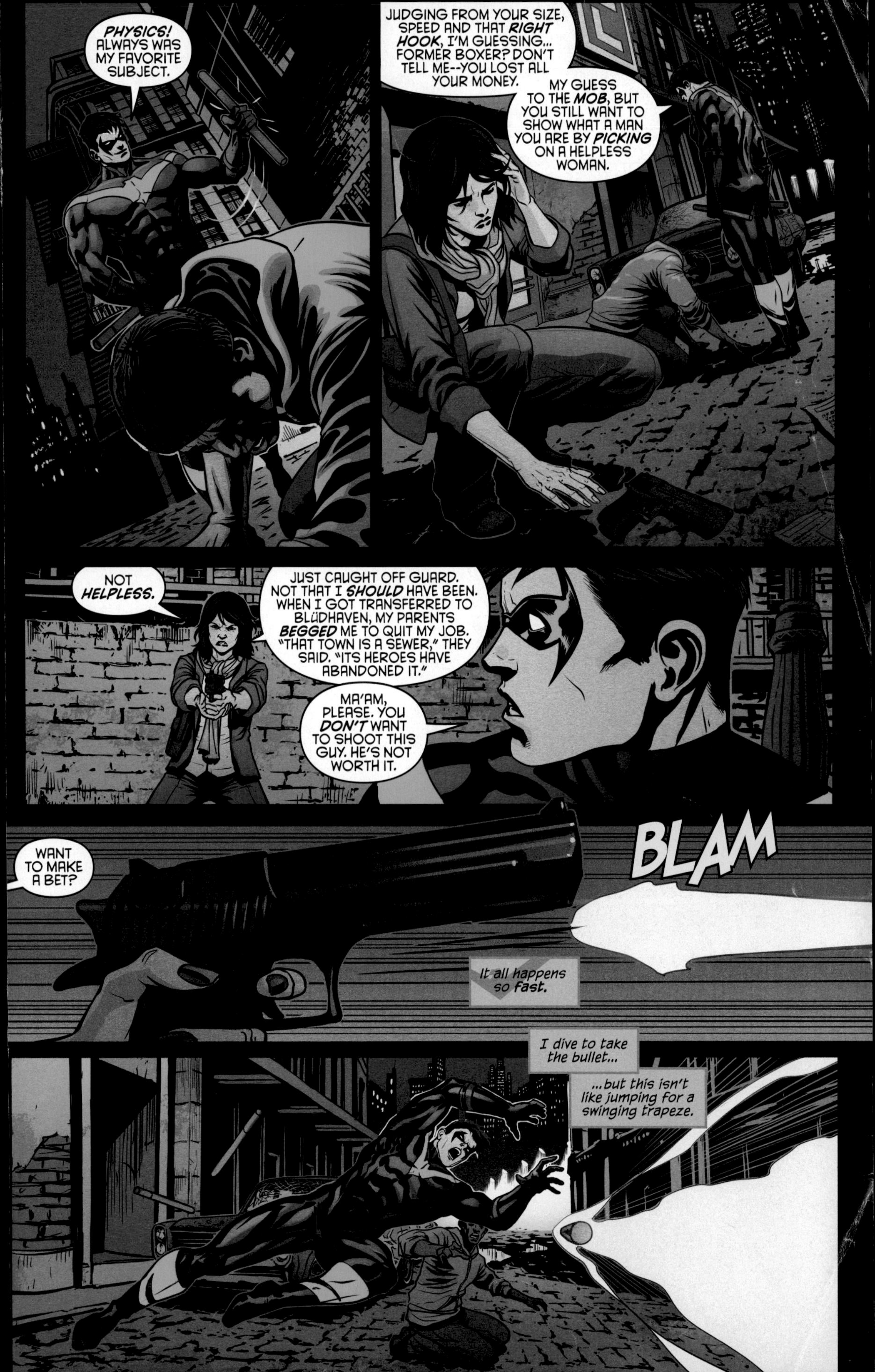
PHYSICS! ALWAYS WAS MY FAVORITE SUBJECT.
JUDGING FROM YOUR SIZE, SPEED AND THAT RIGHT HOOK, I'M GUESSING... FORMER BOXER? DON'T TELL ME--YOU LOST ALL YOUR MONEY.
MY GUESS TO THE MOB, BUT YOU STILL WANT TO SHOW WHAT A MAN YOU ARE BY PICKING ON A HELPLESS WOMAN.
NOT HELPLESS.
JUST CAUGHT OFF GUARD. NOT THAT I SHOULD HAVE BEEN. WHEN I GOT TRANSFERRED TO BLÜDHAVEN, MY PARENTS BEGGED ME TO QUIT MY JOB. "THAT TOWN IS A SEWER," THEY SAID. "ITS HEROES HAVE ABANDONED IT."
MA'AM, PLEASE. YOU DON'T WANT TO SHOOT THIS GUY. HE'S NOT WORTH IT.
WANT TO MAKE A BET?
BLAM
It all happens so fast.
I dive to take the bullet...
...but this isn't like jumping for a swinging trapeze.

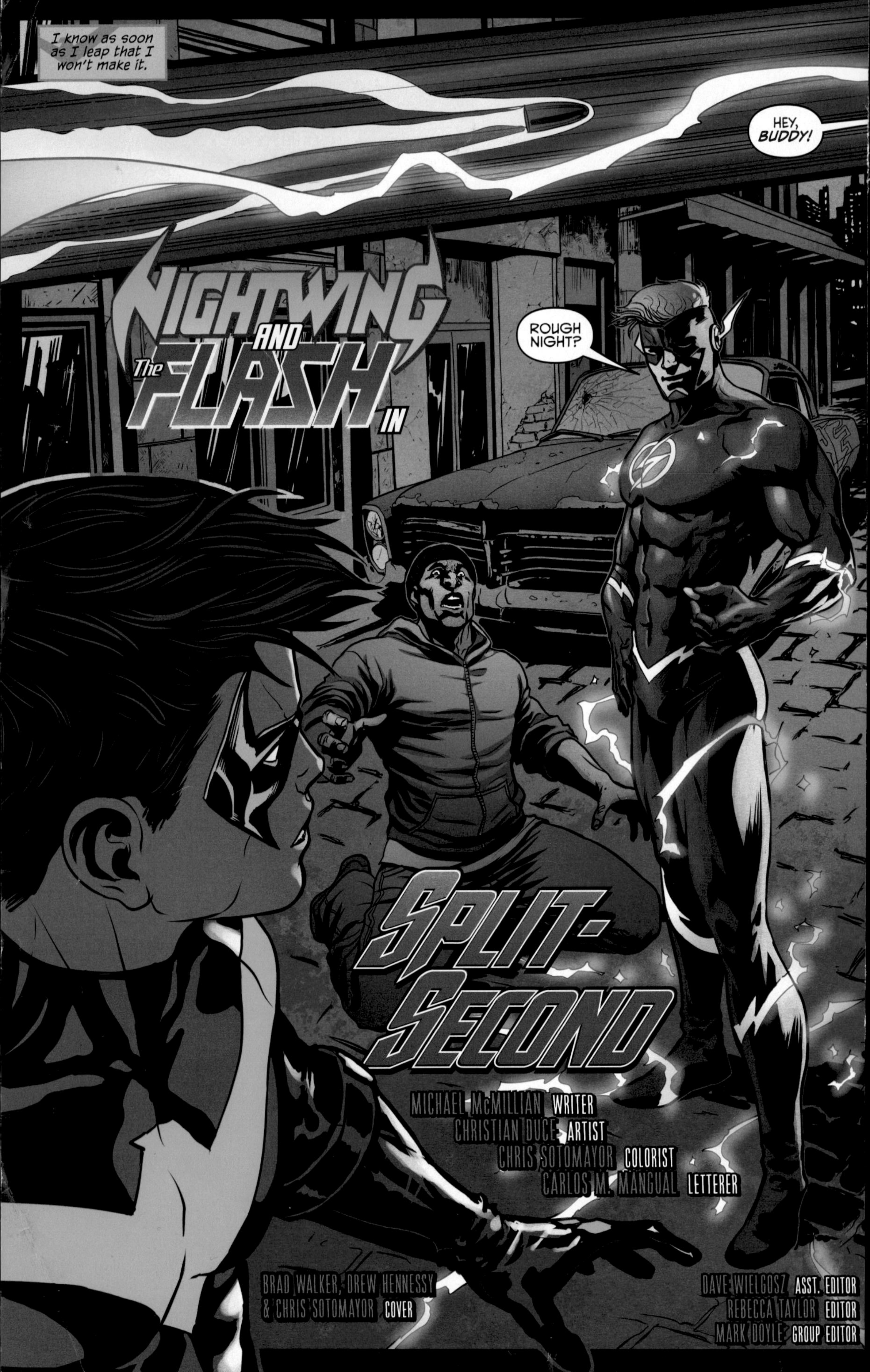
I know as soon as I leap that I won't make it.
HEY, BUDDY!
ROUGH NIGHT?
NIGHTWING AND The FLASH IN
SPLIT-SECOND
MICHAEL McMILLIAN WRITER
CHRISTIAN DUCE ARTIST
CHRIS SOTOMAYOR COLORIST
CARLOS M. MANGUAL LETTERER
BRAD WALKER, DREW HENNESSY & CHRIS SOTOMAYOR COVER
DAVE WIELGOSZ ASST. EDITOR
REBECCA TAYLOR EDITOR
MARK DOYLE GROUP EDITOR

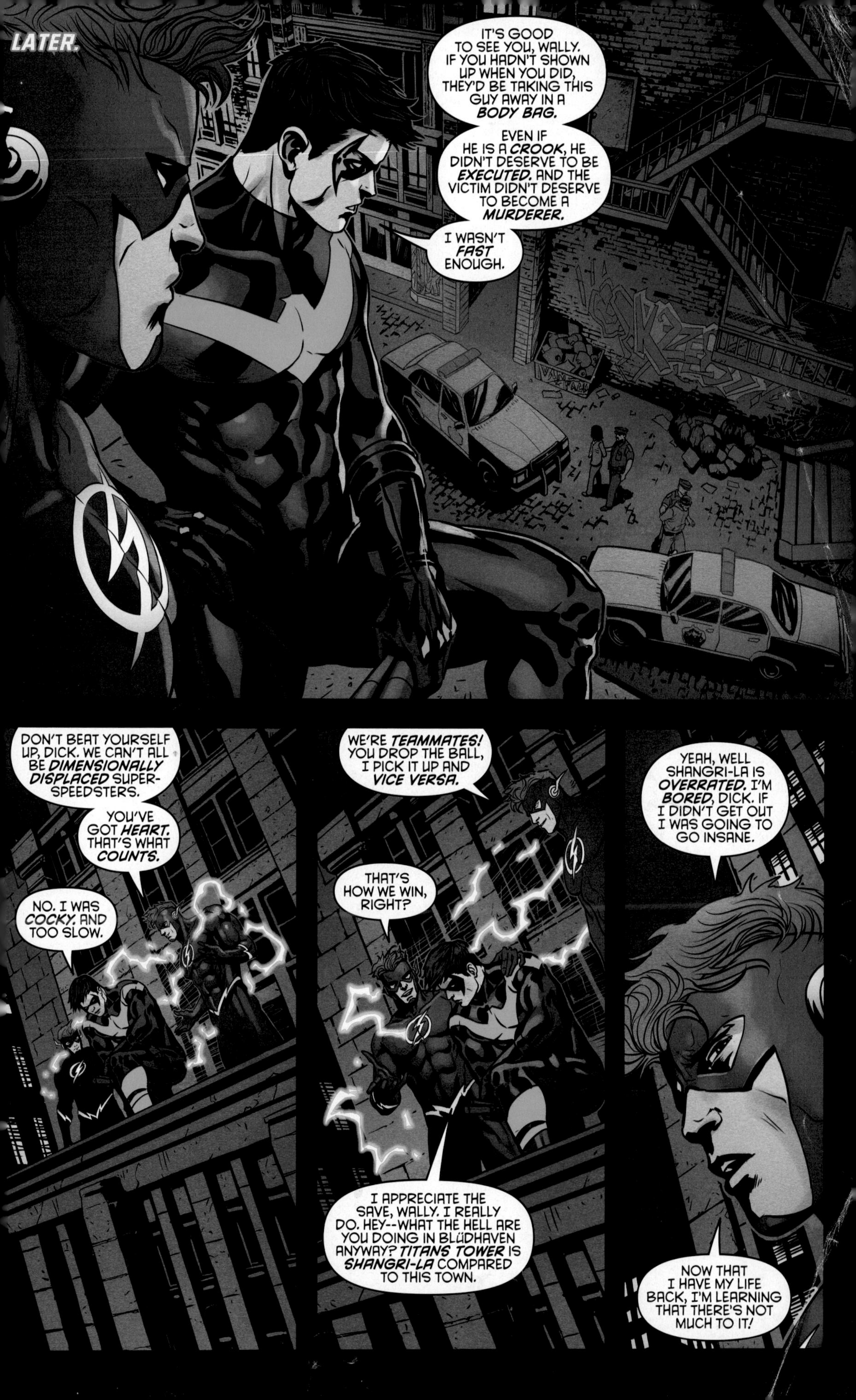

LATER.
IT'S GOOD TO SEE YOU, WALLY. IF YOU HADN'T SHOWN UP WHEN YOU DID, THEY'D BE TAKING THIS GUY AWAY IN A BODY BAG.
EVEN IF HE IS A CROOK, HE DIDN'T DESERVE TO BE EXECUTED. AND THE VICTIM DIDN'T DESERVE TO BECOME A MURDERER.
I WASN'T FAST ENOUGH.
DON'T BEAT YOURSELF UP, DICK. WE CAN'T ALL BE DIMENSIONALLY DISPLACED SUPER-SPEEDSTERS.
YOU'VE GOT HEART. THAT'S WHAT COUNTS.
NO. I WAS COCKY. AND TOO SLOW.
WE'RE TEAMMATES! YOU DROP THE BALL, I PICK IT UP AND VICE VERSA.
THAT'S HOW WE WIN, RIGHT?
I APPRECIATE THE SAVE, WALLY. I REALLY DO. HEY--WHAT THE HELL ARE YOU DOING IN BLÜDHAVEN ANYWAY? TITANS TOWER IS SHANGRI-LA COMPARED TO THIS TOWN.
YEAH, WELL SHANGRI-LA IS OVERRATED. I'M BORED, DICK. IF I DIDN'T GET OUT I WAS GOING TO GO INSANE.
NOW THAT I HAVE MY LIFE BACK, I'M LEARNING THAT THERE'S NOT MUCH TO IT!

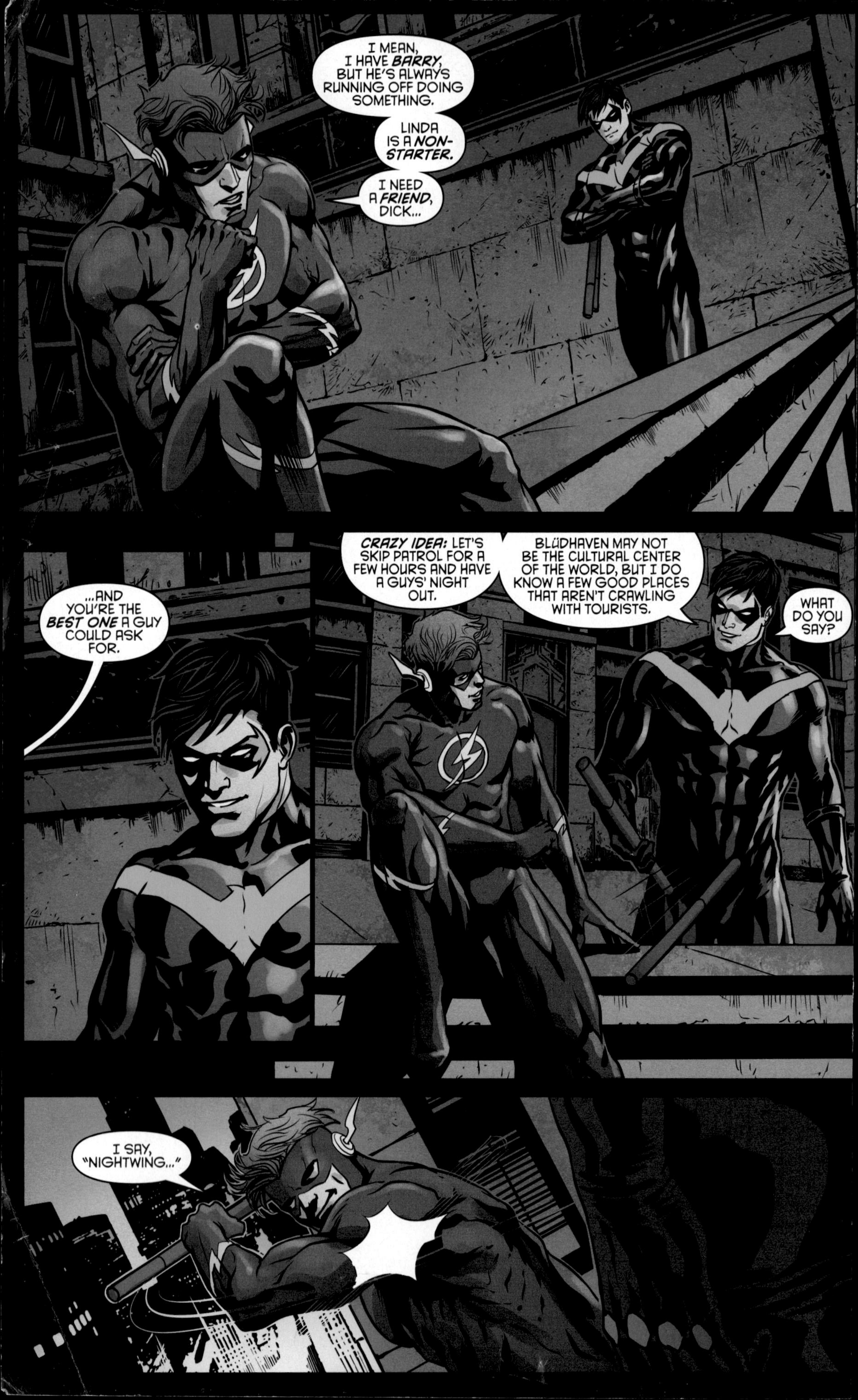
I MEAN, I HAVE BARRY, BUT HE'S ALWAYS RUNNING OFF DOING SOMETHING.
LINDA IS A NON-STARTER.
I NEED A FRIEND, DICK...
...AND YOU'RE THE BEST ONE A GUY COULD ASK FOR.
CRAZY IDEA: LET'S SKIP PATROL FOR A FEW HOURS AND HAVE A GUYS' NIGHT OUT.
BLÜDHAVEN MAY NOT BE THE CULTURAL CENTER OF THE WORLD, BUT I DO KNOW A FEW GOOD PLACES THAT AREN'T CRAWLING WITH TOURISTS.
WHAT DO YOU SAY?
I SAY, "NIGHTWING..."

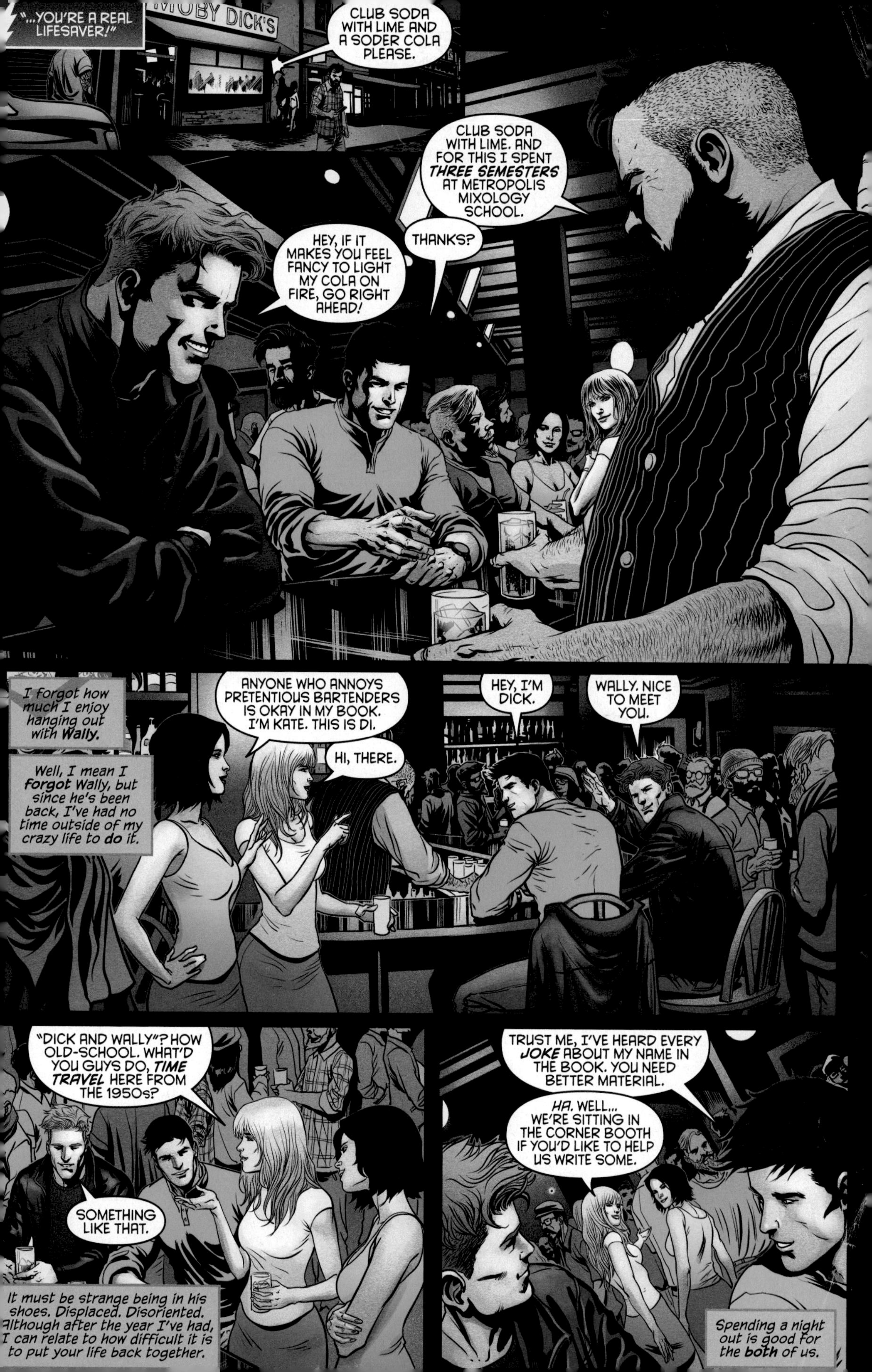
"...YOU'RE A REAL LIFESAVER!"
MOBY DICK'S
CLUB SODA WITH LIME AND A SODER COLA PLEASE.
CLUB SODA WITH LIME. AND FOR THIS I SPENT THREE SEMESTERS AT METROPOLIS MIXOLOGY SCHOOL.
HEY, IF IT MAKES YOU FEEL FANCY TO LIGHT MY COLA ON FIRE, GO RIGHT AHEAD!
THANKS?
I forgot how much I enjoy hanging out with Wally.
Well, I mean I forgot Wally, but since he's been back, I've had no time outside of my crazy life to do it.
ANYONE WHO ANNOYS PRETENTIOUS BARTENDERS IS OKAY IN MY BOOK. I'M KATE. THIS IS DI.
HI, THERE.
HEY, I'M DICK.
WALLY. NICE TO MEET YOU.
"DICK AND WALLY"? HOW OLD-SCHOOL. WHAT'D YOU GUYS DO, TIME TRAVEL HERE FROM THE 1950s?
SOMETHING LIKE THAT.
It must be strange being in his shoes. Displaced. Disoriented. Although after the year I've had, I can relate to how difficult it is to put your life back together.
TRUST ME, I'VE HEARD EVERY JOKE ABOUT MY NAME IN THE BOOK. YOU NEED BETTER MATERIAL.
HA. WELL... WE'RE SITTING IN THE CORNER BOOTH IF YOU'D LIKE TO HELP US WRITE SOME.
Spending a night out is good for the both of us.

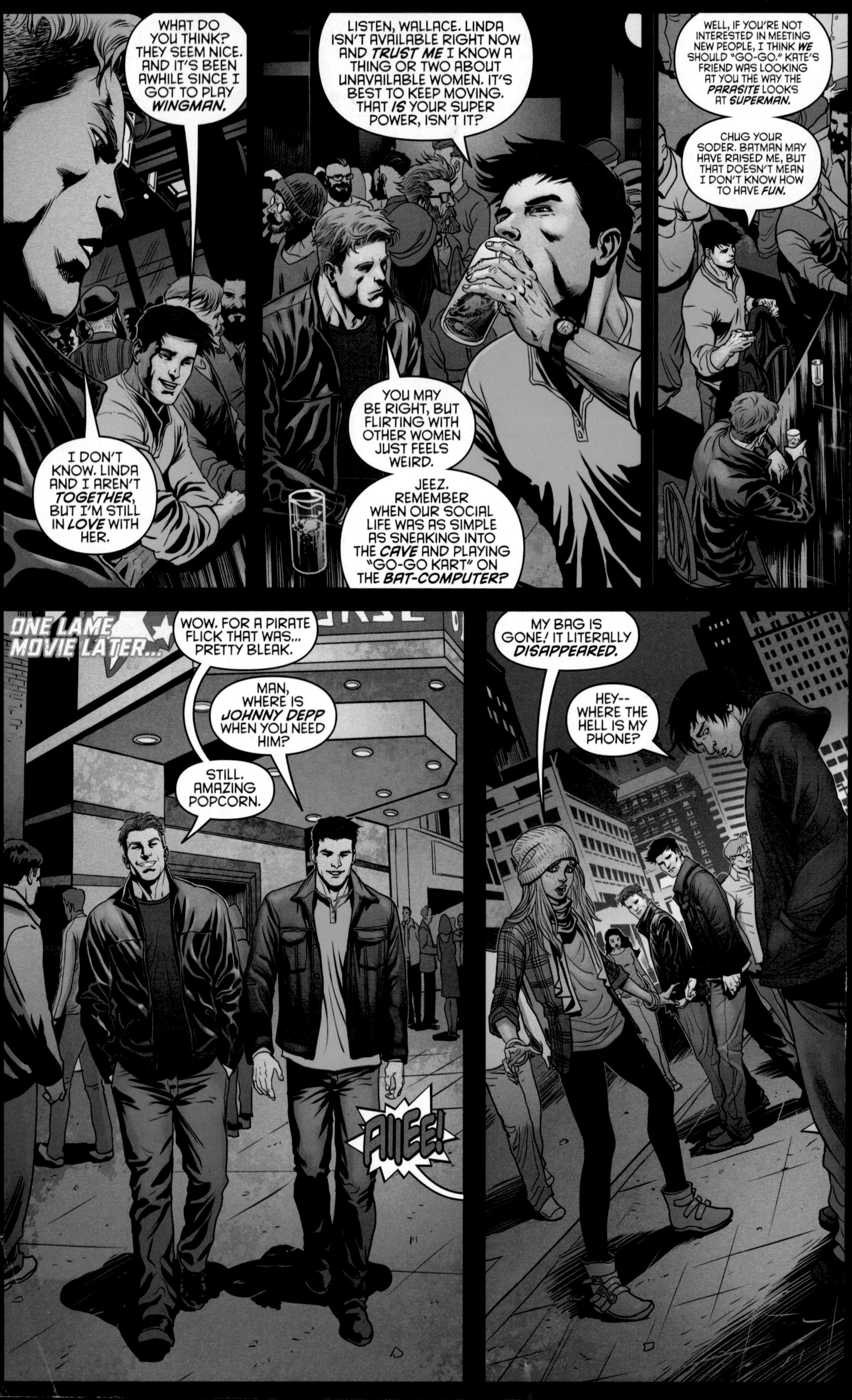
WHAT DO YOU THINK? THEY SEEM NICE. AND IT'S BEEN AWHILE SINCE I GOT TO PLAY WINGMAN.
I DON'T KNOW. LINDA AND I AREN'T TOGETHER, BUT I'M STILL IN LOVE WITH HER.
LISTEN, WALLACE. LINDA ISN'T AVAILABLE RIGHT NOW AND TRUST ME I KNOW A THING OR TWO ABOUT UNAVAILABLE WOMEN. IT'S BEST TO KEEP MOVING. THAT IS YOUR SUPER POWER, ISN'T IT?
YOU MAY BE RIGHT, BUT FLIRTING WITH OTHER WOMEN JUST FEELS WEIRD.
JEEZ. REMEMBER WHEN OUR SOCIAL LIFE WAS AS SIMPLE AS SNEAKING INTO THE CAVE AND PLAYING "GO-GO KART" ON THE BAT-COMPUTER?
WELL, IF YOU'RE NOT INTERESTED IN MEETING NEW PEOPLE, I THINK WE SHOULD "GO-GO." KATE'S FRIEND WAS LOOKING AT YOU THE WAY THE PARASITE LOOKS AT SUPERMAN.
CHUG YOUR SODER. BATMAN MAY HAVE RAISED ME, BUT THAT DOESN'T MEAN I DON'T KNOW HOW TO HAVE FUN.
ONE LAME MOVIE LATER...
WOW. FOR A PIRATE FLICK THAT WAS... PRETTY BLEAK.
MAN, WHERE IS JOHNNY DEPP WHEN YOU NEED HIM?
STILL. AMAZING POPCORN.
AIIEE!
MY BAG IS GONE! IT LITERALLY DISAPPEARED.
HEY-- WHERE THE HELL IS MY PHONE?

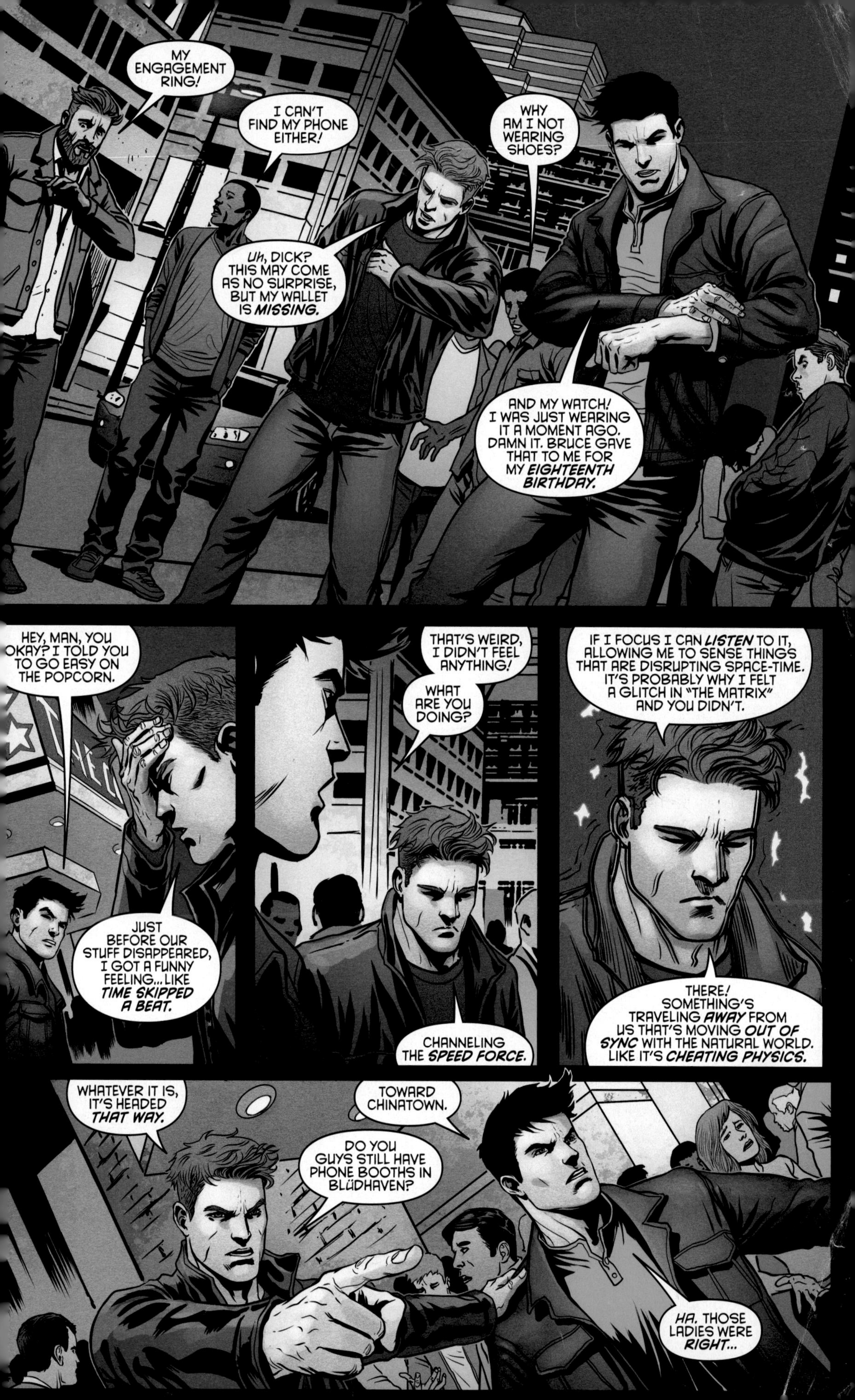

MY ENGAGEMENT RING!
I CAN'T FIND MY PHONE EITHER!
WHY AM I NOT WEARING SHOES?
UH, DICK? THIS MAY COME AS NO SURPRISE, BUT MY WALLET IS MISSING.
AND MY WATCH! I WAS JUST WEARING IT A MOMENT AGO. DAMN IT. BRUCE GAVE THAT TO ME FOR MY EIGHTEENTH BIRTHDAY.
HEY, MAN, YOU OKAY? I TOLD YOU TO GO EASY ON THE POPCORN.
JUST BEFORE OUR STUFF DISAPPEARED, I GOT A FUNNY FEELING... LIKE TIME SKIPPED A BEAT.
THAT'S WEIRD, I DIDN'T FEEL ANYTHING!
WHAT ARE YOU DOING?
CHANNELING THE SPEED FORCE.
IF I FOCUS I CAN LISTEN TO IT, ALLOWING ME TO SENSE THINGS THAT ARE DISRUPTING SPACE-TIME. IT'S PROBABLY WHY I FELT A GLITCH IN "THE MATRIX" AND YOU DIDN'T.
THERE! SOMETHING'S TRAVELING AWAY FROM US THAT'S MOVING OUT OF SYNC WITH THE NATURAL WORLD. LIKE IT'S CHEATING PHYSICS.
WHATEVER IT IS, IT'S HEADED THAT WAY.
TOWARD CHINATOWN.
DO YOU GUYS STILL HAVE PHONE BOOTHS IN BLÜDHAVEN?
HA. THOSE LADIES WERE RIGHT...

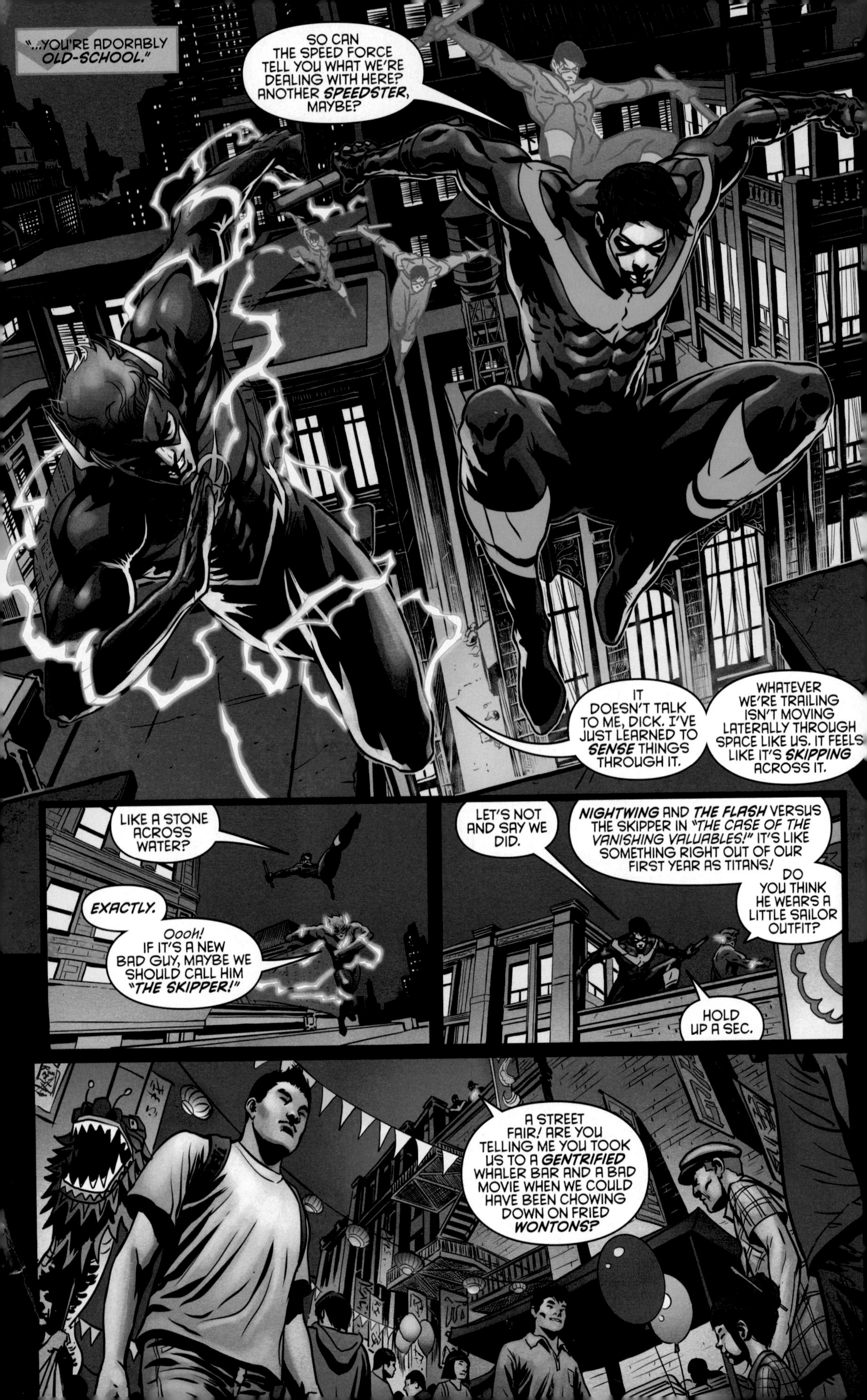
"...YOU'RE ADORABLY OLD-SCHOOL."
SO CAN THE SPEED FORCE TELL YOU WHAT WE'RE DEALING WITH HERE? ANOTHER SPEEDSTER, MAYBE?
IT DOESN'T TALK TO ME, DICK. I'VE JUST LEARNED TO SENSE THINGS THROUGH IT.
WHATEVER WE'RE TRAILING ISN'T MOVING LATERALLY THROUGH SPACE LIKE US. IT FEELS LIKE IT'S SKIPPING ACROSS IT.
LIKE A STONE ACROSS WATER?
EXACTLY.
Oooh! IF IT'S A NEW BAD GUY, MAYBE WE SHOULD CALL HIM "THE SKIPPER!"
LET'S NOT AND SAY WE DID.
NIGHTWING AND THE FLASH VERSUS THE SKIPPER IN "THE CASE OF THE VANISHING VALUABLES!" IT'S LIKE SOMETHING RIGHT OUT OF OUR FIRST YEAR AS TITANS!
DO YOU THINK HE WEARS A LITTLE SAILOR OUTFIT?
HOLD UP A SEC.
A STREET FAIR! ARE YOU TELLING ME YOU TOOK US TO A GENTRIFIED WHALER BAR AND A BAD MOVIE WHEN WE COULD HAVE BEEN CHOWING DOWN ON FRIED WONTONS?

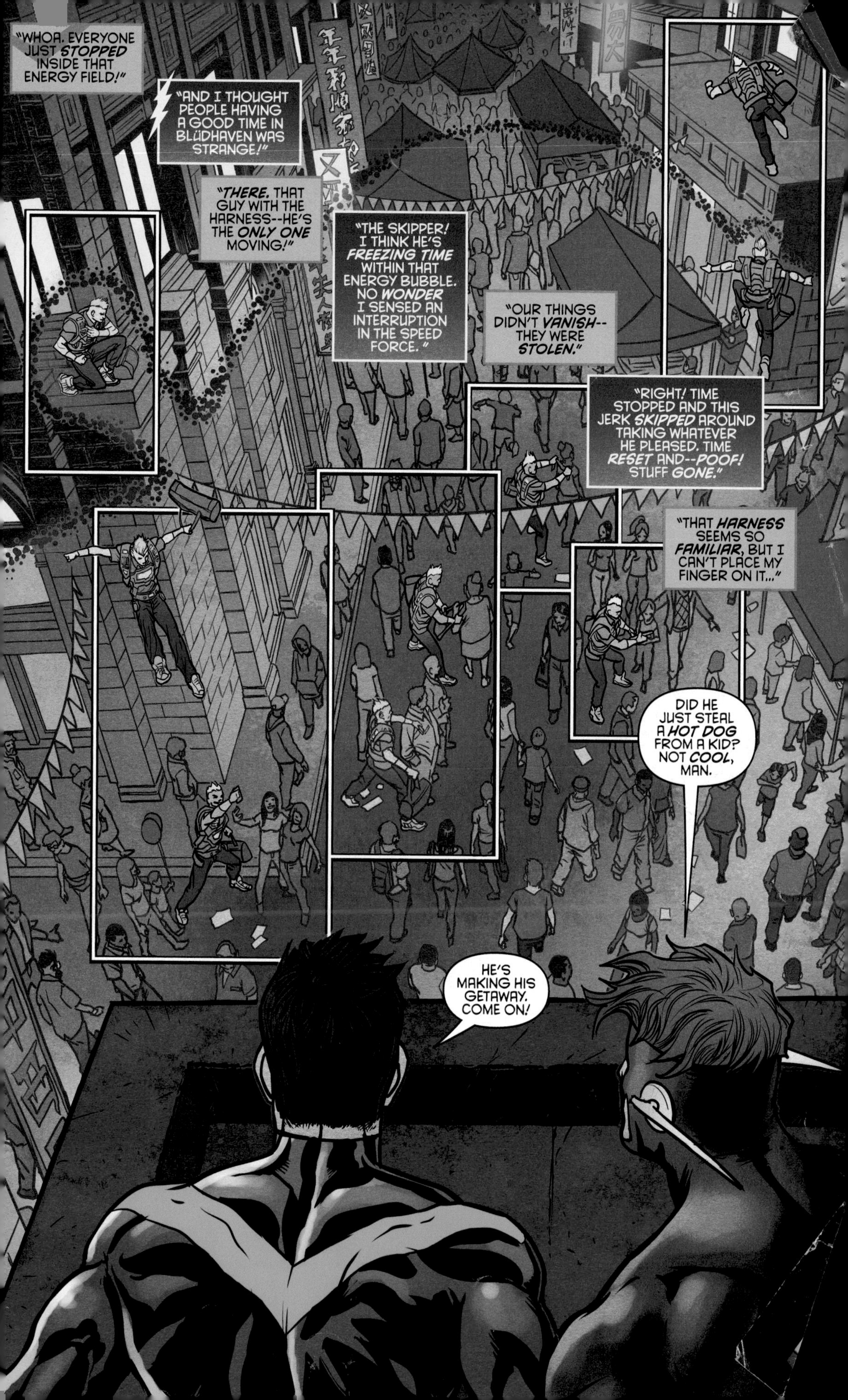
"WHOA. EVERYONE JUST STOPPED INSIDE THAT ENERGY FIELD!"
"AND I THOUGHT PEOPLE HAVING A GOOD TIME IN BLÜDHAVEN WAS STRANGE!"
"THERE. THAT GUY WITH THE HARNESS--HE'S THE ONLY ONE MOVING!"
"THE SKIPPER! I THINK HE'S FREEZING TIME WITHIN THAT ENERGY BUBBLE. NO WONDER I SENSED AN INTERRUPTION IN THE SPEED FORCE."
"OUR THINGS DIDN'T VANISH--THEY WERE STOLEN."
"RIGHT! TIME STOPPED AND THIS JERK SKIPPED AROUND TAKING WHATEVER HE PLEASED. TIME RESET AND--POOF! STUFF GONE."
"THAT HARNESS SEEMS SO FAMILIAR, BUT I CAN'T PLACE MY FINGER ON IT..."
DID HE JUST STEAL A HOT DOG FROM A KID? NOT COOL, MAN.
HE'S MAKING HIS GETAWAY. COME ON!

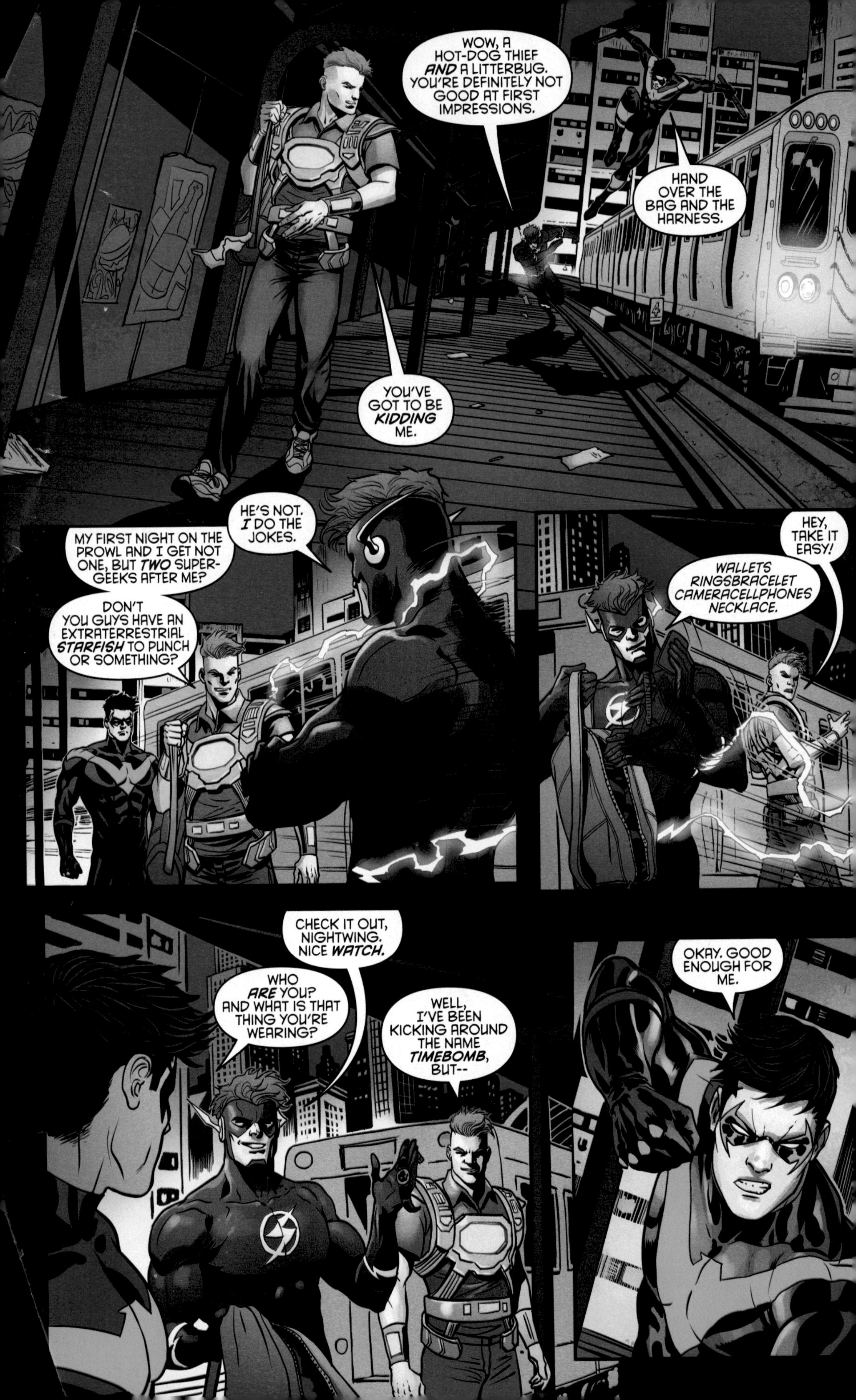
WOW, A HOT-DOG THIEF AND A LITTERBUG. YOU'RE DEFINITELY NOT GOOD AT FIRST IMPRESSIONS.
HAND OVER THE BAG AND THE HARNESS.
YOU'VE GOT TO BE KIDDING ME.
MY FIRST NIGHT ON THE PROWL AND I GET NOT ONE, BUT TWO SUPER-GEEKS AFTER ME?
HE'S NOT. I DO THE JOKES.
DON'T YOU GUYS HAVE AN EXTRATERRESTRIAL STARFISH TO PUNCH OR SOMETHING?
HEY, TAKE IT EASY!
WALLETS RINGSBRACELET CAMERACELLPHONES NECKLACE.
CHECK IT OUT, NIGHTWING. NICE WATCH.
WHO ARE YOU? AND WHAT IS THAT THING YOU'RE WEARING?
WELL, I'VE BEEN KICKING AROUND THE NAME TIMEBOMB, BUT--
OKAY. GOOD ENOUGH FOR ME.

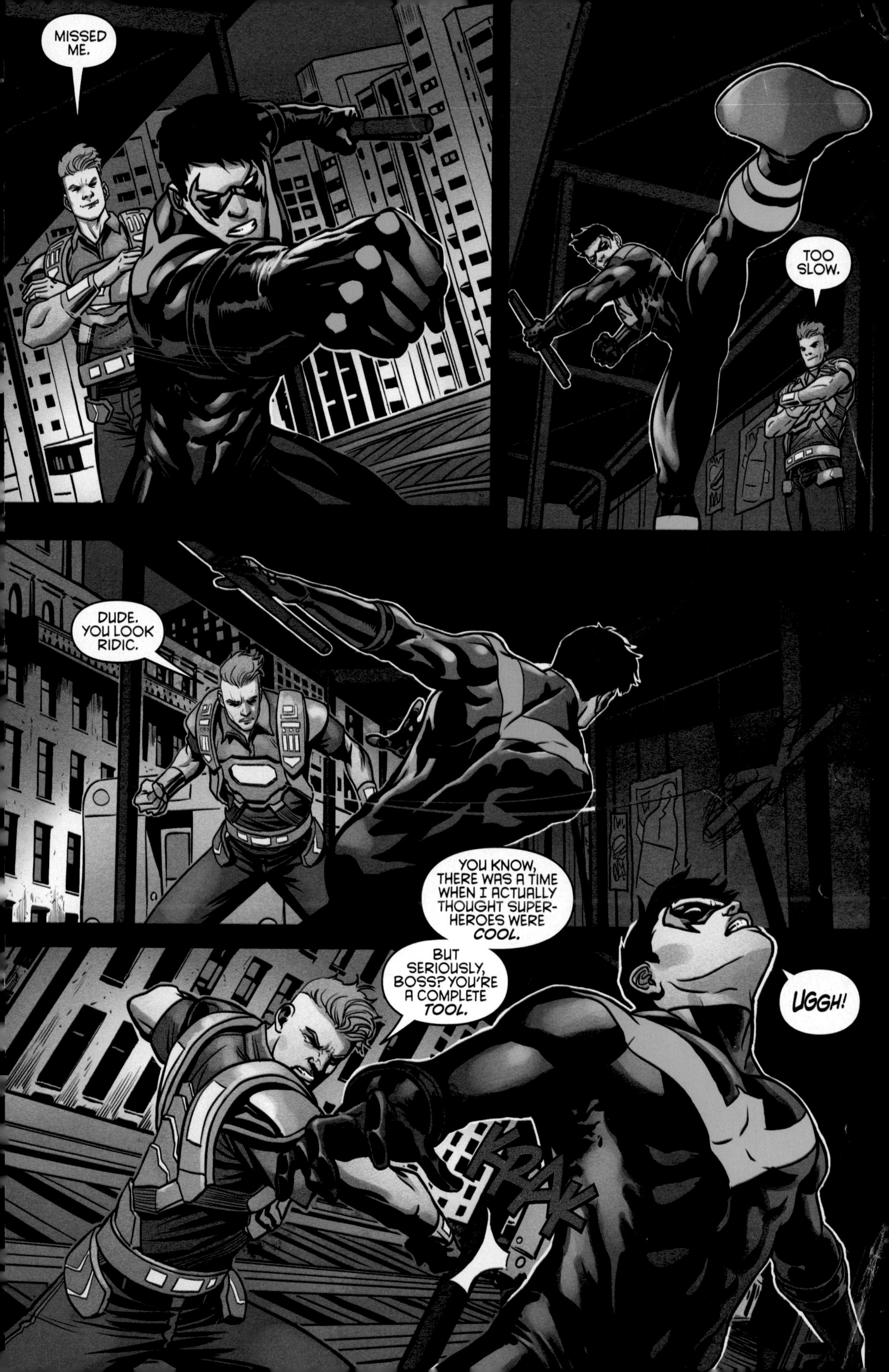
MISSED ME.
TOO SLOW.
DUDE. YOU LOOK RIDIC.
YOU KNOW, THERE WAS A TIME WHEN I ACTUALLY THOUGHT SUPER-HEROES WERE *COOL.*
BUT SERIOUSLY, BOSS? YOU'RE A COMPLETE *TOOL.*
UGGH!
KRAK

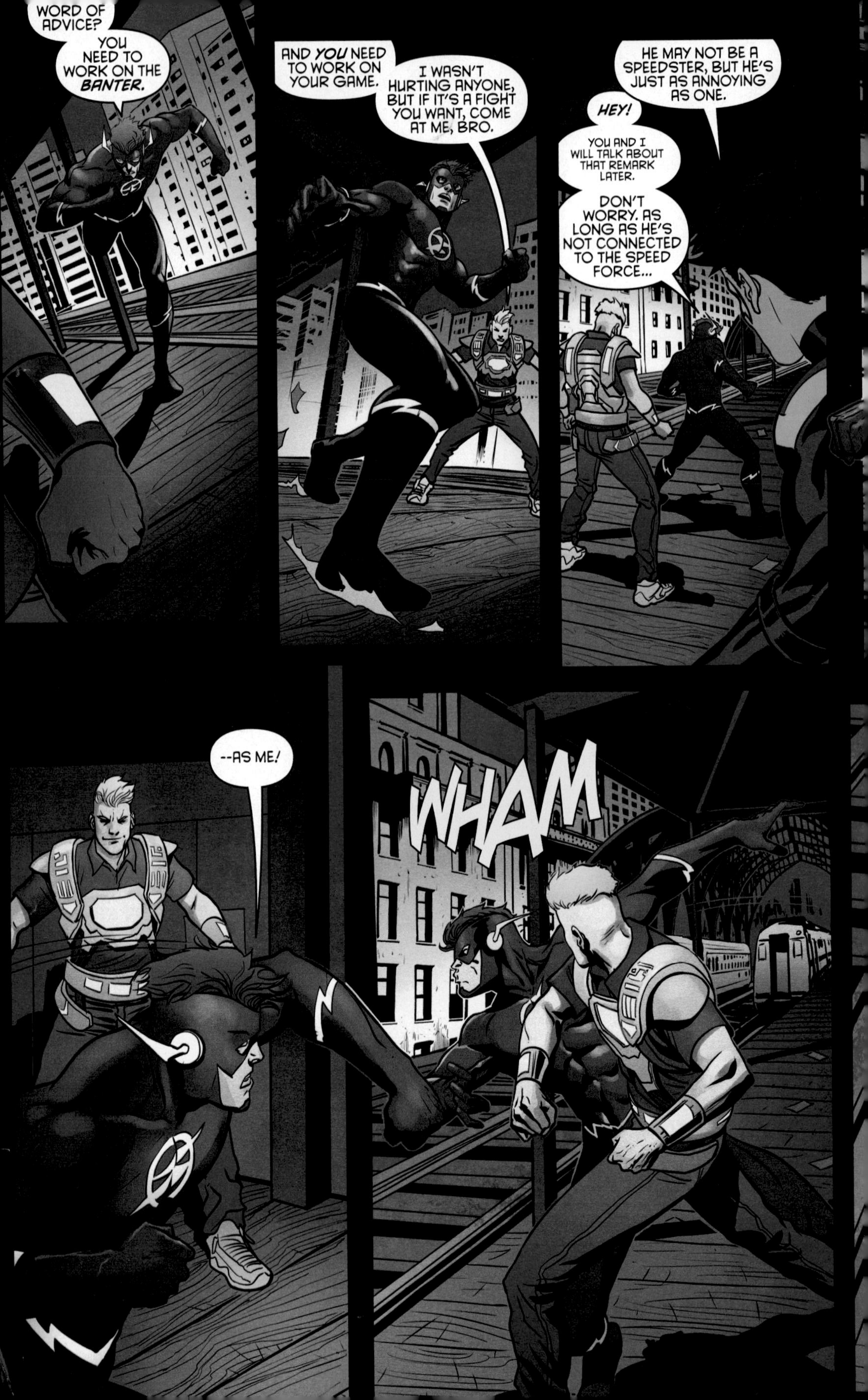

WORD OF ADVICE?
YOU NEED TO WORK ON THE *BANTER.*
AND *YOU* NEED TO WORK ON YOUR GAME.
I WASN'T HURTING ANYONE, BUT IF IT'S A FIGHT YOU WANT, COME AT ME, BRO.
HE MAY NOT BE A SPEEDSTER, BUT HE'S JUST AS ANNOYING AS ONE.
HEY!
YOU AND I WILL TALK ABOUT THAT REMARK LATER.
DON'T WORRY. AS LONG AS HE'S NOT CONNECTED TO THE SPEED FORCE...
--AS ME!
WHAM

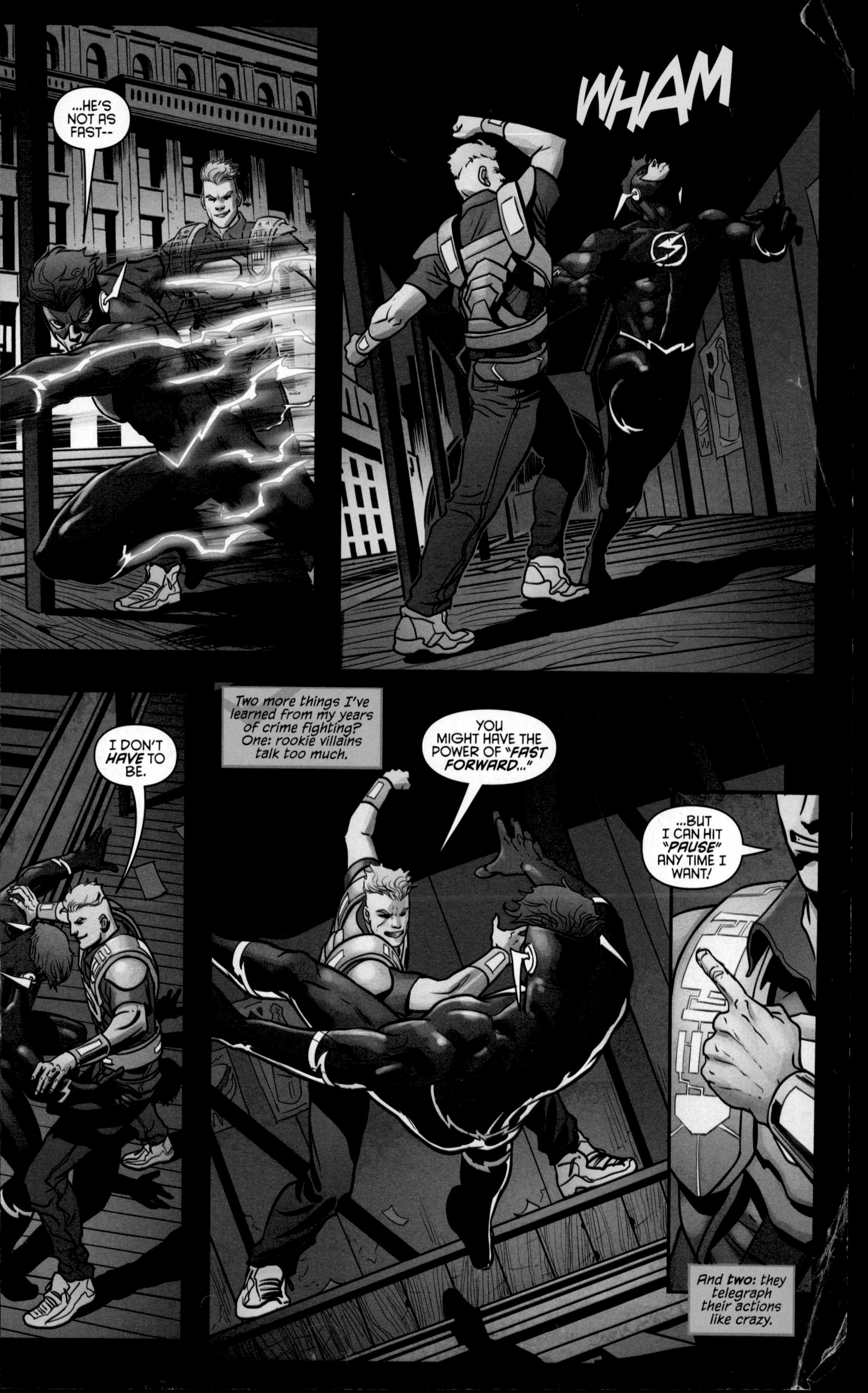
...HE'S NOT AS FAST--
WHAM
I DON'T *HAVE* TO BE.
Two more things I've learned from my years of crime fighting? One: rookie villains talk too much.
YOU MIGHT HAVE THE POWER OF *"FAST FORWARD..."*
...BUT I CAN HIT *"PAUSE"* ANY TIME I WANT!
And two: they telegraph their actions like crazy.

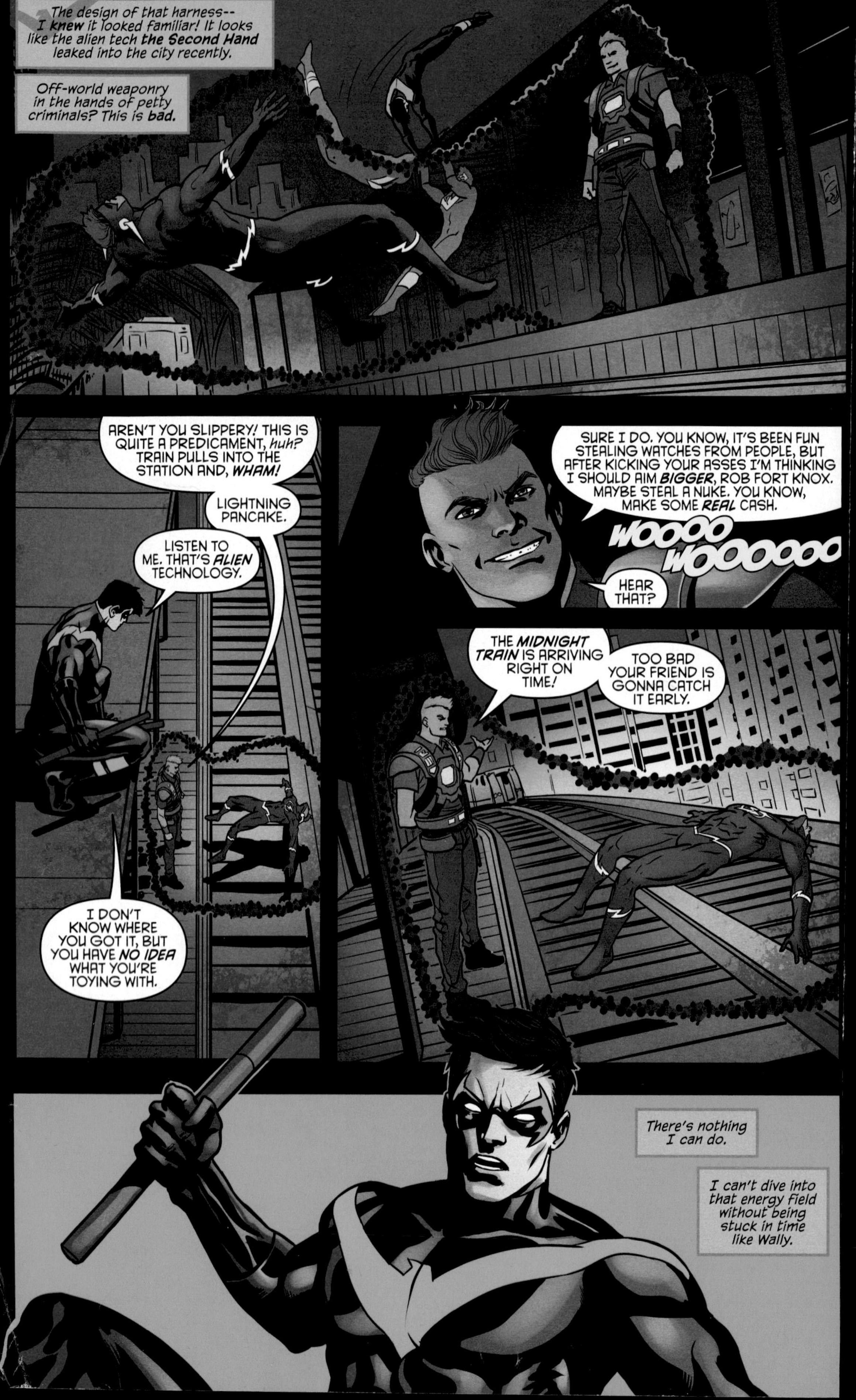
The design of that harness-- I knew it looked familiar! It looks like the alien tech the Second Hand leaked into the city recently.
Off-world weaponry in the hands of petty criminals? This is bad.
AREN'T YOU SLIPPERY! THIS IS QUITE A PREDICAMENT, huh? TRAIN PULLS INTO THE STATION AND, WHAM!
LIGHTNING PANCAKE.
LISTEN TO ME. THAT'S ALIEN TECHNOLOGY.
I DON'T KNOW WHERE YOU GOT IT, BUT YOU HAVE NO IDEA WHAT YOU'RE TOYING WITH.
SURE I DO. YOU KNOW, IT'S BEEN FUN STEALING WATCHES FROM PEOPLE, BUT AFTER KICKING YOUR ASSES I'M THINKING I SHOULD AIM BIGGER, ROB FORT KNOX. MAYBE STEAL A NUKE. YOU KNOW, MAKE SOME REAL CASH.
WOOOO WOOOOOOO
HEAR THAT?
THE MIDNIGHT TRAIN IS ARRIVING RIGHT ON TIME!
TOO BAD YOUR FRIEND IS GONNA CATCH IT EARLY.
There's nothing I can do.
I can't dive into that energy field without being stuck in time like Wally.

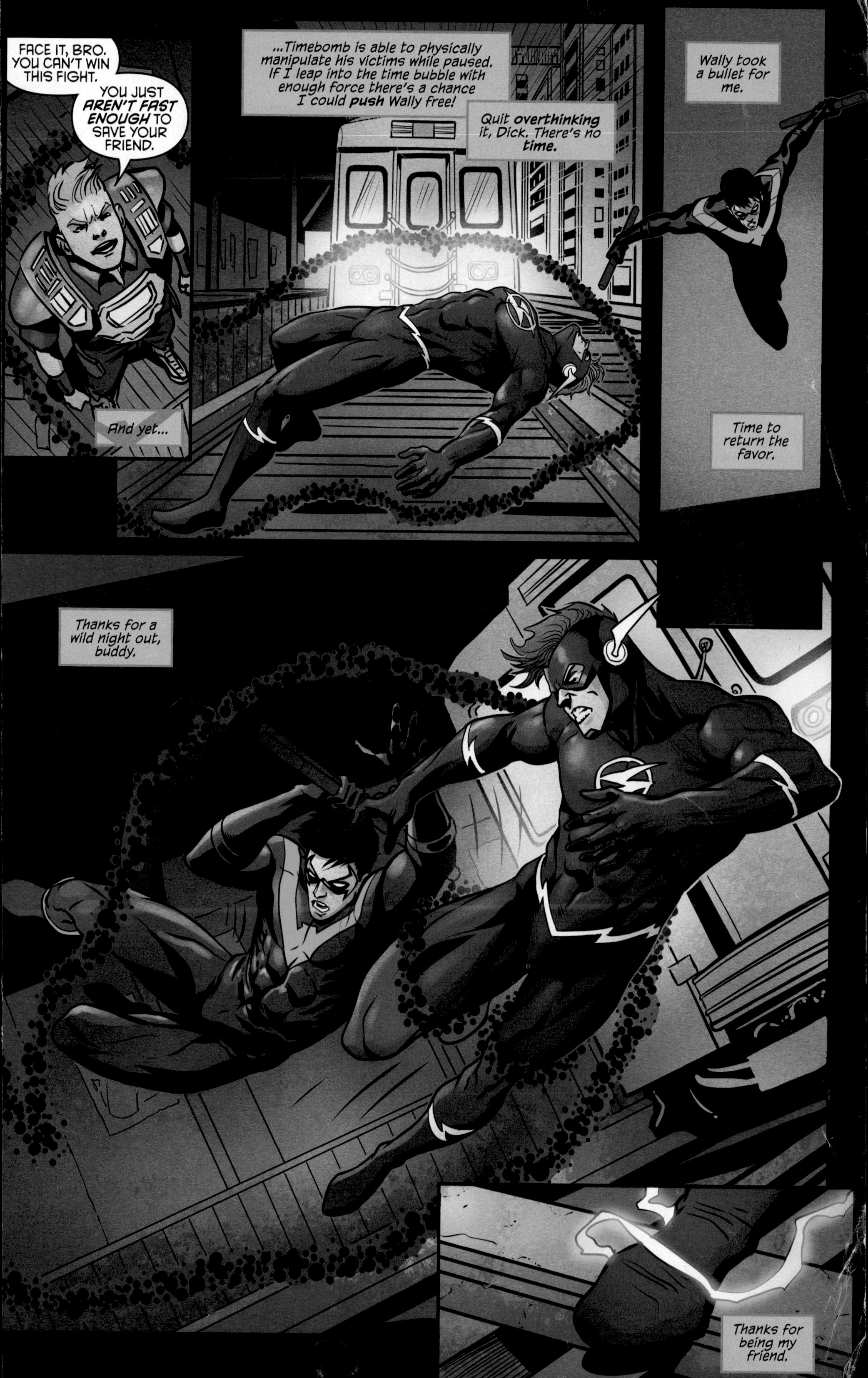
FACE IT, BRO. YOU CAN'T WIN THIS FIGHT.
YOU JUST **AREN'T FAST ENOUGH** TO SAVE YOUR FRIEND.
And yet...
*...Timebomb is able to physically manipulate his victims while paused. If I leap into the time bubble with enough force there's a chance I could **push** Wally free!*
*Quit **overthinking** it, Dick. There's no **time.***
Wally took a bullet for me.
Time to return the favor.
Thanks for a wild night out, buddy.
Thanks for being my friend.

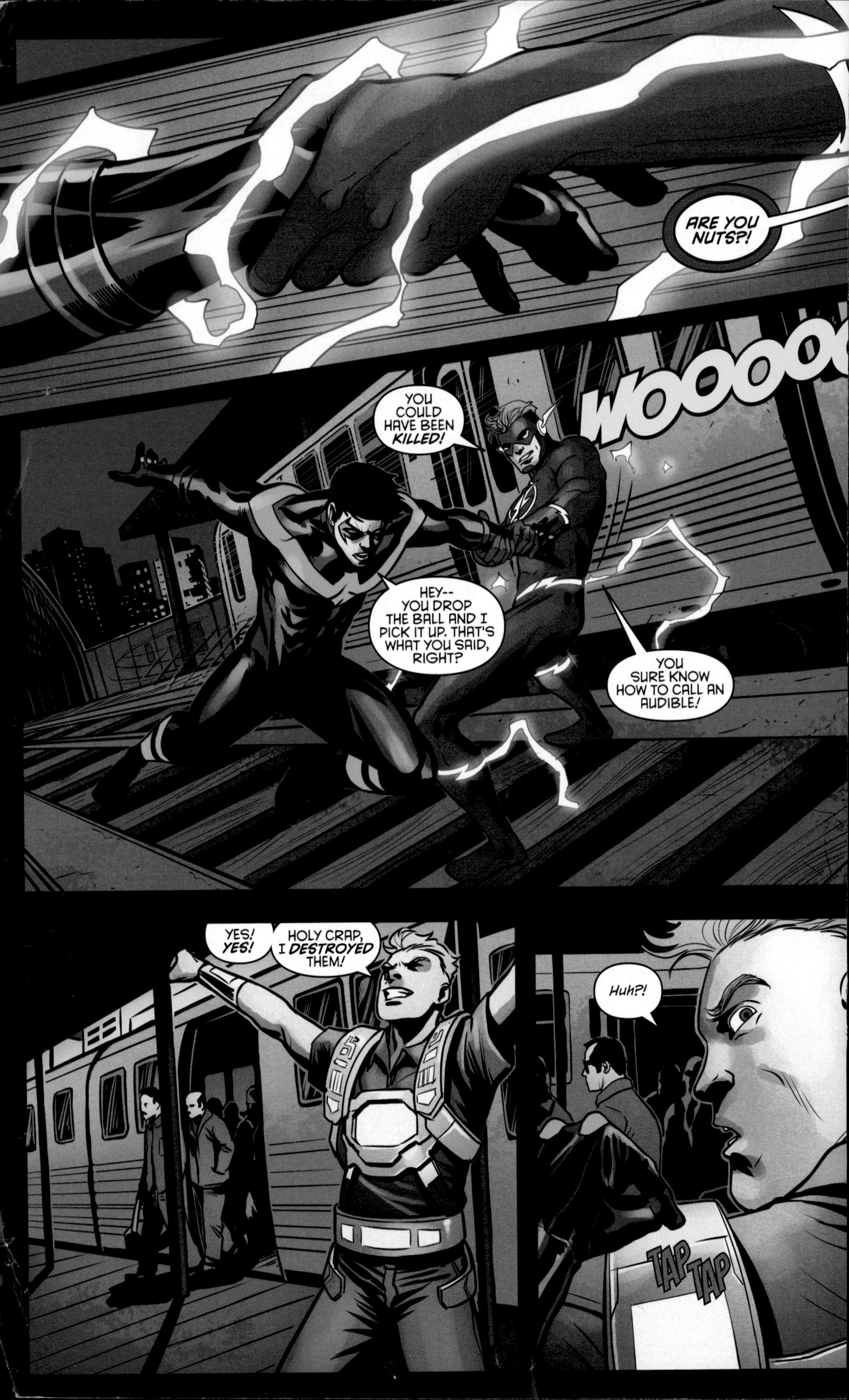
ARE YOU NUTS?!
WOOOOO
YOU COULD HAVE BEEN KILLED!
HEY-- YOU DROP THE BALL AND I PICK IT UP. THAT'S WHAT YOU SAID, RIGHT?
YOU SURE KNOW HOW TO CALL AN AUDIBLE!
YES! YES!
HOLY CRAP, I DESTROYED THEM!
Huh?!
TAP TAP

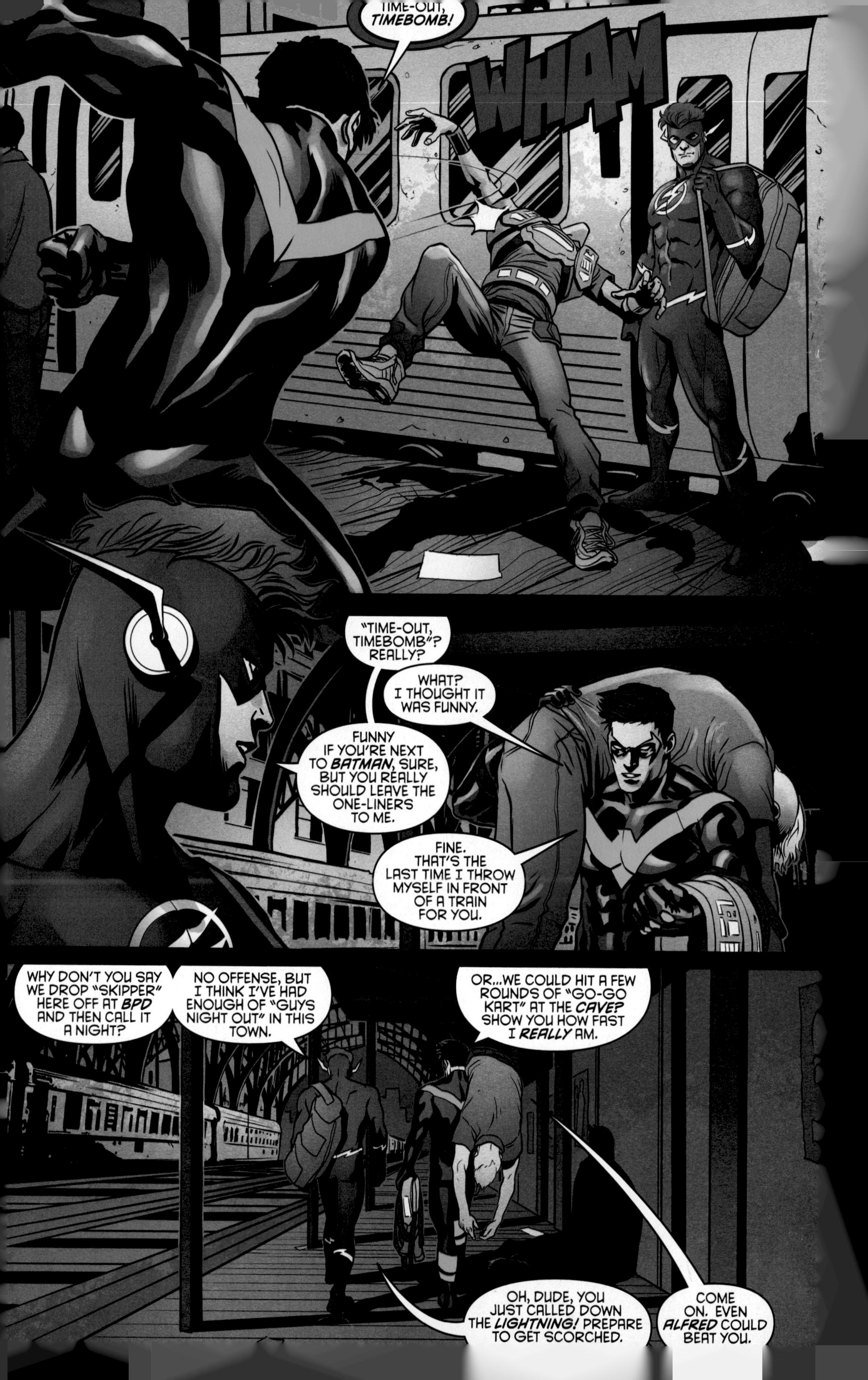
TIME-OUT, TIMEBOMB!
WHAM
"TIME-OUT, TIMEBOMB"? REALLY?
WHAT? I THOUGHT IT WAS FUNNY.
FUNNY IF YOU'RE NEXT TO BATMAN, SURE, BUT YOU REALLY SHOULD LEAVE THE ONE-LINERS TO ME.
FINE. THAT'S THE LAST TIME I THROW MYSELF IN FRONT OF A TRAIN FOR YOU.
WHY DON'T YOU SAY WE DROP "SKIPPER" HERE OFF AT BPD AND THEN CALL IT A NIGHT?
NO OFFENSE, BUT I THINK I'VE HAD ENOUGH OF "GUYS NIGHT OUT" IN THIS TOWN.
OR...WE COULD HIT A FEW ROUNDS OF "GO-GO KART" AT THE CAVE? SHOW YOU HOW FAST I REALLY AM.
OH, DUDE, YOU JUST CALLED DOWN THE LIGHTNING! PREPARE TO GET SCORCHED.
COME ON. EVEN ALFRED COULD BEAT YOU.

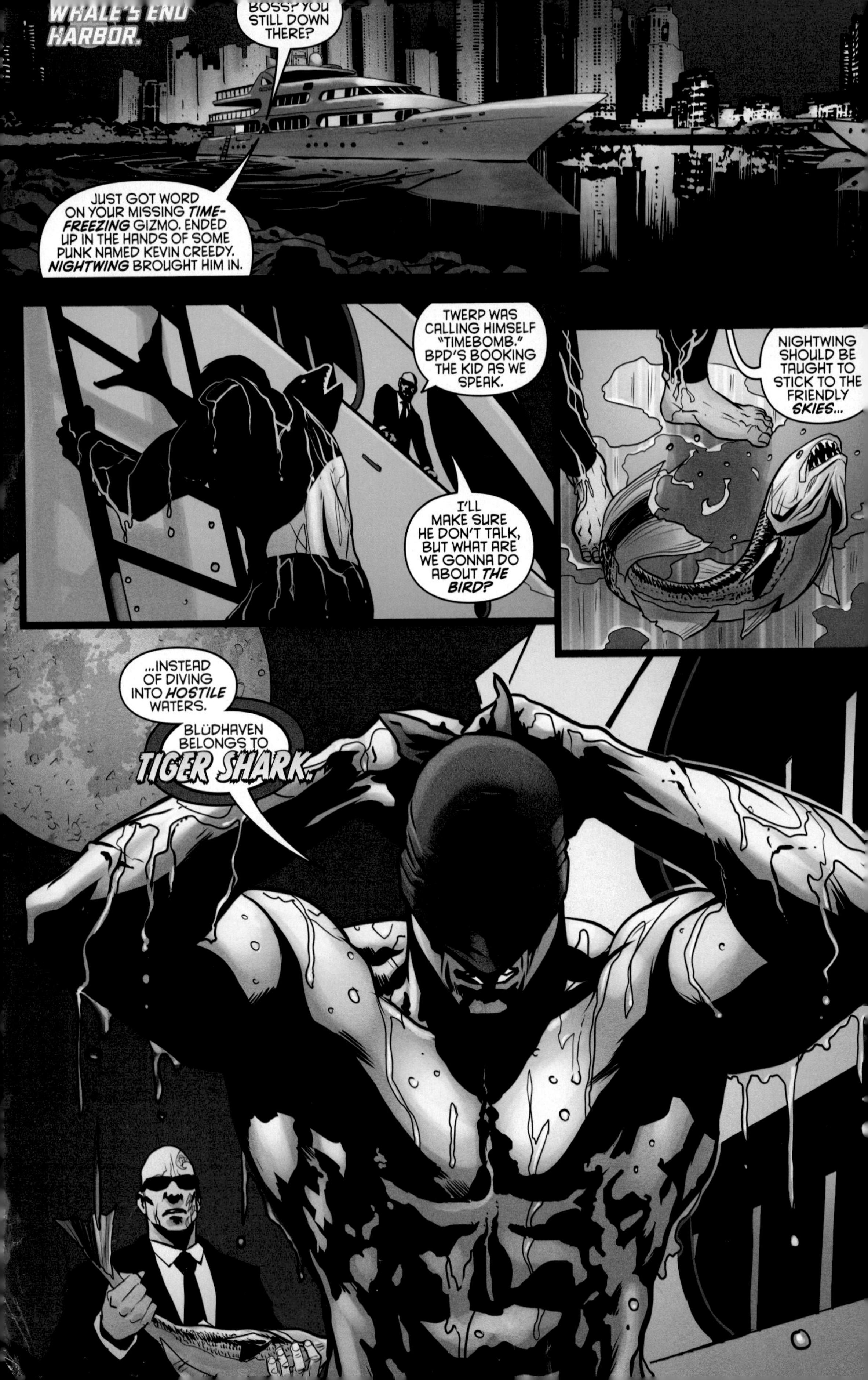
WHALE'S END HARBOR.
BOSS? YOU STILL DOWN THERE?
JUST GOT WORD ON YOUR MISSING TIME-FREEZING GIZMO. ENDED UP IN THE HANDS OF SOME PUNK NAMED KEVIN CREEDY. NIGHTWING BROUGHT HIM IN.
TWERP WAS CALLING HIMSELF "TIMEBOMB." BPD'S BOOKING THE KID AS WE SPEAK.
I'LL MAKE SURE HE DON'T TALK, BUT WHAT ARE WE GONNA DO ABOUT THE BIRD?
NIGHTWING SHOULD BE TAUGHT TO STICK TO THE FRIENDLY SKIES...
...INSTEAD OF DIVING INTO HOSTILE WATERS.
BLÜDHAVEN BELONGS TO
TIGER SHARK.

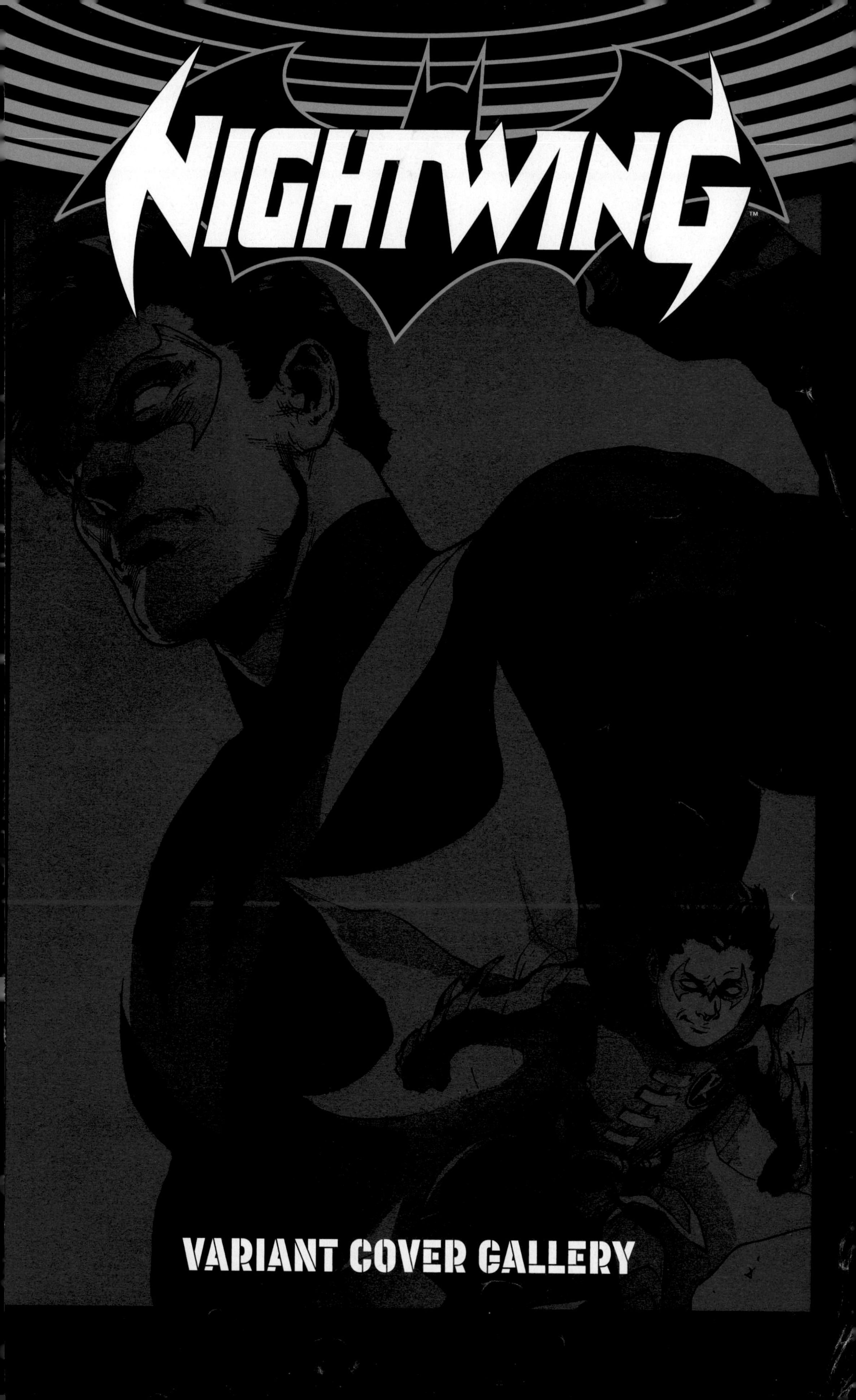
NIGHTWING
VARIANT COVER GALLERY

NIGHTWING #16 Variant by IVAN REIS, OCLAIR ALBERT and SULA MOON

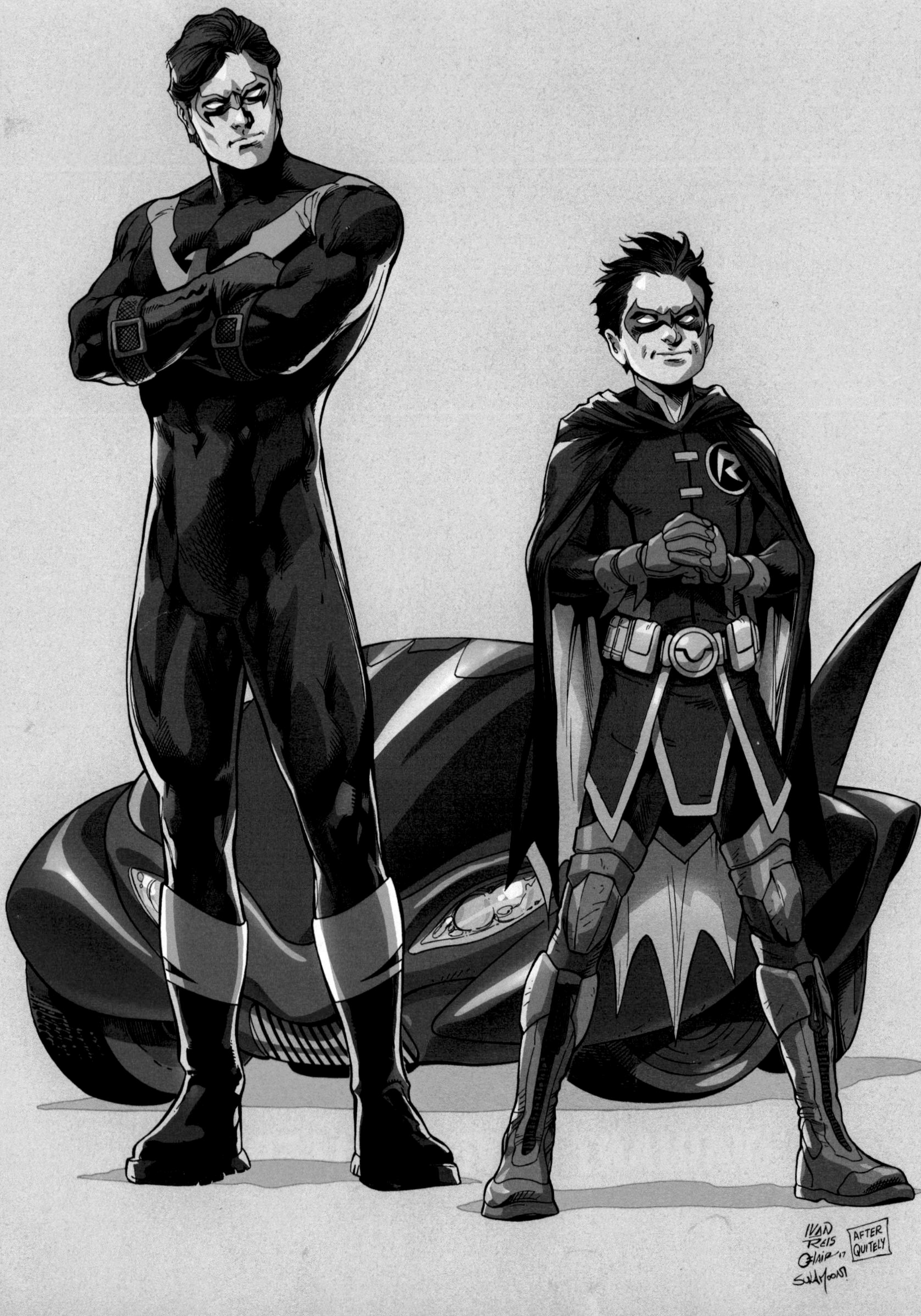
IVAN REIS
AFTER QUITELY

NIGHTWING #17 Variant by IVAN REIS, OCLAIR ALBERT and SULA MOON

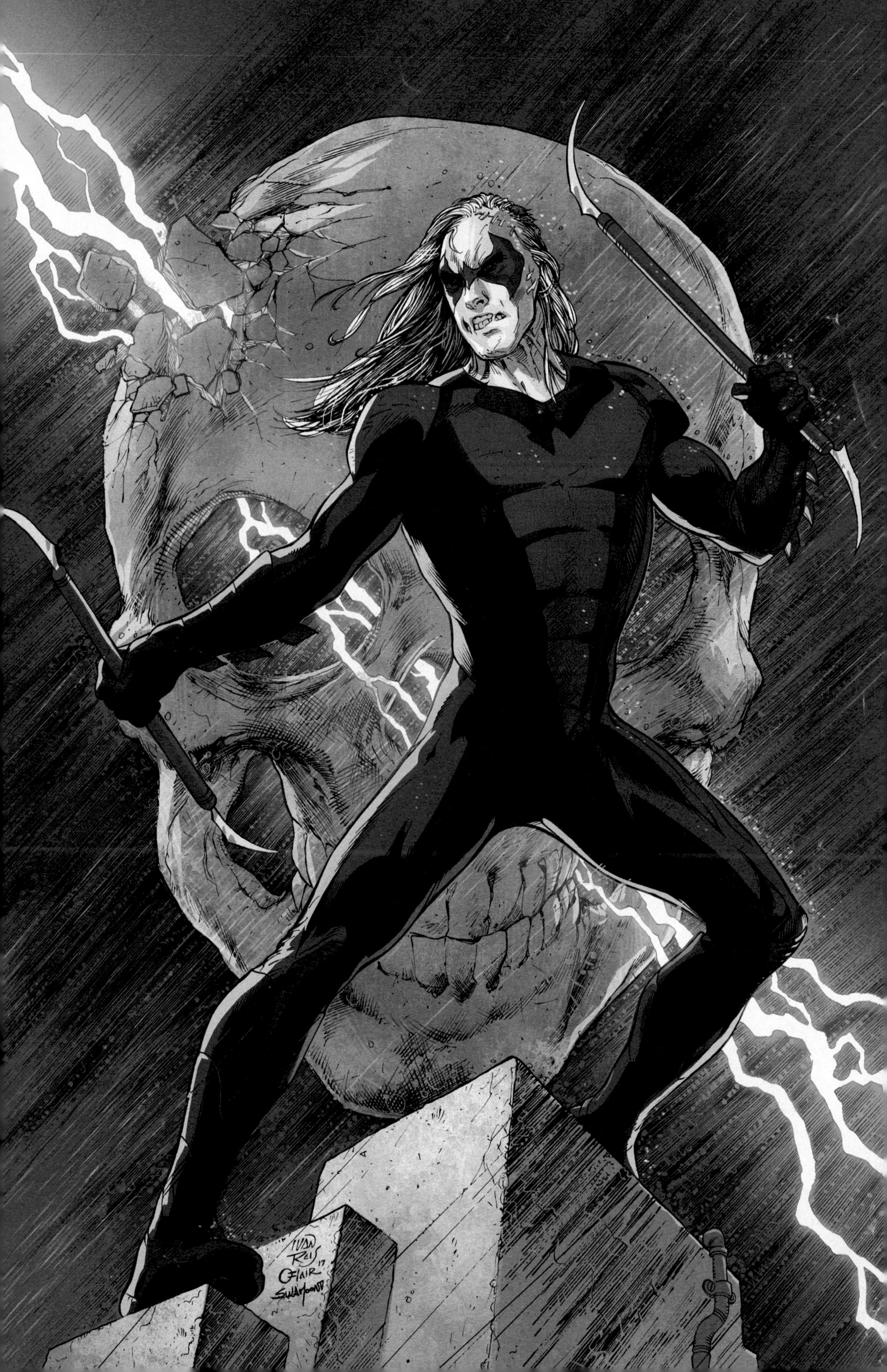

NIGHTWING #18 variant by IVAN REIS,
OCLAIR ALBERT and SULA MOON

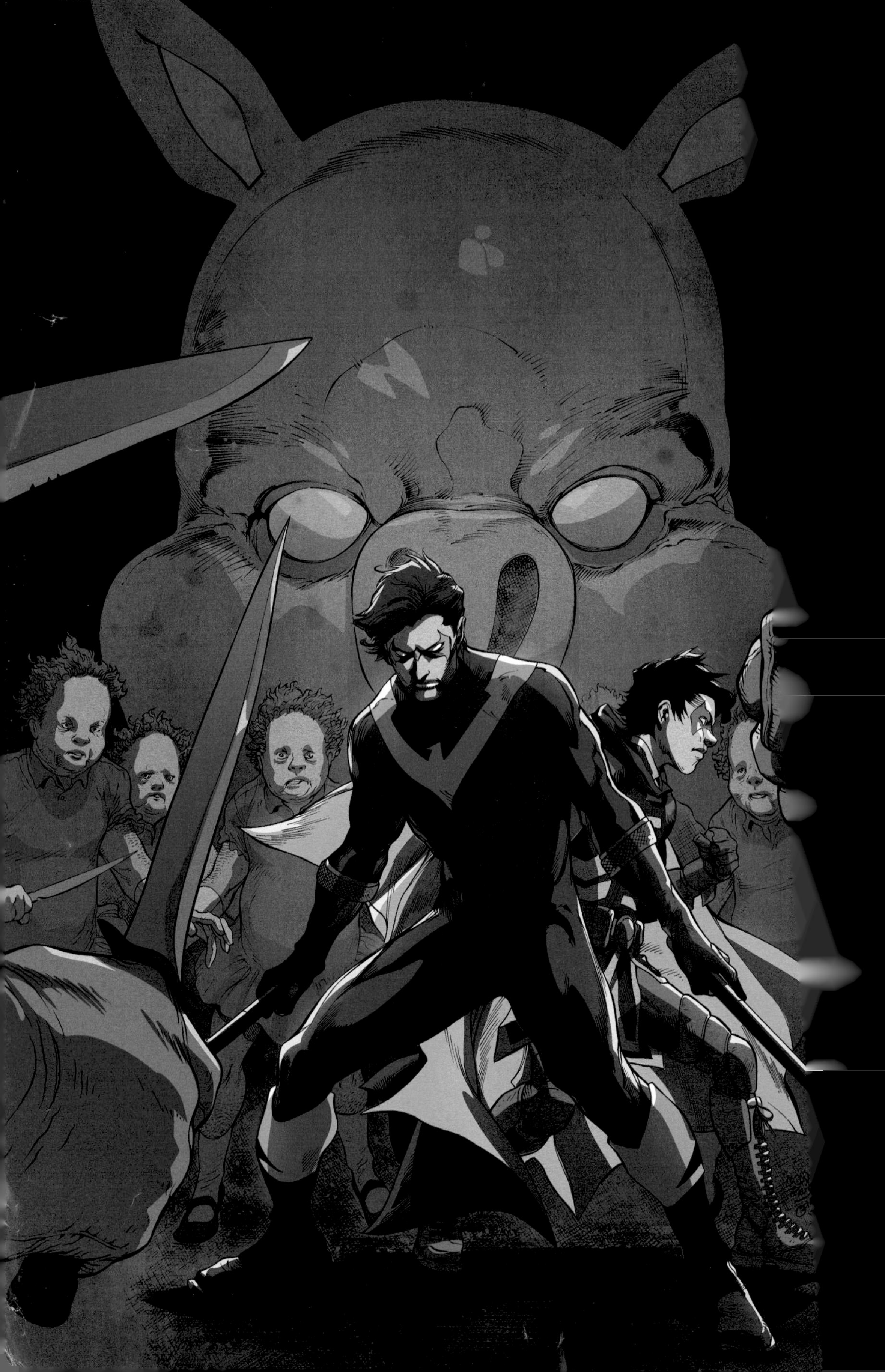

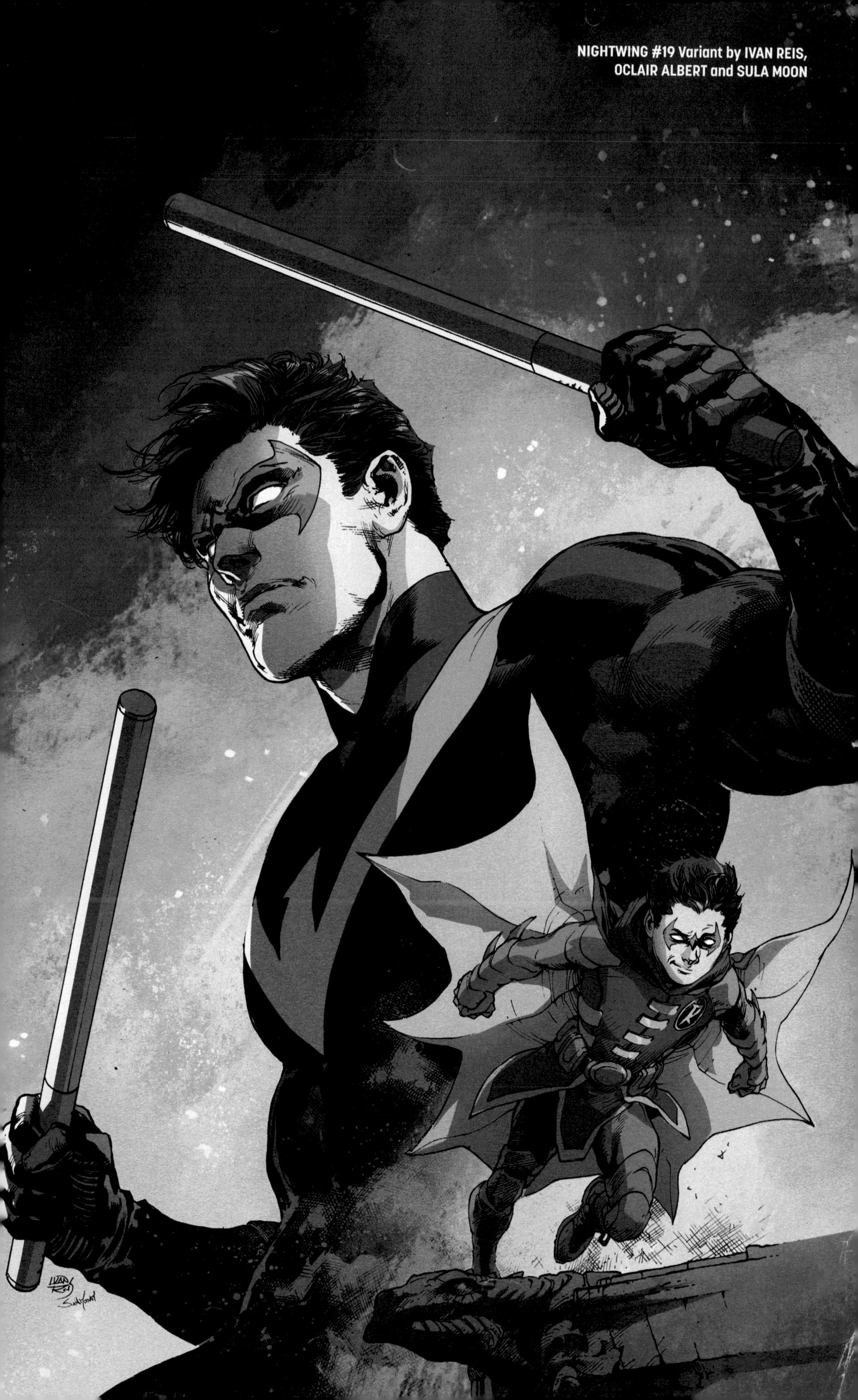

NIGHTWING #19 Variant by IVAN REIS,
OCLAIR ALBERT and SULA MOON

NIGHTWING #20 Variant by CASEY JONES and HI-FI

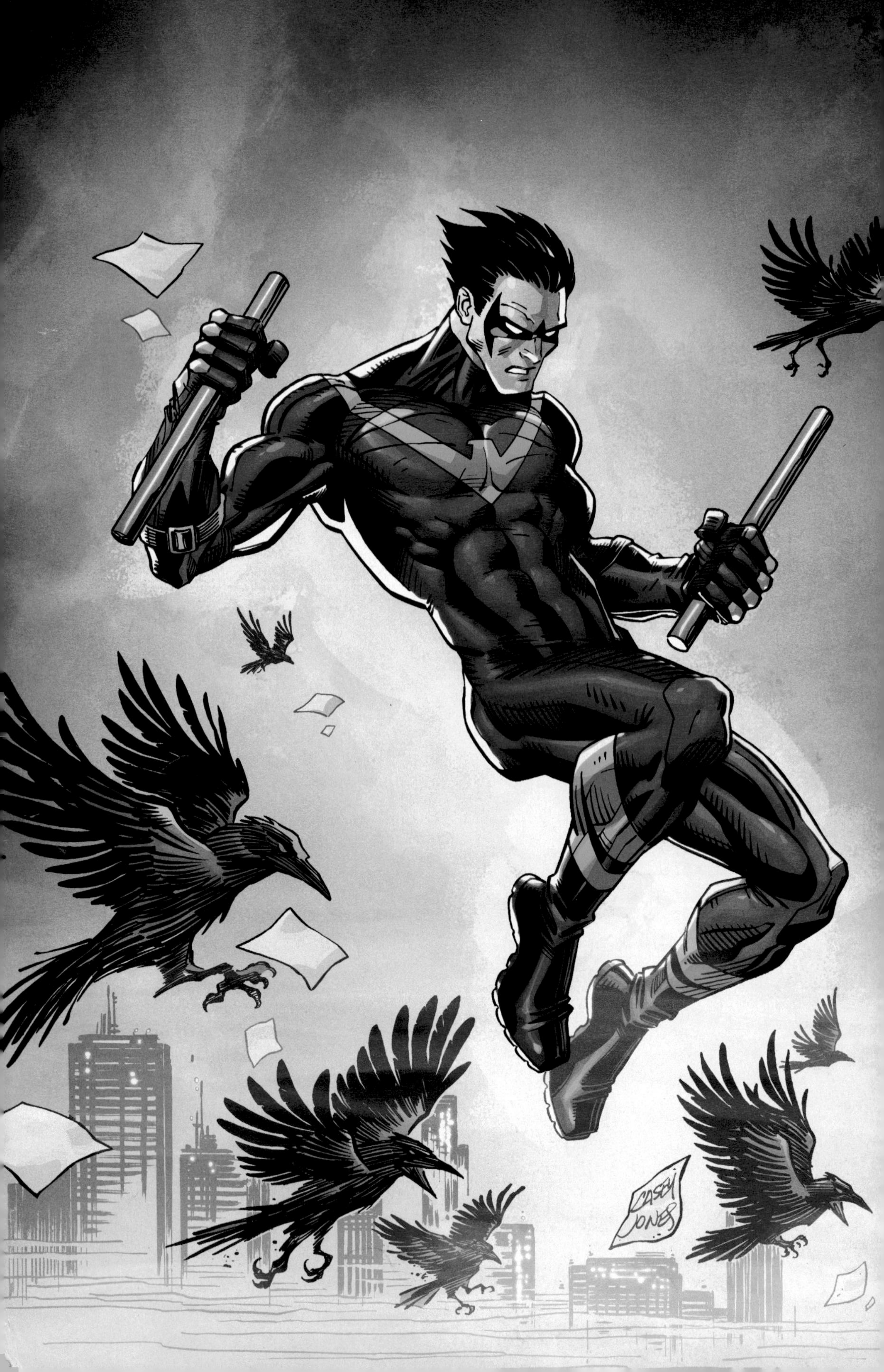
CASEY JONES

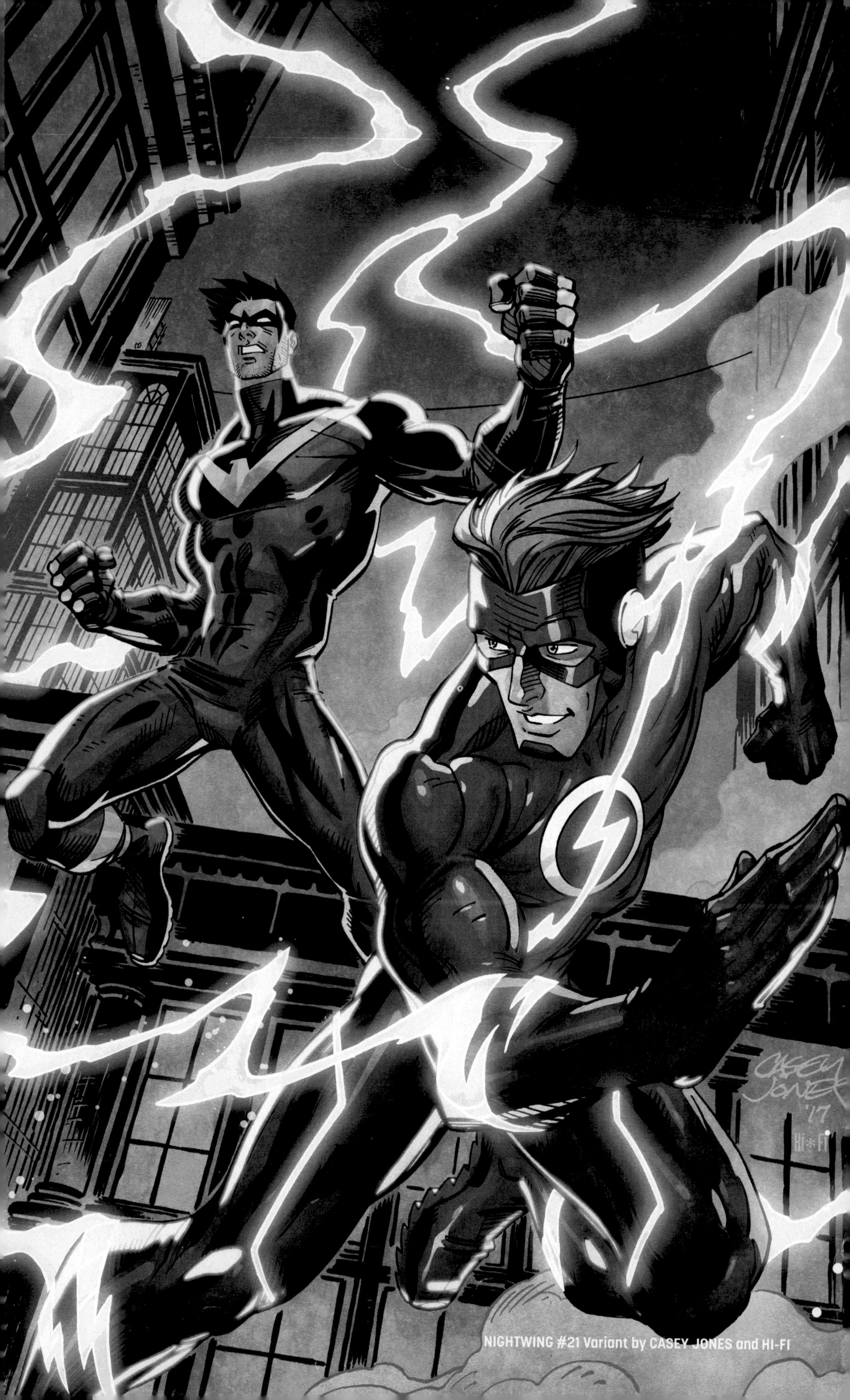
CASEY JONES '17
Hi*FI

NIGHTWING #21 Variant by CASEY JONES and HI-FI

"There's just something about the idea of Dick Grayson returning to the role of Nightwing that feels right." – **IGN**

"Equally weighted between pulse-pounding and heartfelt drama."
– NEWSARAMA

DC UNIVERSE REBIRTH

NIGHTWING

VOL. 1: BETTER THAN BATMAN

TIM SEELEY
with JAVIER FERNANDEZ

VOL.1 **BETTER THAN BATMAN**
TIM SEELEY * JAVIER FERNÁNDEZ * CHRIS SOTOMAYOR

VOL.1 **THE RETURN OF WALLY WEST**
DAN ABNETT * BRETT BOOTH * NORM RAPMUND * ANDREW DALHOUSE

VOL.1 **BEYOND BURNSIDE**
HOPE LARSON * RAFAEL ALBUQUERQUE

VOL.1 **I AM GOTHAM**
TOM KING * DAVID FINCH

**TITANS VOL. 1:
THE RETURN OF WALLY WEST**

**BATGIRL VOL. 1:
BEYOND BURNDSIDE**

**BATMAN VOL. 1:
I AM GOTHAM**

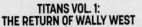

Get more DC graphic novels wherever comics and books are sold!